ELEMENTS OF

D0546877

Patterns, Purpose, and Perspectives

ELEMENTS OF ESSAYS

Patterns, Purpose, and Perspectives

Sue Harper | Douglas Hilker

Harcourt Canada

Toronto Orlando San Diego London Sydney

National Library of Canada Cataloguing in Publication Data

Harper, Sue, 1952-

    Elements of essays : patterns, purpose, and perspectives / Sue Harper,
    Douglas Hilker.

Includes index.

ISBN 0-7747-1589-8

1. Essays. 2. English language--Rhetoric. I. Hilker, Douglas II. Title.

PE1471.H37 2002   808.84   C2002-902640-7

Sue Harper
Cross-Curricular Literacy Head, John Fraser Secondary School, Mississauga, ON, and Developer for the Ontario Secondary School Grade 10 Literacy Test

Douglas Hilker
Writing Team Leader for the Ontario Curriculum Policy Document for English and Lead Developer for the Ontario Secondary School Grade 10 Literacy Test

Editorial Project Manager: Ian Nussbaum
Editor: Brett Savory
Developmental Editor: Sue Mei Ku
Senior Production Editor: Karin Fediw
Production Editor: Susan McNish
Production Coordinator: Cheri Westra
Permissions Editors: Karen Becker/Patricia Buckley
Cover and Interior Design: Sharon Foster Design
Page Composition: Susan Purtell
Cover Illustration: Connie Hayes/The Stock Illustration Source
Illustration: Dorothy Siemens
Printing and Binding: Transcontinental Printing Inc.

∞ Printed in Canada on acid-free paper.
1 2 3 4 5   06 05 04 03 02

Contents

Unit II:

PURPOSE

Unit III:

PERSPECTIVES

Alternative Groupings

PATTERNS

PURPOSE

PERSPECTIVES

Preface to Students

The essay form is described as non-fiction, a literary composition that presents the writer's point of view on a subject. The essays in *Elements of Essays* will entertain, challenge, and inform you. They will provide your class with many ideas and perspectives on those ideas for discussion and debate.

The essays in this textbook will also provide you with models for understanding the effective use of various organizational patterns in essays. You can then use these models to develop your own skill and style when writing essays presenting information and ideas for different audiences and purposes.

Reading and writing essays allow you to demonstrate a wide range of skills including

- thorough and accurate research
- in-depth knowledge and understanding of a topic
- critical and creative thinking
- organization of information and ideas around a central thesis
- clear and effective communication of ideas and development of arguments
- correct and accurate use of written language

As you read the essays in this textbook and write your own essays, consider how the essay form allows you to demonstrate the critical and creative thinking skills described below.

Critical Thinking Skills (Based on Bloom's Taxonomy)

Knowledge (Memory): the ability to recall specific facts and information
Comprehension (Understanding): the ability to understand information, ideas, issues, themes, and arguments
Application: the ability to use information, ideas, and processes in new situations or contexts
Analysis: the ability to break an idea down into its constituent parts

Synthesis: the ability to put together information and ideas to create a whole

Evaluation: the ability to read and assess your own ideas and those of others

Creative Thinking Skills

Fluency: the ability to generate many ideas

Flexibility: the ability to
- view things from different perspectives
- approach a problem in different ways
- change direction of thought

Elaboration: the ability to expand and develop ideas, arguments, and products

Originality: the ability to produce new and unique responses, ideas, solutions, and products

As the Information Age develops, these skills will be in greater demand and will be increasingly important to success.

The Units and Features in This Book

This textbook is organized into three main units, which are in turn divided into smaller subsections, as follows:

- **Unit I Patterns** analyzes the organizational patterns of comparison and contrast, process analysis, definition, classification, cause and effect, and narration.
- **Unit II Purpose** examines the purposes of several types of essays: persuasive and argument, explanation/information, personal, literary, and satirical.
- **Unit III Perspectives** explores the perspectives of essay writers on a variety of topics.

The essays in Units I and II are supported by synopses and information about the writers. They are also supported by activities that assess understanding of content **(Analyzing the Content)** and structure and style

(Structure and Style). Each pattern and purpose concludes with extension activities **(Extending the Pattern/Purpose)**.

Unit III is organized differently from the first two units. The individual essays are not accompanied by activities, allowing you to explore perspectives of writers on your own, with a partner or group, or as a class. The unit ends with cumulative activities **(Extending: Exploring Perspectives)** that provide you with the opportunity to think about and explore your own perspectives on a variety of topics.

The authors and editors of this textbook wish you every success as you prepare for college or university and your eventual participation in the society of the Information Age.

Elements of the Pattern

In a comparison and contrast essay, to *compare* means to explore similarities, whereas to *contrast* means to explore differences. An essay can focus on both or either of these.

When writing a comparison and contrast essay, use the following guidelines:

- **Choose your topic carefully.** A topic that is too narrow will make it difficult for you to say anything beyond the obvious, whereas a topic that is too broad will be impossible to explore satisfactorily. Also, ensure that your comparison is meaningful. For instance, if you were comparing and contrasting two cars for potential buyers, it wouldn't be very meaningful to compare and contrast an economy car with an expensive luxury vehicle. You would need to compare two cars in the potential buyers' price range.

- **Clearly define the points you are going to compare and contrast.** Choose what you believe are the most important points to compare and contrast, and limit your discussion to these points.

- **Choose an appropriate essay structure.** There are two different ways of approaching the comparison and contrast essay:

  1. *Point-by-point method.* In this method, you compare and contrast one aspect of Object A with the same aspect of Object B and then move on to the next aspect. For example, say that you choose to compare and contrast two cars, focusing on the body styles, engine specifications, and warranties. In a point-by-point structure you would first discuss the body styles of *both* cars, then the engine specifications of both cars, and, last, their warranties.

  2. *Block or chunk method.* In this method, you discuss *all* aspects of Object A and then move on to *all* aspects of Object B. Taking the above example, you would first discuss the body style, engine specifications, and warranties of Car A before moving on to the body style, engine specifications, and warranties of Car B.

Am I Blue?

Alice Walker

Elements of the Essay

In this essay from *Living by the Word: Selected Writings 1973–1987* (1988), Alice Walker draws an analogy comparing horses to humans, particularly to enslaved Blacks. Using description and narration, she concludes that humans and horses have much in common, that indeed "human animals and nonhuman animals can communicate quite well."

About the Writer

African-American writer Alice Walker was born in Georgia in 1944. The youngest of eight children, Walker was raised in rural Eatonton, where her parents were sharecroppers. She excelled academically, attending both Spelman College in Atlanta and Sarah Lawrence College in New York on scholarships. While at Spelman she became involved in the civil rights movement and met Dr. Martin Luther King Jr. At Sarah Lawrence her love for writing was nurtured by poet Muriel Ruykeyser and writer Jane Cooper. Since then Walker has published collections of short stories, poetry, essays, and novels, one of which, *The Color Purple* (1982), won a Pulitzer Prize.

"AIN'T THESE TEARS in these eyes tellin' you?"   1

For about three years my companion and I rented a small house in the country that stood on the edge of a large meadow that appeared to run from the end of our deck straight into the mountains. The mountains, however, were quite far away, and between us and them there was, in fact, a town. It was one of the many pleasant aspects of the house that you never really were aware of this.   2

It was a house of many windows, low, wide, nearly floor to ceiling in the living room, which faced the meadow, and it was from one of these that I first saw our closest neighbor, a large white horse, cropping grass,   3 flipping its mane, and ambling about—not over the entire meadow, which stretched well out of sight of the house, but over the five or so fenced-in acres that were next to the twenty-odd that we had rented. I soon learned that the horse, whose name was Blue, belonged to a man who lived in another town, but was boarded by our neighbors next door. Occasionally, one of the children, usually a stocky teenager, but sometimes a much younger girl or boy, could be seen riding Blue. They would appear in the meadow, climb up on his back, ride furiously for ten or fifteen minutes, then get off, slap Blue on the flanks, and not be seen again for a month or more.

4   There were many apple trees in our yard, and one by the fence that Blue could almost reach. We were soon in the habit of feeding him apples, which he relished, especially because by the middle of summer the meadow grasses—so green and succulent since January—had dried out from lack of rain, and Blue stumbled about munching the dried stalks half-heartedly. Sometimes he would stand very still just by the apple tree, and when one of us came out he would whinny, snort loudly, or stamp the ground. This meant, of course: I want an apple.

5   It was quite wonderful to pick a few apples, or collect those that had fallen to the ground overnight, and patiently hold them, one by one, up to his large, toothy mouth. I remained as thrilled as a child by his flexible dark lips, huge, cubelike teeth that crunched the apples, core and all, with such finality, and his high, broad-breasted *enormity;* beside which, I felt small indeed. When I was a child, I used to ride horses, and was especially friendly with one named Nan until the day I was riding and my brother deliberately spooked her and I was thrown, head first, against the trunk of a tree. When I came to, I was in bed and my mother was bending worriedly over me; we silently agreed that perhaps horseback riding was not the safest sport for me. Since then I have walked, and prefer walking to horseback riding—but I had forgotten the depth of feeling one could see in horses' eyes.

6   I was therefore unprepared for the expression in Blue's. Blue was lonely. Blue was horribly lonely and bored. I was not shocked that this should be the case; five acres to tramp by yourself, endlessly, even in the most beautiful of meadows—and his was—cannot provide many interesting events, and once rainy season turned to dry that was about it. No, I was shocked that I had forgotten that human animals and nonhuman animals can communicate quite well; if we are brought up around animals as children we take this for granted. By the time we are

adults we no longer remember. However, the animals have not changed. They are in fact *completed* creations (at least they seem to be, so much more than we) who are not likely to change; it is their nature to express themselves. What else are they going to express? And they do. And, generally speaking, they are ignored.

After giving Blue the apples, I would wander back to the house, aware that he was observing me. Were more apples not forthcoming then? Was that to be his sole entertainment for the day? My partner's small son had decided he wanted to learn how to piece a quilt; we worked in silence on our respective squares as I thought…. 7

Well, about slavery: about white children, who were raised by black people, who knew their first all-accepting love from black women, and then, when they were twelve or so, were told they must "forget" the deep levels of communication between themselves and "mammy" that they knew. Later they would be able to relate quite calmly, "My old mammy was sold to another good family." "My old mammy was _____ _____." Fill in the blank. Many more years later a white woman would say: "I can't understand these Negroes, these blacks. What do they want? They're so different from us." 8

And about the Indians, considered to be "like animals" by the "settlers" (a very benign euphemism for what they actually were), who did not understand their description as a compliment. 9

And about the thousands of American men who marry Japanese, Korean, Filipina, and other non-English-speaking women and of how happy they report they are, "*blissfully*," until their brides learn to speak English, at which point the marriages tend to fall apart. What then did the men see, when they looked into the eyes of the women they married, before they could speak English? Apparently only their own reflections. 10

I thought of society's impatience with the young. "Why are they playing the music so loud?" Perhaps the children have listened to much of the music of oppressed people their parents danced to before they were born, with its passionate but soft cries for acceptance and love, and they have wondered why their parents failed to hear. 11

I do not know how long Blue had inhabited his five beautiful, boring acres before we moved into our house; a year after we had arrived—and had also traveled to other valleys, other cities, other worlds—he was still there. 12

But then, in our second year at the house, something happened in Blue's life. One morning, looking out the window at the fog that lay like 13 a ribbon over the meadow, I saw another horse, a brown one, at the other end of Blue's field. Blue appeared to be afraid of it, and for several days made no attempt to go near. We went away for a week. When we returned, Blue had decided to make friends and the two horses ambled or galloped along together, and Blue did not come nearly as often to the fence underneath the apple tree.

14   When he did, bringing his new friend with him, there was a different look in his eyes. A look of independence, of self-possession, of inalienable *horse*ness. His friend eventually became pregnant. For months and months there was, it seemed to me, a mutual feeling between me and the horses of justice, of peace. I fed apples to them both. The look in Blue's eyes was one of unabashed "this is *it*ness."

15   It did not, however, last forever. One day, after a visit to the city, I went out to give Blue some apples. He stood waiting, or so I thought, though not beneath the tree. When I shook the tree and jumped back from the shower of apples, he made no move. I carried some over to him. He managed to half-crunch one. The rest he let fall to the ground. I dreaded looking into his eyes—because I had of course noticed that Brown, his partner, had gone—but I did look. If I had been born into slavery, and my partner had been sold or killed, my eyes would have looked like that. The children next door explained that Blue's partner had been "put with him" (the same expression that old people used, I noticed, when speaking of an ancestor during slavery who had been impregnated by her owner) so that they could mate and she conceive. Since that was accomplished, she had been taken back by her owner, who lived somewhere else.

16   Will she be back? I asked.

17   They didn't know.

18   Blue was like a crazed person. Blue *was*, to me, a crazed person. He galloped furiously, as if he were being ridden, around and around his five beautiful acres. He whinnied until he couldn't. He tore at the ground with his hooves. He butted himself against his single shade tree. He looked always and always toward the road down which his partner had gone. And then, occasionally, when he came up for apples, or I took apples to him, he looked at me. It was a look so piercing, so full of grief, a look so *human*, I almost laughed (I felt too sad to cry) to think there are people who do not know that animals suffer. People like me who have forgotten, and daily forget, all that animals try to tell us. "Everything you do to us will happen to you; we are your teachers, as

you are ours. We are one lesson" is essentially it, I think. There are those who never once have even considered animals' rights: those who have been taught that animals actually want to be used and abused by us, as small children "love" to be frightened, or women "love" to be mutilated and raped.... They are the great-grandchildren of those who honestly thought, because someone taught them this: "Women can't think," And "niggers can't faint." But most disturbing of all, in Blue's large brown eyes was a new look, more painful than the look of despair: the look of disgust with human beings, with life; the look of hatred. And it was odd what the look of hatred did. It gave him, for the first time, the look of a beast. And what that meant was that he had put up a barrier within to protect himself from further violence; all the apples in the world wouldn't change that fact.

And so Blue remained, a beautiful part of our landscape, very   19
peaceful to look at from the window, white against the grass. Once a friend came to visit and said, looking out on the soothing view: "And it *would* have to be a white horse; the very image of freedom." And I thought, yes, the animals are forced to become for us merely "images" of what they once so beautifully expressed. And we are used to drinking milk from containers showing "contented" cows, whose real lives we want to hear nothing about, eating eggs and drumsticks from "happy" hens, and munching hamburgers advertised by bulls of integrity who seem to command their fate.

As we talked of freedom and justice one day for all, we sat down to   20
steaks. I am eating misery, I thought, as I took the first bite. And spit it out.

After-Reading Activities

Analyzing the Content

1. Find a copy of the lyrics to the song "Am I Blue?" Explain why Alice Walker used an allusion to this song in the title and introduction to this essay.

2. Why does Walker include her friend's comment, "And it *would* have to be a white horse; the very image of freedom" (paragraph 19)? What could she have explained to her friend? Explain why she seems to have just let the comment pass.

3. Explain the significance of the last sentence of this essay. Why do you think Walker chose not to elaborate on its significance in the essay?

Structure and Style

4. If you had to select one sentence from this essay to illustrate its thesis, which one would you choose? Explain your choice.

5. a) Make a chart showing the comparison and contrast structure of this essay.

   b) Explain how this essay also exemplifies the organizational patterns of analogy, description, and narration.

6. Look up the meaning of the suffix "–ness." What is the meaning when "–ness" is combined with an ordinary word like "horse" to form the word "horseness"? What would the word "chairness" refer to?

Canadians and Americans

Elements of the Essays

What is the "Canadian identity"? Who are we in comparison with our American neighbours? These questions have been asked through much of our history. Taking different perspectives, Margaret Atwood and Elizabeth Renzetti explore the Canadian identity and how it is affected by our proximity to the United States. While Atwood uses a metaphor to explain why Canadians "observe, analyze, ponder, snoop and wonder" about their powerful neighbour, Renzetti draws on statistics and personal experiences to argue that the differences we perceive between the two countries are really myths. The question of our identity is complex, but both writers address it in informal and simple language, using everyday experiences as examples to get their points across to their audience.

About the Writers

Poet, novelist, and literary critic Margaret Atwood was born on November 18, 1939, in Ottawa. She received her Bachelor of Arts degree from the University of Toronto and later went on to study at Radcliffe College, Harvard University. Considered one of the greatest literary figures in Canada, Atwood has earned numerous awards and honours. Her first major publication was a collection of poetry, *The Circle Game* (1966), which won the Governor General's Award. Some of her other important works include the literary criticism *Survival: A Thematic Guide to Canadian Literature* (1972), and award-winning novels *The Handmaid's Tale* (1986), *The Robber Bride* (1993), *Alias Grace* (1996), and *The Blind Assassin* (2000). (Note: For an analysis of Chapter 17 of *The Handmaid's Tale*, see pages 196 to 208 of this textbook.)

Canadian freelance writer and journalist Elizabeth Renzetti writes for various publications, including *Maclean's* magazine and *The Globe and Mail*. She has lived in the United States and has since returned to Canada. In 2000, she was voted by readers of *Write* magazine as their favourite freelance writer.

Through the One-Way Mirror

Margaret Atwood

1   THE NOSES OF A GREAT many Canadians resemble Porky Pig's. This comes from spending so much time pressing them against the longest undefended one-way mirror in the world. The Canadians looking through this mirror behave the way people on the hidden side of such mirrors usually do: they observe, analyze, ponder, snoop and wonder what all the activity on the other side means in decipherable human terms.

2   The Americans, bless their innocent little hearts, are rarely aware that they are even being watched, much less by the Canadians. They just go on doing body language, playing in the sandbox of the world, bashing one another on the head and planning how to blow things up, same as always. If they think about Canada at all, it's only when things get a bit snowy or the water goes off or the Canadians start fussing over some piddly detail, such as fish. Then they regard them as unpatriotic; for Americans don't really see Canadians as foreigners, not like the Mexicans, unless they do something weird like speak French or beat the New York Yankees at baseball. Really, think the Americans, the Canadians are just like us, or would be if they could.

3   Or we could switch metaphors and call the border the longest undefended backyard fence in the world. The Canadians are the folks in the neat little bungalow, with the tidy little garden and the duck pond. The Americans are the other folks, the ones in the sprawly mansion with the bad-taste statues on the lawn. There's a perpetual party, or something, going on there—loud music, raucous laughter, smoke billowing from the barbecue. Beer bottles and Coke cans land among the peonies. The Canadians have their own beer bottles and barbecue smoke, but they tend to overlook it. Your own mess is always more forgivable than the mess someone else makes on your patio.

4   The Canadians can't exactly call the police—they suspect that the Americans are the police—and part of their distress, which seems

permanent, comes from their uncertainty as to whether or not they've been invited. Sometimes they do drop by next door, and find it exciting but scary. Sometimes the Americans drop by their house and find it clean. This worries the Canadians. They worry a lot. Maybe those Americans want to buy up their duck pond, with all the money they seem to have, and turn it into a cesspool or a water-skiing emporium.

It also worries them that the Americans don't seem to know who the Canadians are, or even where, exactly, they are. Sometimes the Americans call Canada their backyard, sometimes their front yard, both of which imply ownership. Sometimes they say they are the Mounties and the Canadians are Rose Marie. (All these things have, in fact, been said by American politicians.) Then they accuse the Canadians of being paranoid and having an identity crisis. Heck, there is no call for the Canadians to fret about their identity, because everyone knows they're Americans, really. If the Canadians disagree with that, they're told not to be so insecure.

One of the problems is that Canadians and Americans are educated backward from one another. The Canadians—except for the Québécois, one keeps saying—are taught about the rest of the world first and Canada second. The Americans are taught about the United States first, and maybe later about other places, if they're of strategic importance. The Vietnam War draft dodgers got more culture shock in Canada than they did in Sweden. It's not the clothing that is different, it's those mental noises.

Of course, none of this holds true when you get close enough, where concepts like "Americans" and "Canadians" dissolve and people are just people, or anyway some of them are, the ones you happen to approve of. I, for instance, have never met any Americans I didn't like, but I only get to meet the nice ones. That's what the businessmen think too, though they have other individuals in mind. But big-scale national mythologies have a way of showing up in things like foreign policy, and at events like international writers' congresses, where the Canadians often find they have more to talk about with the Australians, the West Indians, the New Zealanders and even the once-loathed snooty Brits, now declining into humanity with the dissolution of the empire, than they do with the impenetrable and mysterious Yanks.

But only sometimes. Because surely the Canadians understand the Yanks. Shoot, don't they see Yank movies, read Yank mags, bobble around to Yank music and watch Yank telly, as well as their own, when there is any?

9   Sometimes the Canadians think it's their job to interpret the Yanks to the rest of the world; explain them, sort of. This is an illusion: they don't understand the Yanks as much as they think they do, and it isn't their job.

10   But, as we say up here among God's frozen people, when Washington catches a cold, Ottawa sneezes. Some Canadians even refer to their capital city as Washington North and wonder why we're paying those guys in Ottawa when a telephone order service would be cheaper. Canadians make jokes about the relationship with Washington which the Americans in their thin-skinned, bunion-toed way, construe as anti-American (they tend to see any nonworshipful comment coming from that grey, protoplasmic fuzz outside their borders as anti-American). They are no more anti-American than the jokes Canadians make about the weather: it's there, it's big, it's hard to influence, and it affects your life.

11   Of course, in any conflict with the Dreaded Menace, whatever it might be, the Canadians would line up with the Yanks, probably, if they thought it was a real menace, or if the Yanks twisted their arms or other bodily parts enough or threatened a "scorched-earth policy" (another real quote). Note the qualifiers. The Canadian idea of a menace is not the same as the U.S. one. Canada, for instance, never broke off diplomatic relations with Cuba, and it was quick to recognize China. Contemplating the U.S.–Soviet growling match, Canadians are apt to recall a line from Blake: "They became what they beheld." Certainly both superpowers suffer from the imperial diseases once so noteworthy among the Romans, the British and the French: arrogance and myopia. But the bodily-parts threat is real enough, and accounts for the observable wimpiness and flunkiness of some Ottawa politicians. Nobody, except at welcoming-committee time, pretends this is an equal relationship.

12   Americans don't have Porky Pig noses. Instead they have Mr. Magoo eyes, with which they see the rest of the world. That would not be a problem if the United States were not so powerful. But it is, so it is.

(1984)

Hollywood vs. Canada

Elizabeth Renzetti

THE MAN NEARBY AT the rally last December wore a T-shirt showing a maple leaf, dimpled with bullet holes, in the crosshairs of a gun. I didn't tell him he had the hair and forearms of a hockey player. In fact, I didn't open my mouth, lest I say *out* or *about*—and mark myself as the enemy.

In Los Angeles, thanks to "runaway" productions—American films shot north of the border—Canadians are considered thieves, stealing movie-industry jobs that belong in Hollywood. Last week, the trade newspaper *Variety* turned up the heat with a front-page story about jobs lost to Canada, estimating that runaway productions cost America US$1.2-billion and 22,400 jobs over the last three years.

Hence protests like that one. Hence the guy one over from Mr. Bullet Hole, hoisting a sign that read, "Canada Unfair."

That burned. Unfair? Canada? Summon the ghost of Lester Pearson—this man needed a lesson in the essentials of our national character. Such as, "I'm sorry, you stepped on my foot." Or, "You can't laugh at me, I'm laughing at me already."

At least that's what's printed as truth in the gospel of cultural stereotypes, where it says Canadians are fair, learned, ironic. Americans are ... not. These received notions are convenient, and, as far as I can tell, useless. Living in America for two years has overturned my best-loved prejudices. For one, Canadians are, in some small way, villains. We steal American jobs and blow terrorists back their way. For another, Americans are nicer than us. More polite. More courtly. Bigger-hearted.

You don't believe me? Once I, too, wouldn't have believed Americans were anything but brash, potato-brained gun-toters. Within my smug Toronto cocoon, I subscribed to the casual anti-American sentiment around me. (My American-born friend Katherine, who's been biting her tongue around Canadian colleagues for more than 30 years, says, "You can't be an American living in Canada and have a thin skin.")

7   Take my street in Los Angeles, which is, as they say, known to police. The other day, one of the call girls of indeterminate gender who hang out on the corner saw me struggling with a stroller and fistful of bags. She helped me over the curb, smiling through her stubble. This is standard behaviour. I've had more strangers strike up conversations in two years than in 30 years of eye-avoidance on the streets of Toronto. Some other beliefs about Americans that don't stand up to scrutiny:

8   **Myth One.** Americans are patriotic gasbags. Which country's citizens plaster themselves with the Maple Leaf when travelling abroad? Which country has a folk hero called Joe Canadian? It's not as if, say, Miller beer offers up an Andy American, wailing onstage about being misunderstood while wearing eagle-printed underpants.

9   **Myth Two.** Americans are ignorant about themselves and the world. Last year, 63 per cent of Americans passed a test on their history, while 39 per cent of Canadians passed an equivalent quiz. Nine out of 10 Americans correctly identified their first president. Only 54 per cent of Canadians named Sir John A. as our first PM.

10   **Myth Three.** They can't stop flag-waving. Since Sept. 11, America and its giant cars have, with good reason, been wrapped in Old Glory. Before that, with much less excuse, Canadians were at least as obnoxious. Have we forgotten the "flag flap" of five years ago, with Sheila Copps' $23-million program to drape every home in red and white?

11   **Myth Four.** Americans are loud, boorish, wear too-tight shorts and sneakers the size of mattresses: Um, been to Canada's Wonderland lately?

12   Why don't Americans address this calumny? They don't care. The best we can hope from them is that, in the nanosecond they devote to things Canadian, they don't dwell on stereotypes. Fortunately, there's some indication that they don't subscribe to the cliché we fear most, the one that wakes us up in a cold sweat—the idea that as a nation, we're as boring as toast.

13   Instead, the evidence seems to be mounting that Americans think we're … strange. "Canadians are friendly for the most part, but there's something a shade off about them," wrote Tucker Carlson last year in *Talk* magazine. "They remind me of the aliens in sci-fi movies who move about undetected among the human population until they're tripped up by some joke or colloquialism." And then there's the recent *New Yorker* cartoon depicting a woman chatting with a fellow in a bar. She is saying, "You seem familiar yet somehow strange—are you by any chance Canadian?"

Now there's a stereotype we could warm up to. The weird, villainous 14
northern power and its warm, endearing little southern buddy. It could
be the start of a beautiful friendship.

After-Reading Activities

Analyzing the Content

1. Which of these two essays—Margaret Atwood's "Through the One-Way
   Mirror" or Elizabeth Renzetti's "Hollywood vs. Canada"—is more
   insightful about the differences between Americans and Canadians?
   Give reasons for your choice.

2. Identify the significance of the following words and expressions used in
   these two essays. If any are unfamiliar, ask other members of the class
   or your teacher for assistance, or research them using the Internet.

   "Through the One-Way Mirror"

   - "cesspool" (paragraph 4)
   - "Sometimes they say they are the Mounties and the Canadians are
     Rose Marie." (paragraph 5)
   - "Mr. Magoo eyes" (paragraph 12)

   "Hollywood vs. Canada"

   - "*out* or *about*" (paragraph 1)
   - "the ghost of Lester Pearson" (paragraph 4)
   - "nanosecond" (paragraph 12)

Structure and Style

3. Which writer's arguments did you find more convincing? Explain, taking
   into consideration the writer's stylistic techniques.

4. With a partner, make a chart showing the comparison and contrast
   structure of one of these essays. Present your chart to a pair of students
   that made a chart for the other essay.

Extending the Pattern

1. Using Alice Walker's essay "Am I Blue?" as a model, select a line from a popular song as an inspiration to write an essay that makes an important point about life.

2. Read Pico Iyer's essay "Of Weirdos and Eccentrics" (pages 67 to 71). In "Am I Blue?" Alice Walker says, "Blue was like a crazed person." Would Blue be better classified as a weirdo or an eccentric as Iyer defines the terms?

3. Write a letter to either Margaret Atwood or Elizabeth Renzetti explaining why you agree or disagree with her observations.

4. Write your own comparison and contrast essay on one of the following:
   • males and females
   • popular and classical music
   • a scientific and religious view of life
   • life at a particular point in history and life today
   • learning from books and learning from experience
   • television programs made in the United States and those made in Canada
   • a topic of your own choosing

You may need to do additional research. After completing your first draft, work with a partner to revise and edit your essay, focusing on the organization and the strength of your arguments.

Elements of the Pattern

A process analysis essay describes or explains how something works or how something is done, often in a step-by-step manner or chronological order. Its purpose may be to direct the reader's actions in order to help the reader accomplish a task, or it may simply be to provide information. For instance, instructions on how to create and send an e-mail message are intended for the reader to follow and act on. On the other hand, a description of the process by which a bill passes through Parliament into law is not something that will be acted on—it is simply meant to inform.

Because of its purposes, an effective process analysis essay contains clear language to make it easy for readers to move logically from step to step and/or to understand the information. To achieve clarity, writers describing process analyses usually use precise words, an appropriate level of vocabulary, imperative sentences, parallel structures, and transitions.

As well, knowing the audience is key when writing a process analysis essay. As a writer, you will have to make some assumptions about your readers' knowledge. You will have to ask yourself, How familiar are my readers with the subject matter or process? How much detail should I include in the essay? What level of vocabulary should I use? To ascertain whether you have written an effective process analysis essay, try reading it to someone who represents your target audience. See if he or she can follow the instructions or understand the information.

As you read each of the process analysis essays in this section, consider the following:

- What is the intent of the essay? To provide instructions on how to accomplish a task? To provide information? A combination of both?

- Who is the audience? (Consider the level of vocabulary, language, and detail.)

- How successful is the writer in helping his or her audience understand the process?

How I Caused That Story

Doris Kearns Goodwin

Elements of the Essay

The bestselling book *The Fitzgeralds and the Kennedys* (1987) was suddenly caught in controversy in January 2002 when a report accused its author, Doris Kearns Goodwin, of plagiarizing, lifting passages from other sources and using them in the book without giving proper credit. Goodwin responded to the charge with this essay, "How I Caused That Story," to explain how this "plagiarism" could have happened. Are you persuaded by her explanation or viewpoint? Why or why not?

About the Writer

Historian and writer Doris Kearns Goodwin was born on January 4, 1943. Goodwin worked as an aide to President Lyndon Johnson, resulting in a book, *Lyndon Johnson and the American Dream* (1991). This was followed by a biography, *No Ordinary Time: Franklin and Eleanor Roosevelt: The Home Front in World War II* (1994), which received the 1995 Pulitzer Prize for History.

1   I AM A HISTORIAN, WITH the exception of being a wife and mother, it is who I am. And there is nothing I take more seriously.

2   In recent days, questions have been raised about how historians go about crediting their sources, and I have been caught up in the swirl. Ironically, the more intensive and far-reaching a historian's research, the greater the difficulty of citation. As the mountain of material grows, so does the possibility of error.

3   Fourteen years ago, not long after the publication of my book *The Fitzgeralds and the Kennedys*, I received a communication from author Lynne McTaggart pointing out that material from her book on Kathleen Kennedy had not been properly attributed. I realized that she was right. Though my footnotes repeatedly cited Ms. McTaggart's work, I failed to provide quotation marks for phrases that I had taken verbatim, having

assumed that these phrases, drawn from my notes, were my words, not hers. I made the corrections she requested, and the matter was completely laid to rest—until last week, when the *Weekly Standard* published an article reviving the issue. The larger question for those of us who write history is to understand how citation mistakes can happen.

The research and writing for this 900-page book, with its 3,500 footnotes, took place over 10 years. At that time, I wrote my books and took my notes in longhand, believing I could not think well on a keyboard. Most of my sources were drawn from a multitude of primary materials: manuscript collections, private letters, diaries, oral histories, newspapers, periodicals, personal interviews. After three years of research, I discovered more than 150 cartons of materials that had been previously stored in the attic of Joe Kennedy's Hyannis Port house. These materials were a treasure trove for a historian—old report cards, thousands of family letters, movie stubs and diaries, which allowed me to cross the boundaries of time and space. It took me two additional years to read, categorize and take notes on these documents.

During this same period, I took handwritten notes on perhaps 300 books. Passages I wanted to quote directly were noted along with general notes on the ideas and story lines of each book. Notes on all these sources were then arranged chronologically and kept in dozens of folders in 25 banker's boxes. Immersed in a flood of papers, I began to write the book. After each section and each chapter was completed, I returned the notes to the boxes along with notations for future footnoting. When the manuscript was finished, I went back to all these sources to check the accuracy of attributions. As a final protection, I revisited the 300 books themselves. Somehow in this process, a few of the books were not fully rechecked. I relied instead on my notes, which combined direct quotes and paraphrased sentences. If I had had the books in front of me, rather than my notes, I would have caught mistakes in the first place and placed any borrowed phrases in direct quotes.

What made this incident particularly hard for me was the fact that I take great pride in the depth of my research and the extensiveness of my citations. The writing of history is a rich process of building on the work of the past with the hope that others will build on what you have done. Through footnotes you point the way to future historians.

The only protection as a historian is to institute a process of research and writing that minimizes the possibility of error. And that I have tried to do, aided by modern technology, which enables me, having long since moved beyond longhand, to use a computer for both organizing and taking notes. I now rely on a scanner, which reproduces the passages I want to cite, and then I keep my own comments on those books in a separate file so that I will never confuse the two again. But the real miracle occurred when my college-age son taught me how to use the mysterious footnote key on the computer, which makes it possible to insert the citations directly into the text while the sources are still in front of me, instead of shuffling through hundreds of folders four or five years down the line, trying desperately to remember from where I derived a particular statistic or quote. Still, there is no guarantee against error. Should one occur, all I can do, as I did 14 years ago, is to correct it as soon as I possibly can, for my own sake and the sake of history. In the end, I am still the same fallible person I was before I made the transition to the computer, and the process of building a lengthy work of history remains a complicated but honorable task.

After-Reading Activities

Analyzing the Content

1. In your own words, summarize the writer's dilemma and defence against the charges of plagiarism directed at her.

2. Outline the steps that Doris Kearns Goodwin used to ensure that she minimized the possibility of errors.

Structure and Style

3. Assess Goodwin's opening and closing paragraphs. How effective are they to her defence?

4. Examine paragraphs 4 and 5. How does Goodwin try to convince her readers that the task of writing a book is a significant undertaking?

5. Are you convinced by her defence? Why or why not?

6. Who is the audience of this essay? Explain.

7. How does this essay follow the pattern of process analysis? (You may refer back to your response to activity 2.)

How to Eat an Ice-Cream Cone

L . Rust Hills

Elements of the Essay

L. Rust Hills takes a lighthearted but exaggerated look at the simple task of eating an ice-cream cone. With underlying humour, he explains the process one step at a time, using occasionally lofty and technical language, imperative sentences, and diagrams to elevate the importance of this ordinary action.

About the Writer

L. Rust Hills was born in 1924 in Brooklyn, New York. A freelance writer of essays and short stories, he has also been the fiction editor of *Esquire* and *The Saturday Evening Post*. Two of his books are *Great Esquire Fiction: The Finest Stories from the First Fifty Years* (1983), a volume of short stories that he edited, and *Writing in General and the Short Story in Particular: An Informal Textbook* (1987). He has also published "how to" books, including *How to Do Things Right* (1972), in which this essay appeared.

BEFORE YOU EVEN GET the cone, you have to do a lot of planning about it. We'll assume that you lost the argument in the car and that the family has decided to break the automobile journey and stop at an ice-cream stand for cones. Get things straight with them right from the start. Tell them that after they have their cones there will be an imaginary circle six feet away from the car and that no one—man, woman, or especially child—will be allowed to cross the line and reenter the car until his ice-cream cone has been entirely consumed and he has cleaned himself up. Emphasize: Automobiles and ice-cream cones don't mix. Explain: Melted ice cream, children, is a fluid that is eternally sticky. One drop of it on a car-door handle spreads to the seat covers, to trousers, to hands, and thence to the steering wheel, the gearshift, the rearview mirror, all the knobs of the dashboard—spreads *everywhere* and

1

lasts *forever*, spreads from a nice old car like this, which might have to be abandoned because of stickiness, right into a nasty new car, in secret ways that even scientists don't understand. If necessary, even make a joke: "The family that eats ice-cream cones together sticks together." Then let their mother explain the joke and tell them you don't mean half of what you say, and no, we won't be getting a new car.

2   Blessed are the children who always eat the same flavor of ice cream or always know beforehand what kind they will want. Such good children should be quarantined from those who want to "wait and see what flavors there are." It's a sad thing to observe a beautiful young child who has always been perfectly happy with a plain vanilla ice-cream cone being subverted by a young schoolmate who has been invited along for the weekend—a pleasant and polite visitor, perhaps, but spoiled by permissive parents and scarred by an overactive imagination. This schoolmate has a flair for contingency planning: "Well, I'll have banana if they have banana, but if they don't have banana then I'll have peach, if it's fresh peach, and if they don't have banana or fresh peach I'll see what else they have that's like that, like maybe fresh strawberry or something, and if they don't have that or anything like that that's good I'll just have chocolate marshmallow chip or chocolate ripple or something like that." Then—turning to one's own once simple and innocent child, now already corrupt and thinking fast—the schoolmate invites a similar rigmarole. "What kind are *you* going to have?"

3   I'm a great believer in contingency planning, but none of this is realistic. Few adults, and even fewer children, are able to make up their minds beforehand what kind of ice-cream cone they'll want. It would be nice if they could all be lined up in front of the man who is making up the cones and just snap smartly when their turn came, "Strawberry, please," "Vanilla, please," "Chocolate, please." But of course it never happens like that. There is always a great discussion, a great jostling and craning of necks and leaning over the counter to see down into the tubs of ice cream, and much interpersonal consultation—"What kind are *you* having?"—back and forth, as if that should make any difference. Until finally the first child's turn comes and he asks the man, "What kinds do you have?"

4   Now, this is the stupidest question in the world, because there is always a sign posted saying what kinds of ice cream they have. As I tell the children, that's what they put the sign up for—so you won't have to ask what kinds of ice cream they have. The man gets sick of telling everybody all the different kinds of ice cream they have, so they put a

sign up there that *says*. You're supposed to read it, not ask the man.

"All right, but the sign doesn't say strawberry."   5

"Well, that means they don't have strawberry."   6

"But there *is* strawberry, right there."   7

"That must be raspberry or something." (Look again at the sign.   8
Raspberry isn't there, either.)

When the child's turn actually comes, he says, "Do you have   9
strawberry?"

"Sure."   10

"What other kinds do you have?"   11

The trouble is, of course, that they put up that sign saying what   12
flavors they have, with little cardboard inserts to put in or take out
flavors, way back when they first opened the store. But they never
change the sign—or not often enough. They always have flavors that
aren't on the list, and often they don't have flavors that *are* on the list.
Children know this—whether innately or from earliest experience it
would be hard to say. The ice-cream man knows it, too. Even grownups
learn it eventually. There will always be chaos and confusion and mind-
changing and general uproar when ice-cream cones are being ordered,
and there has not been, is not, and will never be any way to avoid it.

Human beings are incorrigibly restless and dissatisfied, always in   13
search of new experiences and sensations, seldom content with the
familiar. It is this, I think, that accounts for people wanting to have a
taste of your cone, and wanting you to have a taste of theirs. "*Do* have a
taste of this fresh peach—it's delicious," my wife used to say to me, very
much (I suppose) the way Eve wanted Adam to taste her delicious apple.
An insinuating look of calculating curiosity would film my wife's eyes—
the same look those beautiful, scary women in those depraved Italian
films give a man they're interested in. "How's *yours?*" she would say. For
this reason, I always order chocolate chip now. Down through the years,
all those close enough to me to feel entitled to ask for a taste of my
cone—namely, my wife and children—have learned what chocolate chip
tastes like, so they have no legitimate reason to ask me for a taste. As for
tasting other people's cones, never do it. The reasoning here is that if it
tastes good, you'll wish you'd had it; if it tastes bad, you'll have had a
taste of something that tastes bad; if it doesn't taste either good or bad,
then you won't have missed anything. Of course no person in his right
mind ever *would* want to taste anyone else's cone, but it is useful to have
good, logical reasons for hating the thought of it.

14   Another important thing. Never let the man hand you the ice-cream cones for the whole group. There is no sight more pathetic than some bumbling disorganized papa holding four ice-cream cones in two hands, with his money still in his pocket, when the man says, "Eighty cents." What does he do then? He can't hand the cones back to the man to hold while he fishes in his pocket for the money, for the man has just given them to *him*. He can start passing them out to the kids, but at least one of them will have gone back to the car to see how the dog is doing, or have been sent round in back by his mother to wash his hands or something. And even if papa does get them distributed, he's still going to be left with his own cone in one hand while he tries to get his money with the other. Meanwhile, of course, the man is very impatient, and the next group is asking him, "What flavors do you have?"

15   No, never let the man hand you the cones of others. Make him hand them out to each kid in turn. That way, too, you won't get those disgusting blobs of butter pecan and black raspberry on your own chocolate chip. And insist that he tell you how much it all costs and settle with him *before* he hands you your own cone. Make sure everyone has got paper napkins and everything *before* he hands you your own cone. Get *everything* straight before he hands you your own cone. Then, as he hands you your own cone, reach out and take it from him. Strange, magical, dangerous moment! It shares something of the mysterious, sick thrill that soldiers are said to feel on the eve of a great battle.

16   Now, consider for a moment just exactly what it is that you are about to be handed. It is a huge, irregular mass of ice cream, faintly domed at the top from the metal scoop, which has first produced it and then insecurely balanced it on the uneven top edge of a hollow inverted cone made out of the most brittle and fragile of materials. Clumps of ice cream hang over the side, very loosely attached to the main body. There is always much more ice cream than the cone could hold, even if the ice cream were tamped down into the cone, which of course it isn't. And the essence of ice cream is that it melts. It doesn't just stay there teetering in this irregular, top-heavy mass; it also melts. And it melts *fast*. And it doesn't just melt—it melts into a sticky fluid that *cannot* be wiped off. The only thing one person could hand to another that might possibly be more dangerous is a live hand grenade from which the pin had been pulled five seconds earlier. And of course if anybody offered you that, you could say, "Oh. Uh, well—no thanks."

17   Ice-cream men handle cones routinely, and are inured. They are like

professionals who are used to handling sticks of TNT; their movements are quick and skillful. An ice-cream man will pass a cone to you casually, almost carelessly. Never accept a cone on this basis! Too many brittle sugar cones (the only good kind) are crushed or chipped or their ice-cream tops knocked askew, by this casual sort of transfer from hand to hand. If the ice-cream man is attempting this kind of brusque transfer, keep your hands at your side, no matter what effort it may cost you to overcome the instinct by which everyone's hand goes out, almost automatically, whenever he is proffered something delicious and expected. Keep your hands at your side, and the ice-cream man will look up at you, startled, questioning. Lock his eyes with your own, and *then*, slowly, calmly, and above all deliberately, take the cone from him.

Grasp the cone with the right hand firmly but gently between thumb and at least one but not more than three fingers, two-thirds of the way up the cone. Then dart swiftly away to an open area, away from the jostling crowd at the stand. Now take up the classic ice-cream-cone-eating stance: feet from one to two feet apart, body bent forward from the waist at a twenty-five-degree angle, right elbow well up, right forearm horizontal, at a level with your collar-bone and about twelve inches from it. But don't start eating yet! Check first to see what emergency repairs may be necessary. Sometimes a sugar cone will be so crushed or broken or cracked that all one can do is gulp at the thing like a savage, getting what he can of it and letting the rest drop to the ground, and then evacuating the area of catastrophe as quickly as possible. Checking the cone for possible trouble can be done in a second or two, if one knows where to look and does it systematically. A trouble spot some people overlook is the bottom tip of the cone. This may have been broken off. Or the flap of the cone material at the bottom, usually wrapped over itself in that funny spiral construction, may be folded in a way that is imperfect and leaves an opening. No need to say that through this opening—in a matter of perhaps thirty or, at most, ninety seconds—will begin to pour hundreds of thousands of sticky molecules of melted ice cream. You know in this case that you must instantly get the paper napkin in your left hand under and around the bottom of the cone to stem the forthcoming flow, or else be doomed to eat the cone far too rapidly. It is a grim moment. No one wants to eat a cone under that kind of pressure, but neither does anyone want to end up with the bottom of the cone stuck to a messy napkin. There's one other alternative—one that takes both skill and courage: Forgoing any cradling

18

action, grasp the cone more firmly between thumb and forefinger and extend the other fingers so that they are out of the way of the dripping from the bottom, then increase the waist-bend angle from twenty-five degrees to thirty-five degrees, and then eat the cone, *allowing* it to drip out of the bottom onto the ground in front of you! Experienced and thoughtful cone-eaters enjoy facing up to this kind of sudden challenge.

19   So far, we have been concentrating on cone problems, but of course there is the ice cream to worry about, too. In this area, immediate action is sometimes needed on three fronts at once. Frequently the ice cream will be mounted on the cone in a way that is perilously lopsided. This requires immediate corrective action to move it back into balance—a slight pressure downward with the teeth and lips to seat the ice cream more firmly in and on the cone, but not so hard, of course, as to break the cone. On other occasions, gobs of ice cream will be hanging loosely from the main body, about to fall to the ground (bad) or onto one's hand (far, far worse). This requires instant action, too; one must snap at the gobs like a frog in a swarm of flies. Sometimes, trickles of ice cream will already (already!) be running down the cone toward one's fingers, and one must quickly raise the cone, tilting one's face skyward, and lick with an upward motion that pushes the trickles away from the fingers and (as much as possible) into one's mouth. Every ice-cream cone is like every other ice-cream cone in that it potentially can present all of these problems, but each ice-cream cone is paradoxically unique in that it will present the problems in a different order of emergency and degree of severity. It is, thank God, a rare ice-cream cone that will present all three kinds of problems in exactly the same degree of emergency. With each cone, it is necessary to make an instantaneous judgment as to where the greatest danger is, and to *act!* A moment's delay, and the whole thing will be a mess before you've even tasted it *(Fig. 1)*. If it isn't possible to decide between any two of the three basic emergency problems (i.e., lopsided mount, dangling gobs, running trickles), allow yourself to make an arbitrary adjudication; assign a "heads" value to one and a "tails" value to the other, then flip a coin to decide which is to be tended to first. Don't, for heaven's sake, *actually* flip a coin— you'd have to dig in your pocket for it, or else

(Fig. 1)

have it ready in your hand before you were handed the cone. There isn't remotely enough time for anything like that. Just decide *in your mind* which came up, heads or tails, and then try to remember as fast as you can which of the problems you had assigned to the winning side of the coin. Probably, though, there isn't time for any of this. Just do something, however arbitrary. Act! *Eat!*

In trying to make wise and correct decisions about the ice-cream cone in your hand, you should always keep the objectives in mind. The main objective, of course, is to get the cone under control. Secondarily, one will want to eat the cone calmly and with pleasure. Real pleasure lies not simply in eating the cone but in eating it *right*. Let us assume that you have darted to your open space and made your necessary emergency repairs. The cone is still dangerous—still, so to speak, "live." But you can now proceed with it in an orderly fashion. First, revolve the cone through the full three hundred and sixty degrees, snapping at the loose gobs of ice cream; turn the cone by moving the thumb away from you and the forefinger toward you, so the cone moves counterclockwise. Then, with the cone still "wound," which will require the wrist to be bent at the full right angle toward you, apply pressure with the mouth and tongue to accomplish overall realignment, straightening and settling the whole mess. Then, unwinding the cone back through the full three hundred and sixty degrees, remove any trickles of ice cream. From here on, some supplementary repairs may be necessary, but the cone is now defused.

At this point, you can risk a glance around you. How badly the others are doing with their cones! Now you can settle down to eating yours. This is done by eating the ice cream off the top. At each bite, you must press down cautiously, so that the ice cream settles farther and farther into the cone. Be very careful not to break the cone. Of course, you never take so much ice cream into your mouth at once that it hurts your teeth; for the same reason, you never let unmelted ice cream into the back of your mouth. If all these procedures are followed correctly, you should shortly arrive at the ideal—the way an ice-cream cone is always pictured but never actually is when it is handed to you *(Fig. 2)*. The ice cream should now form a small dome whose circumference exactly coincides with the large circumference

(Fig. 2)

20

21

of the cone itself—a small skullcap that fits exactly on top of a larger, inverted dunce cap. You have made order out of chaos; you are an artist. You have taken an unnatural, abhorrent, irregular, chaotic form, and from it you have sculpted an ordered, ideal shape that might be envied by Praxiteles or even Euclid.

22   Now at last you can begin to take little nibbles of the cone itself, being very careful not to crack it. Revolve the cone so that its rim remains smooth and level as you eat both ice cream and cone in the same ratio. Because of the geometrical nature of things, a constantly reduced inverted cone still remains a perfect inverted cone no matter how small it grows, just as a constantly reduced dome held within a cone retains *its* shape. Because you are constantly reshaping the dome of ice cream with your tongue and nibbling at the cone, it follows in logic—and in actual practice, if you are skillful and careful—that the cone will continue to look exactly the same, except for its size, as you eat it down, so that at the very end you will hold between your thumb and forefinger a tiny, idealized replica of an ice-cream cone, a thing perhaps one inch high. Then, while the others are licking their sticky fingers, preparatory to wiping them on their clothes, or going back to the ice-cream stand for more paper napkins to try to clean themselves up—*then* you can hold the miniature cone up for everyone to see, and pop it gently into your mouth.

After-Reading Activities

Analyzing the Content

1. Explain what the illustrations (Fig. 1 and Fig. 2) add to this essay. Suggest and draw an idea for a third figure, and explain where it would be placed in the essay.

2. Create a rubric for eating an ice-cream cone based on the criteria presented in this essay.

Structure and Style

3. What do you think is L. Rust Hills' main purpose in this essay?

4. Describe the tone of this essay. How does Hills create this tone? Assess

whether the tone is appropriate for the subject matter of the essay. Is it appropriate for the main purpose of the essay you identified in activity 3? Would any other tone be appropriate?

5. Considering its subject matter, this essay contains some difficult vocabulary. Make a list of challenging or unfamiliar words in the essay. Give reasons to explain why the writer might have included them.

6. Assess the length of this essay. Is it too long for the topic? If you were the editor of the magazine in which it appeared, what, if anything, would you cut?

7. How does the writer use analogy and narration in this essay?

How to Write a Test

Eileen A. Brett

Elements of the Essay

While L. Rust Hills' "How to Eat an Ice-Cream Cone" approaches an ordinary task with exaggeration and humour, Eileen A. Brett's "How to Write a Test" approaches a serious task with lightheartedness. Providing tips on writing a test, Brett takes the reader logically through each step from entering the classroom and choosing a seat to waiting for the test results. Her point of view and tone draw in her audience while she proves that "writing tests need not be a frightening experience."

About the Writer
Eileen Brett was a student at the University of British Columbia when she wrote this essay and submitted it for publication to *Contest: Essays by Canadian Students*, Second Edition, edited by Robert Hookey and Joan Pilz (1994).

1 I T IS THE DAY OF THE final exam or perhaps it is just a unit quiz. (Of course, in today's academic courses, when entire grades are sometimes comprised of quiz marks, there is no such thing as a mere quiz.) Whether quiz, test, or examination, does the very suggestion of being tested induce fear and panic? Rest assured; writing tests need not be a frightening experience. If you sit in a place without distractions, bring the right tools, relax, think positively, and organize yourself, you will survive the experience. You may even surprise yourself by doing well on the test.

Question opener

Controlling idea

Blueprint for how the essay will be organized

2 As you enter the classroom the day of the test, your first priority should be to choose where to sit. The important point here is not to find the most comfortable seat but to avoid windows. When a task of importance is unpleasant, eyes tend to wander toward windows and

Before the test. Develops #1 in blueprint

scenes of interest outside. When this happens, inevitably, concentration is relaxed. Equally distracting can be a seat at the back of the room where the back view of any number of attractive blondes or rugged athletes will be in your direct line of vision. Always choose a seat in the front row.

Develops #2 in blueprint

To be prepared you will have brought with you at least two pens and one pencil accompanied by a bottle of correction fluid, an eraser, and a watch. Often I have forgotten this last item and suffered tremendously from judging incorrectly how much time remained. These are the essential tools of any test. The pencil may be used substantially more than the pen, for reasons that will be discussed later. One pencil is sufficient, since the walk to the pencil sharpener provides a practical excuse to exercise leg muscles. I stress, however, that this is not an opportunity to cheat. The walk over to the pencil sharpener is not only a form of physical release, it is also a "brain break." However short this walk may be, the brain welcomes the chance to escape deep mental concentration for the non-strenuous act of sharpening a pencil.

3

Develops #3 in blueprint

Many students spend the remaining few minutes before the test cramming crucial bits of information into their heads. This effort is wasteful since, in my experience, last minute cramming serves to confuse and is not actually remembered anyway. Why not, instead, spend those moments in mental relaxation and deep breathing? At the same time, analyze the mood in the room. If absolutely everyone else, not having read these helpful hints, is deeply engrossed in last minute preparation, this is a fairly positive indication that the exam will be a difficult one. In this case, it is best that you breathe deeply rather than analyze. If, on the other hand, the majority is calm, cool, and collected, either the test is going to be easy or you have got the date wrong. In both cases, you have nothing to worry about.

4

Develops #4 in blueprint

The interval between the time the test is placed in front of you and the time you are told you may begin is the time to take the Attitude Adjustment Approach,

5

which concerns the mindset in which you will commence writing the exam. During this time, students who want only to scrape by will decide to put minimum effort into the exam. In contrast, students who want a good, if not exceptional, grade will use this time to prepare mentally for the challenge ahead.

6   As the examination begins, take a moment to glance through the test. The decision as to where to start is yours. However, a word to the wise: multiple choice questions should be attacked first for two reasons. First, tidbits of information can often be gleaned from them and then reworked to fit nicely (and inconspicuously) into sentence answers or essays. Second, since the answer is right in front of you, multiple choice questions are the least painful way of easing into the task ahead.

As the test begins

7   In examinations, an organized student has the advantage over a disorganized student. An organized system for writing tests involves using a pen or pencil, depending on how confident you are with the material. Those answers of which you are fairly certain should be answered in pen. Otherwise, pencils are ideal for answering tests because answers can be changed easily. However, since numerous studies have found that, particularly with multiple choice, the first answer chosen is most often the correct one, be 110 percent sure before you change an answer. Should time permit double-checking, it will be necessary to review only those answers in pencil as answers in pen are likely to be correct. If an answer is elusive, make a mark beside the question so you will be able to quickly identify those questions to which you did not know the answers. Then move on and go back to them later.

During the test (paragraphs 7 to 9). Develops #5 in blueprint

8   A few techniques have been developed for writing essays. Of course, understanding exactly what the question is asking is essential. If, for example, there is more than one essay question, ideas may flow more freely if you switch back and forth among them. When I begin to get frustrated for lack of ideas, often new

thoughts will surface as I answer another question and I will quickly jot them down. Still, other people find staying with one essay until it is completed more beneficial. If all else fails, use the technique of free-writing: write on anything that is even remotely connected with the essay topic until you feel inspired. But perhaps you should take a brain break.

The technique you choose is of less importance, though, than the interest level of your essays. Not many teachers enjoy perusing forty essay exams on "The Effect of Green Pesticides on Small Herbivores." If you want a good mark, you will strive to keep the professor not only awake but also excited at your discussion of genetic differences in field mice. Imagination is a wonderful asset, but if it is not one of yours, description or examples are also effective. Easy reading is also enhanced by grammatically correct writing.

Finishing the test

Before you finish the exam, remember to finish those multiple choice questions that you had found impossible to answer. If the process of elimination does not yield an answer that is satisfactory, depending on the amount of time remaining, one of two options is open: count up how many *A* answers you have, how many *B*, etc., and choose the letter that has the least number of answers; or take a reasonable guess. If all else fails, write your professor a note telling him or her of the immense satisfaction and enjoyment you derived from doing the exam, and extend holiday greetings. Then, with hope, you wait for the results and you trust that:

Humorous conclusion

(a) Without your knowledge, your teacher has sent in several of your essays from the examination to Mensa, which extends the honour of membership to you.

(b) The test was for the government, which does not care anyway.

(c) The teacher appreciated your note.

After-Reading Activities

Analyzing the Content

1. Identify the most and least valuable advice presented in the essay, and explain your choices.

Structure and Style

2. What do you think is Brett's main purpose in this essay?

3. Examine the margin annotations in this essay. What do they tell you about how the writer has organized her essay? What other order might have been used?

4. Describe the tone Brett has used in this essay. Is it an appropriate tone for presenting this advice to senior students?

Extending the Pattern

1. In a style similar to the one used by Eileen Brett, write a paragraph presenting an additional piece of advice on how to write a test. Identify where your paragraph would best be placed if it were to be integrated into Brett's essay.

2. Write your own process analysis essay providing advice on one of the following:
   - how to write a research essay with proper documentation
   - how to do homework
   - how to buy a car
   - how to select a mate
   - how to eat a peach
   - a topic of your own choosing

   You may need to do additional research. After completing your first draft, work with a partner to revise and edit your essay, focusing on the logic of your organization and the clarity of your language.

Elements of the Pattern

A definition essay provides an extended explanation, or a definition, of a term, object, or concept. When writing this type of essay, you can help your reader by moving from the general to the specific. When any term is defined, it is common to begin by placing it in a context that is familiar to the reader. This is achieved by defining the term in relation to a larger "class" of objects or ideas. For instance, to define the word "tabby," you might begin by saying that a tabby is a type of cat. Since readers probably know what a cat is, they immediately gain a fuller understanding of what a tabby is. You would then proceed to describe the characteristics that are specific to a tabby.

One strategy for providing the specifics is to use examples or analogies (comparisons that focus on similarities between two objects that are otherwise not the same). Once again, this strategy is an attempt to give readers a familiar context. When using this strategy, provide one example per paragraph. Present the example, and then explain why it is a good representation of the term being defined. Another strategy is to use "negation." This is a strategy of providing an example of what your term is *not*. When using negation, pair it with a statement describing what your term *is*. For example, you might say, "A tabby is not a big cat like a cougar, lion, or tiger. It is a small domesticated cat that may be kept as a pet in a home."

The essays in this section define "television addiction," "trompe-l'oeil," and "victims and agents." As you read each essay, note the strategies that the writer uses to establish familiar contexts to help readers understand the term, object, or concept being discussed.

Television Addiction

Marie Winn

Elements of the Essay

Excerpted from a chapter in Marie Winn's book *The Plug-In Drug: Television, Computers, and Family Life*, 25th Anniversary Edition (2002), this essay defines and examines the modern phenomenon of television addiction. Using a combination of definition and comparison and contrast structures, Winn presents an analysis of television addiction. (Note: For another discussion of the effects of television watching, see Philip Marchand's essay, "We're Mesmerized by the Flickering Tube," pages 153 to 157.)

About the Writer

Born in Czechoslovakia, Marie Winn has lived in the United States much of her life. A writer who explores a wide range of topics, she has written books about children, and columns for *The Wall Street Journal* about nature and bird watching. Her interest in the latter has resulted in a book of fiction, *Red-Tails in Love: A Wildlife Drama in Central Park* (1998). Besides writing, she has also translated books written in Czech.

THE WORD "ADDICTION" IS often used loosely and wryly in conversation. People will refer to themselves as "mystery-book addicts" or "cookie addicts." E.B. White wrote of his annual surge of interest in gardening: "We are hooked and are making an attempt to kick the habit." Yet nobody really believes that reading mysteries or ordering seeds by catalogue is serious enough to be compared with addictions to heroin or alcohol. In these cases the word "addiction" is used jokingly to denote a tendency to overindulge in some pleasurable activity.

People often refer to being "hooked on TV." Does this, too, fall into the lighthearted category of cookie eating and other pleasures that people pursue with unusual intensity? Or is there a kind of television viewing that falls into the more serious category of destructive addiction?

Not unlike drugs or alcohol, the television experience allows the participant to blot out the real world and enter into a pleasurable and passive mental state. To be sure, other experiences, notably reading, also provide a temporary respite from reality. But it's much easier to stop reading and return to reality than to stop watching television. The entry into another world offered by reading includes an easily accessible return ticket. The entry via television does not. In this way, television viewing, for those vulnerable to addiction, is more like drinking or taking drugs—once you start it's hard to stop.

4   Just as alcoholics are only vaguely aware of their addiction, feeling that they control their drinking more than they really do ("I can cut it out any time I want—I just like to have three or four drinks before dinner"), many people overestimate their control over television watching. Even as they put off other activities to spend hour after hour watching television, they feel they could easily resume living in a different, less passive style. But somehow or other while the television set is present in their homes, it just stays on. With television's easy gratifications available, those other activities seem to take too much effort.

5   A heavy viewer (a college English instructor) observes:

> I find television almost irresistible. When the set is on, I cannot ignore it. I can't turn it off. I feel sapped, will-less, enervated. As I reach out to turn off the set, the strength goes out of my arms. So I sit there for hours and hours.

6   Self-confessed television addicts often feel they "ought" to do other things—but the fact that they don't read and don't plant their garden or sew or crochet or play games or have conversations means that those activities are no longer as desirable as television viewing. In a way, the lives of heavy viewers are as unbalanced by their television "habit" as drug addicts' or alcoholics' lives. They are living in a holding pattern, as it were, passing up the activities that lead to growth or development or a sense of accomplishment. This is one reason people talk about their television viewing so ruefully, so apologetically. They are aware that it is an unproductive experience, that by any human measure almost any other endeavor is more worthwhile.

7   It is the adverse effect of television viewing on the lives of so many people that makes it feel like a serious addiction. The television habit distorts the sense of time. It renders other experiences vague and curiously unreal while taking on a greater reality for itself. It weakens relationships by reducing and sometimes eliminating normal

opportunities for talking, for communicating.

And yet television does not satisfy, else why would the viewer continue to watch hour after hour, day after day? "The measure of health," wrote the psychiatrist Lawrence Kubie, "is flexibility ... and especially the freedom to cease when sated."[1] But heavy television viewers can never be sated with their television experiences. These do not provide the true nourishment that satiation requires, and thus they find that they cannot stop watching. ...

8

In the early 1980s Robin Smith, a graduate student at the University of Massachusetts in Amherst, conducted a research study on television addiction as part of a doctoral dissertation.[2] Setting out to discover whether television viewing can truly be classified as an addiction according to a particular, narrow definition she had constructed from the work of various social scientists, Smith sent out a questionnaire to 984 adults in Springfield, Massachusetts, in which they were asked to rate their own behavior in regard to television viewing. Using a number of statistical tests to analyze the responses, the author concluded that the results failed to confirm that television addiction exists. "Television addiction does not appear to be a robust phenomenon," Smith wrote in that poetic yet obscure way academics sometimes have of expressing things.

9

Striving to understand why television is so widely considered an addiction, in the conclusion of her research paper Smith noted:[3]

10

... the popularity of television as "plug-in drug" is enduring. One possible source of this image lies in the nature of viewing experience. The only study to date that examines the nature of the viewing experience in adults found that television watching, of all life activities measured in the course of one week, was the least challenging, involved the least amount of skill, and was most relaxing.

If television viewing is so bereft of value by most measures of well-being, and yet takes up the greatest part of people's leisure hours, it becomes moot whether it is defined as an addiction or simply a powerful habit. As psychologists Robert Kubey and Mihaly Csikszentmihalyi concluded in their book about the television experience: "A long-held habit becomes so ingrained that it borders on addiction. A person may no longer be watching television because of simple want, but because he or she virtually has to. Other alternatives may seem to become progressively more remote. What might have been a choice years earlier is now a necessity."[4]

11

Robert Kubey explains further: "While television can provide

12

relaxation and entertainment ... it still rarely delivers any lasting fulfillment. Only through active engagement with the worlds we inhabit and the people in them can we attain for ourselves the rewards and meaning that lead to psychological well-being."[5]

Notes

[The following are Winn's notes.]

1. Lawrence Kubie, *Neurotic Distortion and the Creative Process*. Lawrence: University of Kansas Press, 1958.
2. Robin Smith, "Television Addiction," in Jennings Bryant and Dolf Zillmann's *Perspectives on Media Effects*. Hillsdale, NJ: Lawrence Erlbaum Associates, 1986.
3. Source of Smith's definition of addiction: Solomon R.L. and Corbit J.D., "An opponent-process theory of motivation: I. Temporal dynamics of affect." *Psychological Review*, 81, 1974.
4. Robert Kubey and Mihaly Csikszentmihalyi, *Television and the Quality of Life: How Viewing Shapes Everyday Experiences*. Hillside, NJ: Lawrence Erlbaum, 1990.
5. Robert Kubey, "A Body at Rest Tends to Remain Glued to the Tube," *The New York Times*, August 5, 1990.

After-Reading Activities

Analyzing the Content

1. Explain how television addiction is like alcohol or drug addiction.

2. What does the writer mean when she says television cannot provide the "true nourishment that satiation requires" (paragraph 8)?

Structure and Style

3. Assess Marie Winn's opening paragraph. How effective is she in establishing her topic and drawing her readers' attention?

4. Why does the writer use quotations from other people within her essay? Is each one used effectively?

5. Reread the essay and note the types of transitions that Winn uses to link her ideas between paragraphs. Consider word transitions, thought transitions, and structural transitions.

6. Explain why it is more effective to use both definition and comparison and contrast as patterns of development rather than using definition by itself.

Eye Tricks

Mark Kingwell

Elements of the Essay

What is *trompe-l'oeil*? Why do artists pursue it in their work? What do philosophers think of it? These are the questions that Mark Kingwell explores in his essay, "Eye Tricks." The essay is structured as an extended definition, loosely following a chronological order, to explain the concept of *trompe-l'oeil*, "the trick on the eye." The essay, with its technical language and references to artists and philosophers, assumes a certain level of knowledge among its audience and may pose a challenge to the average reader.

About the Writer

Born in Toronto in 1963, philosopher and cultural critic Mark Kingwell studied at the University of Toronto, Edinburgh University, and Yale University. He currently teaches philosophy at the University of Toronto. He has published several books, notably, *Better Living: In Pursuit of Happiness from Plato to Prozac* (1998), which was awarded the Drummer-General's Award for Non-Fiction, and *Canada: Our Century* (1999), a commercially successful photographic history of Canada that he co-wrote.

T HE FALL FASHION RUNWAYS were mysteriously filled with it: painted lapels and false pockets from Cacharel, the shadows of buttons or false seams embroidered on a blazer by Anna Sui or a dress from Carol Christian Poell, fake stitched-on hands clasping the waist on a François Lesage couture belt, Elsa Schiaparelli's full-length dress with various illusory rips and tears painted and screened on the fabric. Meanwhile, the interior designs of Mark Paradine Cullup and John Carter, the same thing: lush landscapes glued to the flat wall, sly details (a dog's bone, a footprint) painted onto a kitchen floor, a London flat made to resemble a Renaissance Italian palazzo. For £10,000, in fact, Carter will paint Gabrielle and her sister bathing naked in your tub.

   In an era in which illusion and reality are supposed to be thoroughly

1

2

entwined—when the old metaphysical distinction between appearance and reality is no longer supposed to apply—we are suddenly fetched by *trompe-l'oeil*, the oldest trick in the book. You might even call it the trick that wrote the book, in fact, because *trompe-l'oeil*—the trick on the eye—is the implied motive of all representational art: the rendering in two dimensions of what is usually encountered in three, otherwise known as painting the world. Plato may have condemned mimetic art for its deceptiveness, its declension from Reality, but in so doing he succeeded only in lighting the fuse on a firebomb of metaphysical speculation and aesthetic invention. The history of Western civilization can thus be viewed as a series of successive, ever more elaborate attempts to turn the trick of representation: to make things present again through depiction or description, through art or science.

3   *Trompe-l'oeil* lies at the logical extreme of this grand mimetic project, the region where imitation goes a little too far and becomes split-second substitution. Here flat pigmented representation is so faithful to the non-flat original as to create a momentary optical illusion. The point is actually to fool the viewer into thinking the painted object—which is not an object at all, just the appearance of one—is real. Here re-presentation is indistinguishable from, well, presentation: the metaphysics of presence achieved through a piece of painterly sleight of hand. *Trompe-l'oeil* thus always threatens to become the slapstick end of art's spectrum, a mere pratfall. It is also a feat of representation whose surface success (the little trick) works paradoxically to expose the deep failure of all mimeses (the big trick): in a contest between the world and its representation, the former must always win. But in the right hands, *trompe-l'oeil* invites a deeper reflection. It interrogates the nature of reality, and the reality of nature.

4   Like all tricks, *trompe-l'oeil* has a cheerful exterior and a heart of cold, hard stone. Pliny the Elder relates the story of an ancient *trompe-l'oeil* competition in which the artist Zeuxis deceived half-starved birds into thinking his painted grapes were real, and Shaftesbury tells a story of a slain-rabbit painting so life-like it drove the artist's hungry dog to tear it to pieces. The impecunious apprentices of Giotto's studio bent over to pick up dropped coins—only to find them painted on the floor. Gotcha! But that cruelty cuts both ways. Zeuxis came second in that particular contest when he tried to lift a drape partially covering the canvas of his rival Parrhasios, only to find it was painted on. Giorgio Vasari, the Renaissance critic and pupil of Michelangelo, tells us that Giotto fooled

his own master Cimabue into trying to brush away a painted fly. No, no, gotcha back!

Illusionism was a staple of seventeenth-century Dutch and Flemish   5
art, a key element of that era of highly skilled landscape and still-life painting. Contemporary advances in the sciences of optics, zoology and botany, combined with new precision and range in oil-based pigments, made *trompe-l'oeil* techniques popular within a repertoire of optical-illusion projects of the period, including the perspective box and the camera obscura. Insect specimens were painted to throw shadows on cream-coloured canvas parchments; gorgeous vistas beckoned through non-existent windows and arches.

But this was no longer mere sleight of hand, trickery for its own sake.   6
The pious artists of the period saw their imitations as inherently devotional, microcosmic tributes to the glory of God's creation. Deception, or the creation of falsely ideal images, was actually a form of praise for the bounty of the Supreme Being. Even the most perfect still-lifes took care to include reminders of worldly evanescence, such *memento mori* as wilted flowers among blooming ones, worms eating the flesh of nearly rotten fruit, and transient drops of dew.

The artist Samuel van Hoogstraten, a pupil of Rembrandt, made   7
these devices a specialty, among other things painting a famous view of a corridor, showing a progression of spacious rooms that the London merchant Thomas Povey had installed behind the door to a very small room. Povey would throw the door open for visitors, and the false perspective, complete with apparently startled dog and cat, actually startled his guests. "A perfect painting," wrote van Hoogstraten, is "a mirror of Nature, which makes the things that do not exist, appear to exist, and which deceives in an allowed, amusing and praiseworthy manner."

Play with perspective, brushwork and light was also, in its way, the   8
exact painterly illustration of the period's regnant philosophical debates. René Descartes, writing at the very time van Hoogstraten was setting out from Rembrandt's studio for stays in Rome, Vienna and London, began his epistemological project of radical doubt by considering the everyday problem of optical illusions. Our senses can deceive us, Descartes says, making a square tower appear round at a distance, or a straight stick appear broken in water. This unsettles trust in our own experience, pitching us into epistemological vertigo. What was a visual fascination for van Hoogstraten, Fabritius, and De Gheyn was for

Descartes a signal that deceptive appearances needed to be probed, that even commonplace knowledge must be shored up by some deeper certainty that the apparently real was really real. (He found this in his certain knowledge of himself and so, with God's help, got the world back. But not everyone is so sure.)

9   In the centuries that follow, the technique moved in and out of fashion, always popular but never entirely respectable. *Trompe-l'oeil* was a prominent feature of nineteenth-century French art, for example, when questions of appearance and reality once more raged. Parisian practitioners of the *trompe-l'oeil* art peddled their wares—detailed renderings of household objects, the contents of trouser pockets or desk drawers—near the city's famous Pont Neuf. There it joined a new generation of devices of optical illusion in the realm of popular entertainment, including the stereopticon and the panorama, those early precursors of 3-D movies and VR-generators, which brought views of natural wonders and distant skylines to everyone.

10   But over the past century, to paraphrase Tom Wolfe, artists have been more interested in painting the word than the world. Even representational art is, today, rarely preoccupied with the kind of exact imitation that is essential for *trompe-l'oeil*. Many painters simply lack the intricate skill required to erase the traces of human agency in the finished canvas or mural. Paint is more often spackled or splattered, sometimes to the point of becoming itself three-dimensional. Mimesis may be the origin of art, but in a world dominated by non-mimetic fashions—expressionist, conceptual, ironic—*trompe-l'oeil* seems little more than an outmoded party piece, a smart-alecky jape.

11   And yet, even in a swirl of post-modern trickery the basic lesson is still alive, if only as the implied limit case of all pigment-on-canvas efforts. The broken violin and recognizable hinges, doorknobs, or keyholes of early Picasso and Braque are little *trompe-l'oeil* flourishes, grace-note reminders of the very mimetic imperatives that are at the same time flouted in Cubism's larger project of fracturing the frame. De Chirico's loopy architecture and Magritte's second-order ironies—the exquisitely detailed *trompe-l'oeil* pipe which we are told is not a pipe at all—are, in their fractured way, deliberate allusions to those everyday objects depicted in earlier *trompe-l'oeil* efforts sold in the stalls along the Pont Neuf. Magritte's *The Titanic Days* shows the figure of a man attacking a woman, both superimposed on a single painted body, and his

Red Model depicts shoes complete with painted feet already in them—a conceit that inspired Pierre Cardin's actual 1986 shoes, bringing the fine art of painting back to the applied one of fashion.

Contemporary artists like David Bierk, who appropriates fragments of old high-realist images and frames them in concrete, rusted iron or brushed steel, keep the game alive after a different fashion: a deliberate use of mimetic art in non-mimetic ways, drawing attention to skill through the deployment of skill, and to ideas through the deployment of contextual shifts and sly commentary. (In many early works, Bierk would paint a big-idea word—Reality, Memory, Nature—on the appropriated image or detail, destabilizing its representational status and, at the same time, our comfort as viewers of recreated scenes and figures. Memory is never simple.)   12

Philosophy, for its part, has also largely abandoned the project of representation begun by Plato 25 centuries ago. The American philosopher Richard Rorty, author of an influential 1979 book called *Philosophy and the Mirror of Nature*, urged philosophers to give up the misleading picture of language and science as reflections or models of something "out there." Worlds, Rorty suggested in this now-classic statement of postmodernism, are made, not found; all so-called representations are really just inventions. In fact, the issue goes even deeper than that. Copies of copies of copies now proliferate to such an extent that the logic of original and copy, of reality and appearance, is obsolete. A long-standing, interlinked project of remembering and re-presenting is now overtaken by simulacral profusion and an attendant, general vertigo that is larger (and more encompassing, more all-pervasive) than the little joke of making two dimensions play at being three for an instant or two. The simulacrum is not a representation of anything; it is a free-floating signifier, a node of visual allusiveness without anything particular to allude to.   13

This Baudrillardian end game, the triumph of dizzying hyper-reality, would seem to render simple *trompe-l'oeil* superfluous or unworthy of our attention, its attempt at irony either too obvious or not quite up to scratch. And yet, a joke never gets old if you find new ways to make it. Perhaps that is why the trick on the eye resurfaces now as a fashionable technique amid pervasive visual confusion, a bravura performance, often in those zones that lie outside the museum or gallery: fashion, wallpaper, architecture, and urban art. These efforts work to push the epistemological envelope, to dislocate and amuse, not just imitate.   14

15   The artist Richard Haas, for example, recreates absent façades and long-gone shadows in huge *trompe-l'oeil* murals in downtown buildings, jarring the workaday perceptions of city dwellers. His painted backdrop for the Byham Theater in Pittsburgh shows the interior of a steel mill, a reminder of the city's gritty foundation. The mural on Toronto's Flatiron Building, of wallpaper peeling away from the façade, is a small-scale version of the same thing.

16   There is a risk here, certainly. *Trompe-l'oeil* works its magic only if there is some chance of deception, however small. Accustomed to distortions and manipulations of the visual field, we are perhaps not as likely as Zeuxis or Cimabue to be actually fooled. We have, moreover, lived through unfortunate developments like the long-sleeved tuxedo T or the chambray shirt with a stitched pair of Ray-Bans in the pocket—things that tend to give *trompe-l'oeil* a bad name. That's why some of the recent *trompe-l'oeil*, in the fashion spreads and would-be witty interior designs, seems to have surrendered the original appearance/reality mediation, that little frisson of sensory doubt, in favour of kitsch or camp efforts that draw self-conscious, sometimes overbearing attention to the fakery. The purported trickery is not even a real attempt at deception, in other words. We have not an appearance masquerading as a reality, only an appearance of an appearance of doing so. We get the joke before the joke even has a chance to get us.

17   This can be charming, but the larger gag is now on everybody. Predictable or too-knowing *trompe-l'oeil* threatens to become a device deployed to no purpose, illusion drained of wonder. A trick should never be just a trick. Surrender yourself and take *trompe-l'oeil's* challenge a little more seriously. Trumping the eye even for a moment reminds us that the truly interesting proliferation in the visual realm is not of copies, but of questions. What's real? What's apparent? Can we ever make a distinction? The mesmerizing possibility raised by *trompe-l'oeil* is not that optical illusion might succeed—that, after all, is easy—but rather that knowledge itself might not. Double gotcha!

After-Reading Activities

Analyzing the Content

1. a) What is the most basic definition of *trompe-l'oeil* found in this essay?
   b) Summarize the ways *trompe-l'oeil* has changed since its inception.

2. a) Look up and define the following words contained in this essay, stating the etymology of each word where possible: "mimesis" (mimetic) (paragraph 2); "metaphysical" (paragraph 2); "aesthetic" (paragraph 2); "impecunious" (paragraph 4); "regnant" (paragraph 8); "epistemological" (paragraph 8); "jape" (paragraph 10); "simulacral" (paragraph 13); "frisson" (paragraph 16).
   b) Using print or electronic sources, look up the description of the following devices: perspective box and camera obscura (paragraph 5), stereopticon and panorama (paragraph 9).

Structure and Style

3. In your own words, write the thesis of this essay.

4. a) Identify the essay's purpose and intended audience, supporting your answer with specific examples from the essay.
   b) Describe the aspects of this essay that present challenges to the average reader, considering vocabulary, sentence structure and length, prior knowledge, and tone.

5. Comment on the effectiveness of the opening sentence in attracting the attention of the reader, introducing the topic, and sustaining interest to encourage the reader to finish the essay.

6. Mark Kingwell frequently uses colons in his writing. Find each occurrence and decide whether or not he could have used a different structure to achieve the clarity he was seeking.

7. This essay develops a definition of *trompe-l'oeil* by loosely following a chronological order. Is this an effective structure for the essay? Support your opinion.

Victims and Agents

Martha Nussbaum

Elements of the Essay

Martha Nussbaum's essay, "Victims and Agents," analyzes Sophocles' lead character in *Philoctetes*, an ancient Greek tragedy produced in 409 B.C., and applies the analysis to the modern world. Nussbaum moves back and forth between the ancient and the contemporary, defining the terms "victim" and "agent" in the context of law and society. Combining an extended definition with analogies and examples, and appealing to authorities as well as her personal experience for support, Nussbaum argues that society needs to develop a sense of human tragedy in order to have compassion for victims and agents.

About the Writer

Martha Nussbaum was born in 1947. She was educated at New York University and at Harvard University. She is noted for her study of feminist issues and ancient Greek philosophy, which are reflected in this essay. A multiple-award winner for her non-fiction books, Nussbaum has also written an award-winning novel, *Cultivating Humanity* (1998). Her most recent book is *Sex and Social Justice* (2000). Nussbaum is currently a professor of Law and Ethics at the University of Chicago.

---

1   THE PRINCIPAL CHARACTERS IN ancient Greek tragedy are often depicted as victims of circumstances beyond their control. They ask for compassion and help by pointing out that they are victims, that they did not bring disaster (enslavement, rape, hunger, death of loved ones) upon themselves. Consider one central case, Sophocles' *Philoctetes*, produced in 409 B.C. at a time when Athens, involved in a costly war, had good reason to ponder the toll taken on human beings by disasters not of their own making.

2   Philoctetes was a good man and a good soldier. On his way to Troy to fight with the Greeks in the Trojan War, he had a terrible accident.

He stepped by mistake into a sacred shrine, and his foot was bitten by the serpent who guarded the shrine. It began to ooze with a foul-smelling pus, and his cries of agony disrupted the religious observances of the troops. The commanders therefore abandoned him on a deserted island, with no resources but his bow and arrows. Ten years later, having learned that they cannot win the war without him, they return, determined to trick him into rejoining them. Sick, lonely, hungry, exhausted from hunting his own food, Philoctetes still longs for friendship and activity. He greets his visitors with joy, delighted that he can interact with others after his long solitude. And he asks them to have compassion for him, seeing the troubles that life has brought him, troubles from which no human is safe:

> … Have compassion for me.
> Look how men live, always precariously
> balanced between good and bad fortune.
> If you are out of trouble, watch for danger.
> And when you live well, then think the hardest
> About life, lest ruin take you unawares.

Compassion proves crucial to the subsequent plot. The younger of the two leaders, Neoptolemus, witnesses an attack of Philoctetes' terrible pain. At this point, he is seized by what he calls "a fearful compassion," a compassion that strikes terror into him because it makes him see that the plan to snare Philoctetes into helping the Greek war effort by deceit is morally wrong. Reflecting, he recognizes that they ought not to use this man merely as a means of political ends. Seeing Philoctetes in his pain, he sees him as human and therefore worthy of respect. Sympathy for weakness and respect for human agency are allies, because once Neoptolemus understands the magnitude of Philoctetes' suffering, he can no longer regard him as simply a thing to be manipulated, or an animal to be pushed around. He cries out in pain himself, with a sharp cry of *moral* pain (guilt at his deception) that mimics Philoctetes' inarticulate cry of bodily pain. From then on he refuses to lie to him, insisting that Philoctetes must be treated as someone entitled to decide without being manipulated.

In our society today, we often hear that we have a stark and binary choice between regarding people as agents and regarding them as victims. We hear this contrast in debates about social welfare programs: it is said that to give people various forms of social support is to treat

3

them as mere victims of life's ills, rather than to respect them as agents, capable of working to better their lot.

4   We hear the same contrast in recent feminist debates, where we are told that respecting women as agents is incompatible with a strong concern to protect them from rape, sexual harassment, and other forms of unequal treatment. To protect women is to presume that they can't fight on their own against this ill treatment: this, in turn, is to undermine their dignity by treating them as mere victims. For Katie Roiphe, for example, "the image that emerges from feminist preoccupations with rape and sexual harassment is that of women as victims,"[1] an image that reinforces an antiquated perception of women as frail and helpless. Betty Friedan, similarly, criticizes the rape-crisis movement: "Obsession with rape, even offering Band-Aids to its victims, is a kind of wallowing in that victim state, that impotent rage, that sterile polarization."[2] Naomi Wolf decries a "victim feminism" that "[c]harges women to identify with powerlessness."[3]

5   We hear the same contrast, again, in debates about criminal sentencing, where we are urged to think that any sympathy shown to a criminal defendant on account of a deprived social background or other misfortunes such as child sexual abuse is, once more, a denial of the defendant's human dignity. Supreme Court Justice Clarence Thomas, for example, went so far as to say, in a 1994 speech, that when black and poor people are shown sympathy for their background when they commit crimes, they are being treated like children, "or even worse, treated like animals without a soul."[4]

6   Interestingly, we do not take this attitude in all areas. Even if we believe that people are capable of much resourcefulness under adversity, we still hold that law should protect them against many of life's ills. We all know that writers and artists are capable of extraordinary resourcefulness and cunning when their freedom of speech is suppressed by a brutal regime: and yet we do not hold that we are undermining their dignity, or turning them into soulless victims, when we defend strong legal protections for the freedoms of speech and press, protections that make it unnecessary for them to struggle against tyranny in order to publish their work. Some people have held this: the philosopher Friedrich Nietzsche wrote that liberties of speech and press undermine "the will to assume responsibility for oneself," making people "small, cowardly, and hedonistic." Calling John Stuart Mill a "flathead," he pronounced that "[t]he highest type of free men should be sought where the highest

resistance is constantly overcome: five steps from tyranny, close to the threshold of the danger of servitude."[5] But we do not accept Nietzsche's view about liberty. Legal guarantees, we think, do not erode agency: they create a framework within which people can develop and exercise agency.

Again, we do not believe that strong law enforcement in the area of personal property turns property-holders into victims without dignity. Laws protect citizens from theft and fraud: these laws are backed up by state power, in the form of a police force supported by tax money. Nonetheless, we usually do not hear arguments that such uses of public money turn property owners into victims. Even though we are of course aware that people are sometimes capable of fighting to defend their homes and their possessions from theft, we think it's a lot better for law and the police to get involved, so people don't have to spend all their time fending off attack, and can get on with their other business. Often, Americans support even stronger protections of personal property, without thinking that in that way they are turning property owners into helpless victims. Those who support a repeal of the capital gains tax do not hold that this handout from the government would turn investors into victims without honor. Even though they are aware that investors are quite capable of doing pretty well even with current tax levels, they do not regard this legal change as producing passivity or turning people into soulless animals. If, then, we hear political actors saying such things about women, and poor people, and racial minorities, we should first of all ask why they are being singled out: what is there about the situation of being poor, or female, or black that turns help into condescension, compassion into insult?

The *Philoctetes*, I believe, helps us to understand this issue better. Greek tragedy is preoccupied with the portrayal of human beings as victims. As Aristotle says, its governing emotions, the emotions that hold the audience to the plot, are compassion and fear. Compassion, as he tells us, requires three thoughts: that the suffering we see is significant, has "size": that the suffering person did not deserve to suffer to this extent; and that we too share certain general human possibilities with the suffering person—so we too, or people we know and care about, may suffer similar catastrophes. The occasions for compassion that he mentions are the common bases of tragic plots: illness, old age, hunger, disability, solitude, loss of one's friends, loss of one's children, loss of one's citizenship or money or well-being. Sometimes people face such disasters because of their own wickedness: but, as Aristotle says, tragedy focuses on cases where this is not so, where a pretty good person gets hit very hard by life. Our compassion itself acknowledges that Philoctetes doesn't deserve to suffer as he does; and our fear acknowledges that something similar might happen to us, or someone dear to us.

9   So, that means, we are seeing Philoctetes as a victim. And so, commonly, we see a host of other tragic characters: women who get raped in wartime, little children who are sold into slavery, men who lose their families or see their loved ones being raped, and so on. When we see them as victims, we are seeing something true about them and about life: we see that people can be harmed on a large scale, in ways that even the best efforts cannot prevent. As the *Philoctetes* suggests, this gives people of good will strong incentives for doing something about such disasters, and bringing relief to the afflicted.

10   And further, the *Philoctetes* suggests that the victim shows us something about our own lives: we see that we are not any different from the people whose fate we are watching, that we too are vulnerable to misfortune, and that we therefore have reason to fear a similar reversal. But if we are ourselves vulnerable, we had better think about what we would wish if we were to find ourselves in a situation of tragic reversal. If people think themselves exempt from misfortune, they can easily harden themselves to the cry of the afflicted. But if they truly see their own vulnerability, they will move close in thought to the victims they see, and this very movement will lead them to want structures that provide support for people against life's ungovernable disasters. Rousseau puts it this way:

> Human beings are by nature neither kings nor nobles nor courtiers nor rich. All are born naked and poor, all are subject to the misfortunes of life, to difficulties, ills, needs, pains of all sorts. Finally, all are condemned to death.... Each may be tomorrow what the one whom he helps is today.... Do not, therefore, accustom your pupil to regard the sufferings of the unfortunate and the labors of the poor from the height of glory.... Make him understand well that the fate of these unhappy people can be his, that all their ills are there in the ground beneath his feet.... Show him all the vicissitudes of fortune.[6]

Rousseau thought that to focus on the pain of others, through stories that arouse emotion, was a good way of reminding people of the truth of their own condition and of giving them incentives to make the lot of the victim less bad than it would otherwise be.

But isn't this treating people as passive rather than active? Is this   11
victim role compatible with being seen as an agent? Entirely compatible,
as we see from Philoctetes' story. We see him as a victim, in the sense
that we see his loneliness, his poverty, his illness as things that he did not
bring upon himself. But we also are led by the play to see him as capable
of activity of many kinds. We hear him reason, we see his commitments
to friendship and justice. Seeing that he can't be active in some parts of
his life is fully compatible with observing that in other ways he remains
very active. Seeing this, we are led to admire the dignity with which he
confronts these ills, and to notice the yearning for full activity that he
displays even in the most acute misery.

It is precisely this combination of dignified agency with disaster out   12
of which the tragic response is made. If we just saw the hero as a worm
or an ant, a pathetic low creature grovelling in the mud, we would not
have the intense concern we do have with the forces that have inflicted
suffering on him. Sophocles takes great pains to show Philoctetes'
suffering as fully human: even when he screams out in unbearable pain,
his cry is metrical—a human cry of pain. What inspires our compassion
(and also our self-interested fear) is in fact this combination of human
dignity with disaster. It is because we respect his humanity that we come
to hate the forces that bear down upon him, and to think that
something ought to be done about them. It is precisely because
Philoctetes is shown to be capable of a human use of his faculties that
Neoptolemus eventually shrinks from treating him like an animal or a
thing. Tragedy shows us that disasters do strike at the heart of human
action: they don't just cause superficial discomfort, they impede
mobility, planning, citizenship, ultimately life itself. On the other hand,
when we see that such a disaster strikes a human being, it is then that we
feel the sense of tragic compassion: for we don't want humanity to be
wasted, or even callously pushed around.

Let me now return to the three contemporary issues, and see how   13
tragedy helps us think about them. We should begin by observing that
all Americans in countless ways receive financial assistance from the
government, and are highly dependent on that assistance. State money
and state power support laws without which most of us would not know
how to live: laws protecting public order, personal safety, private
property, the ability to make a binding contract, freedoms of assembly,
worship, speech, and press. Of course people could learn to live without

the expenditure of public money protecting those rights, but as a society we have decided that we think human agency is worthy of a basic concern that involves protecting these rights as prerequisites of meaningful human action.

14   Take the case of poverty and welfare reform. There are of course many complex empirical questions in this area, and this is why every society must experiment with programs and policies to understand their effects. It's not evident that direct relief is the best way to promote flourishing lives, and we should explore other alternatives. But there is one thing we should not say. We should not say that financial assistance for basic food, child welfare, and other prerequisites of meaningful human life is a way of dehumanizing people or turning them into passive victims. Human beings can struggle against all sorts of obstacles; frequently they succeed. But middle-class parents typically reveal in their own lives the belief that young children should not be hungry or neglected, that they should have the basic necessities of life provided to them so that they can develop their agency richly and fully. It is strange that we so often speak differently about the poor, suggesting that cutting off basic social support is a way of encouraging agency in poor mothers and children and improving their character, rather than a way of stifling agency, or stunting it before it gets a chance to develop. If we do respect agency and its dignity, we owe it a chance to develop and flourish.

15   The late Justice William Brennan made precisely this connection between dignity and luck in one of his most memorable opinions—in *Goldberg v. Kelly* (1970), a case that established that welfare rights could not be abridged without a hearing:

> From its founding the Nation's basic commitment has been to foster the dignity and well-being of all persons within its borders. We have come to recognize that forces not within the control of the poor contribute to their poverty.... Welfare, by meeting the basic demands of subsistence, can help bring within the reach of the poor the same opportunities that are available to others to participate meaningfully in the life of the community.... Public assistance, then, is not mere charity, but a means to "promote the general Welfare, and secure the Blessings of Liberty to ourselves and our Posterity."

It is certainly legitimate, and even desirable, for states to experiment with different welfare strategies. But something more sinister is currently in the air, a backing away from the "basic commitment" to dignity and well-being that Brennan finds, plausibly, at the heart of our traditions.

Think now of women who demand more adequate enforcement of laws against rape and sexual harassment. They are asking the state to do something about this problem. Are they therefore asking to be treated as people who have no ability to stand up for their rights? Of course not. Women do manage to struggle against sexual harassment. Most working women of my generation have done so—sometimes with relatively little damage to their careers, sometimes with great damage. But should women be required to wage this struggle? Or do we think that a woman's dignity demands that she not have to fight this struggle all the time, that part of the respect we owe to a woman as an agent is to let her get on with her work in an atmosphere free from such intimidation and pressure? It seems plausible that women will be more productive in the economy and in their homes with these pressures minimized.

Finally, let us consider Justice Thomas's observations about criminal defendants. This is the most difficult of the cases we have before us: it requires us to depart from the comfortable framework of ancient tragedy. Sophocles shows us good people whose suffering was not their own fault. Even in tragedy, however, we now notice, the distinction between innocent and blameworthy conduct is not always terribly clear. Aristotle insisted that the hero should not be shown as falling through wickedness, or deep-seated defect of character. He preferred plots where the bad consequence came about through a chain that involved a mistake of some type made by the leading character, sometimes innocent, but sometimes at least partly blameworthy. His general attitude to such errors was that we should be forgiving of people who go wrong, seeing the difficulty of judging well in circumstances of great complexity. So we may begin our response to Justice Thomas by pointing out that even basically good people go wrong, and that a forgiving attitude may be appropriate to the general frailty and weakness of human judgment. In judging a person's blameworthy errors in a forgiving spirit, we record that we ourselves are not perfect in judgment, even when we have the best intentions.

But what if the person who is asking for our sympathy is a criminal who has done bad things from a genuinely bad character? Justice Thomas says that it is insulting to a black defendant to treat him as not responsible for his criminal acts on account of a bad social background. To deny responsibility is to treat the criminal as no more than a "soulless animal." And this claim seems plausible if we were to say that people who

16

17

18

grow up in the inner city will all, as a group, be treated as not guilty by reason of insanity, that would indeed be to negate their human potential.

19   But this is not the way the issue typically comes up in the law. The law typically uses a conventional standard of sanity when assessing guilt or innocence, and introduces the deprived background in a separate phase of the trial, the sentencing phase, in order to plead for some leniency. And in fact, there is a long tradition in the law that this sympathetic assessment of the defendant's life story in the penalty phase, far from treating people like animals, is an essential part of treating them as fully human. An opinion written by Justice Potter Stewart in a 1976 capital sentencing case, *Woodson v. North Carolina*, held that a process lacking this opportunity to hear the life story

> excludes from consideration … the possibility of compassionate or mitigating factors stemming from the diverse frailties of humankind. It treats all persons convicted of a designated offense not as uniquely individual human beings, but as members of a faceless, undifferentiated mass.…

So Stewart is claiming more or less the opposite of what Thomas claimed: he says that when we *do not* take the opportunity to show compassion to a defendant's background, we treat that person as not fully human. What does he mean? The law's two-stage process asks us to assess guilt or innocence by looking to the state of mind with which the person did the act: if the person is not insane, he is responsible. But it says, as well, that people are not always fully in control of the factors that form their state of mind. And here we get back to tragedy. The standard tragic hero, like Philoctetes, grows to adulthood, becomes a good person, and then gets clobbered by life. But people get clobbered by life, sometimes, before they become good and grow to adulthood. The sentencing process recognizes that we may at times encounter a criminal who meets the conditions of basic responsibility, but whose moral development was subject to unusual hardships, and who therefore deserves to be seen as a kind of victim of life, one who did not get the support that life should have provided. When we recognize the "diverse frailties of humankind" and the way in which these are brought out by social circumstances, we recognize that few human beings are so firm that they can resist temptations to wrong, even under the prolonged effect of extremely bad circumstances. Sometimes they will make the type of error that is compatible with a basically good character. But sometimes damage has set in earlier, and the character itself is deformed by what it has encountered. Even this type of criminal defendant can be regarded as not a breed apart, intrinsically evil, but a human being like us, with diverse frailties and weaknesses, who has encountered circumstances— whether personal or social—that bring out those weaknesses in the worst possible way. And this, of course, creates incentives, once again, to think hard about those circumstances, so that we do not put people under pressures that many normal agents cannot stand.

In November 1996, I was mugged while walking from my office to a meeting on the other side of the Midway at 5 o'clock in the evening. My assailant was a short, timid, young black man, only about 5'2", wearing a thick parka and a blue wool hat. He said he had a gun, although I wasn't sure this was true: he seemed very inexperienced and tentative in his actions. After a certain amount of negotiation, I managed to get away losing only the cash in my wallet. But I spent some hours the next day in the police station, looking at hundreds of mug shots and talking to Officer Queenola Smith about the crime. I didn't find my suspect, and Officer Smith was not surprised. Given the recent cutbacks in welfare support and the high unemployment, she said, so many people have no money for their families, no warm clothes, and not enough food as winter approaches and the holidays draw close. So there are many new offenders.

Officer Smith was a very zealous officer; she boasted to me of the dangerous felons she had apprehended, the high-stakes chases she had conducted with aplomb. But she also had a sense of tragedy. And she saw these criminals not as a breed apart, but as members of her own community and her own race, who deserved a chance to exercise basic human agency, and therefore deserved the basic support to make that possible. Most who lose that support are like Philoctetes, good people hammered by circumstances, and it is—or at least it should be—easy to sympathize with them. But some get pushed harder and earlier, and don't resist the temptation to commit a crime. She did not deny that the mugger was responsible for his act. But she thought it was a humanly comprehensible act, an act many of us would have committed had we faced similar pressures. She saw my assailant as both victim and agent: someone trying to get a job, to support a family, someone hit hard by all kinds of circumstances, from the welfare cuts to unemployment to the harshness of the Chicago winter. She said in effect, see how hard it is to

20

21

be good, with adversities like these. Now Queenola Smith didn't think we should stop arresting these criminals—as I say, she was proud of her work. But, she argued, we should think hard about our own responsibility in creating a situation in which some people so unequally face poverty and closed doors, and also, therefore, the temptation to do wrong. That's what it would mean to take their human agency seriously, and not to treat them as animals who could not help being bad.

22   A few days later the president of the university phoned me and said, "I heard about this terrible thing that happened." And I felt that we were talking about the wrong event—for the loss of $40 by a professor was a trivial thing, compared to the tragedy that was going on all around us in our community. Who is the victim, and who the agent?

23   As a society we are in grave danger of losing our sense of tragedy. I am arguing that if we lose this sense of tragic compassion for people who unequally suffer the misfortunes of life—including both those who remain good and those who turn to the bad—we are in danger of losing our own humanity. We are in danger of forgetting something central about ourselves—that we don't become agents automatically; that our own relatively comfortable lives typically need, but also get, much support from government and from the material world; that we too would suffer terribly, and perhaps even become worse, were that support to be withdrawn. By thinking like the audience at an ancient tragedy, we may possibly move closer to building a community that does indeed "foster the dignity and well-being of all persons within its borders." "Thus from our weakness," Rousseau observed, "our fragile happiness is born."

Notes

[The following are Nussbaum's notes.]
1. Katie Roiphe. *The Morning After: Sex, Fear, and Feminism* (Boston: Little, Brown, 1993), p. 6.
2. Betty Friedan. *The Second Stage* (New York: Summit Books, 1981), p. 362.
3. Naomi Wolf. *Fire With Fire: The New Female Power and How to Use It* (New York: Fawcett, 1993), p. 136.
4. "Justice Thomas blames 'rights revolution' for increase in black crime." *Chicago Tribune*, 17 May 1994.
5. Friedrich Nietzsche, "Skirmishes of an Untimely One," from *Twilight of the Idols.* in *The Viking Portable Nietzsche*, ed. and trans. Walter Kaufmann (New York: Viking Penguin, 1959), section 38.
6. Jean Jacques Rousseau. *Emile*, trans. Allan Bloom (New York: Basic Books, 1979), pp. 222, 224. I have altered Bloom's translation in several places, in particular substituting "human being" for "man." [Nussbaum's note.]

After-Reading Activities

Analyzing the Content

1. Define the words "agents" and "agency" as they are used in this essay. Why is it important to double-check the meanings of familiar words?

2. Write a summary of "Victims and Agents." Start with the main point of the essay and show how the writer supports that point.

3. Why does the writer choose social welfare programs, protection of women, and criminal sentencing as the central foci of her discussion of victims and agents?

4. According to Martha Nussbaum, we do not believe that laws in support of freedom of speech or laws against theft or fraud create victims (paragraphs 6 and 7). Why not?

Structure and Style

5. Explain why Nussbaum has used Greek tragedy as a device to define "victims" and "agents."

6. Describe the tone of this essay. Use examples of the writing to support your opinion.

7. In her essay, Nussbaum appears to balance her position by presenting counterarguments to some of her points (paragraphs 3, 4, and 5; paragraphs 13 and 14). How does she control the counterarguments so that they do not outweigh her own points?

8. Nussbaum adds a personal anecdote at the end of this essay. What effect does this have on the reader? How does it enhance, or detract from, her thesis?

Extending the Pattern

Choose one of the following:

- Using Marie Winn's essay as a model, write an essay on addiction to the Internet. You may need to do additional research to develop your ideas and arguments.
- Find an example of a *trompe-l'oeil*, and write a review of it. Use definition and one other pattern of development in your review.
- Using print and/or electronic sources, find information on Stendahl's syndrome. Write an information essay (see pages 152 to 170) on this phenomenon using definition as your basic pattern but building in one of the other patterns from this book.
- Using definition as the primary organizational pattern, write about one of these topics: music popular with young people; cliques in schools; the best kind of pet; a bad hair day.
- Aristotle says that compassion and fear hold the audience's interest in a tragedy. Research a tragic story that has garnered public interest. Using Aristotle's definition of the essential elements of tragedy, write an essay explaining why the incident you have chosen has held the public's (the audience's) interest.

After completing your first draft, work with a partner to revise and edit your essay, focusing on the organization and the clarity of your definition.

Elements of the Pattern

A classification essay groups together similar items that share common characteristics in order to help readers gain a better understanding of these items. For example, when writing about cars, you might classify them into luxury, mid-range, and economy cars, and then define and describe each. You can help your readers by providing examples that fall within each class.

An important aspect of writing an effective classification essay is the careful definition of *distinct* categories. That is, you must ensure that the object you are defining *cannot* fit into more than one of the classes. For instance, say you were writing an essay about cars and you grouped them into luxury cars, economy cars, and imported cars. Such a classification is ineffective because it causes an overlap in that an import could be either a luxury car or an economy car.

As you read the following classification essays, take note of the categories the writers have used. How effective are they? Do they give you a better understanding of the subject?

It's Only a Paper World

Kathleen Fury

Elements of the Essay

Have computers cut down the amount of paper that we use in the workplace? This question is as pertinent today as it was when Kathleen Fury wrote "It's Only a Paper World" in 1986. With humour, she argues that offices have more paper now than ever before. Using analogies and caricatures, she describes and compares different types of individuals in the office and how each deals with paper. This essay is an effective model of the use of classification as an organizational pattern and has been studied by many students since its publication.

About the Writer

Kathleen Fury was born in 1941 in New York. She has been an editor and contributing writer for a variety of magazines, notably, *Ladies Home Journal* and *Working Woman*, the latter in which "It's Only a Paper World" first appeared. In 1989, Fury was acknowledged by Barbara Bush for her article about the former first lady's fight against illiteracy in America.

---

1   MANY EXPERTS CLAIMED THAT the computer age heralded the advent of the paperless office. Clearly, this is not to be. If anything, offices are overwhelmed by even more paper, much of it now with sprocket holes.

2   Humankind is adapting, fortunately. According to the dictates of our varied individual natures, we have developed ways of coping with our changing ecosystem.   Controlling idea

3   The <u>beaver</u> uses paper to build. It may not be exactly clear to observers just what she's building, but deep in her genetic code she knows.   Office Worker #1

4   On one side of the typical beaver's desk leans a foot-high stack of papers. Close by is a vertical file stuffed

with bulging folders, some waving in the air, unable to touch bottom. In between, the beaver constructs a clever "dam" to prevent the entire structure from falling over: Her two-tier In/Out box supports the pile and allows movement of papers from one place to another.

Incredibly, to nonbeaver observers, the beaver has an 5 uncanny ability to locate a two-month-old report buried within the pile. With deft precision, she can move her hand four millimeters down the pile and extract what she's looking for, confident that the dam will hold.

In this way, the beaver has evolved a protective 6 mechanism that makes her invaluable within the organization, for nobody else, including her secretary, can find anything on her desk. When the beaver goes away on vacation, her department simply ceases work until she returns. She is thus assured that the cliché "nobody's indispensable" doesn't apply to her.

The squirrel's desk, by contrast, is barren. 7 Throughout the year, in all kinds of weather, the squirrel energetically stores away what her brain tells her she may need someday. In her many file cabinets, drawers and bookcases she neatly stores memos, letters, printouts and receipts she believes will nourish her in the months and years to come.

Unlike her co-worker the beaver, the squirrel does 8 not always know exactly where she has hidden a particular item. She knows she *has* it but is not skilled at remembering the exact location.

Like the maple tree, which produces enough seeds to 9 reforest a continent, the squirrel illustrates nature's method of "overkill." By saving and storing everything, she increases her chance of retrieving something.

Of necessity, squirrels have developed the ability to 10 move through a wide territorial range. When a squirrel moves on to another job, as she tends to do rather often due to lack of space, management must hire a special team of search-and-destroy experts to go through her files.

Nature's scavengers, her "clean-up crew," crows are 11

Linking word to previous idea; transition
Office worker #2

Links to paragraphs 5 and 7; transition

Repetition of an idea to link paragraphs 10 and 11

Office worker #3

regarded with wary admiration by squirrels and beavers, who recognize their contribution to keeping the corporate ecosystem tidy.

12   Crows are responsible for such paper-management advice as "Act on it—or throw it away." They are deeply drawn to paper shredders, trash compactors and outsized waste receptacles and will buy them if they happen to work in purchasing.

13   Crows belie the common epithet "birdbrained," for it has taken centuries of evolution to create a mind disciplined enough to know with certainty that it is OK to throw the CEO's Statement of Corporate Policy in the wastebasket after a glance.

14   Other species, who must adapt to the corporate food chain, quickly learn not to address any crow with a sentence that begins, <u>"Do you have a copy of ... ?</u> The clever bees are among the wonders of the corporate world. A <u>bee</u> neither hoards nor destroys paper; she redistributes it, moving from office to office as if between flowers.

Idea links to previous three workers
Office worker #4

15   Her methods are various and unpredictable, but there is no madness in them. Sometimes she arrives in an office with paper in hand and, distracting a colleague with conversation, simply leaves the paper inconspicuously on his desk. Sometimes she moves paper through seemingly legitimate channels, sending it through interoffice mail with ingenious notes like "Please look into this when you get a chance." More often, she employs the clever notation invented by bees, "FYI."

16   Whatever her method, she ensures that paper floats outward and does not return to her. Students of human behavior have come to call this cross-pollination "delegation," though to the bee it is simply a genetic imperative.

Idea links to the four previous office workers

17   <u>While others of the species hoard, distribute and destroy paper,</u> the <u>possum</u> follows the evolutionary dictates of all marsupials and carries it with her.

Office worker #5

18   Instead of a pouch, the office possum has a

briefcase—in some cases, several. It is large and soft sided to accommodate her needs. Some possums, as an auxiliary system, carry handbags large enough to hold legal-size files. When a possum needs to retrieve paper, she goes not to a file cabinet or an In box but to her bags. She protects her paper by carrying it with her at all times—to her home, to the health club, to lunch.

Though she has no natural predators, the possum's habits create special risks. She must spend considerable time at the lost-and-found department of theaters and restaurants and knows by heart the telephone number of the taxi commissioner. One of her arms is longer than the other.

19

Conclusion refers to all other office workers as well as to the piece of paper that is essential to the office

But in nature, all things serve a purpose. And if the office burned down, the lowly possum would be the sole possessor of the paper that is the raison d'être of all the other animals.

20

After-Reading Activities

Analyzing the Content

1. Explain the description, "much of it now with sprocket holes" (paragraph 1). How does this description date the essay?

2. a) Kathleen Fury refers to the group of people she's describing as "the species" (paragraph 17). Define this species.
   b) Create a chart that lists the members of the species and the attributes of each.

Structure and Style

3. Who is the audience for this essay? Explain your answer.

4. How has the writer used hyperbole, sarcasm, caricature, and visual language to create humour in the essay?

5. What is the function of paragraph 11? Show how the writer has made this paragraph function effectively.

6. Examine the margin annotations in this essay. How do they help or hinder your understanding of the organizational pattern of the essay?

7. As well as classification, what other organizational pattern has the writer used? Why does the combination of the patterns work well to develop the ideas in the essay?

8. The writer always uses feminine pronouns when referring to the animals. What effect does this single gender reference have on the reader?

Of Weirdos and Eccentrics

Pico Iyer

Elements of the Essay

"Of Weirdos and Eccentrics" takes a look at the differences between two classes of people: "weirdos" and "eccentrics." Pico Iyer defines and examines these social misfits, beginning with a specific example of each. Note the parallel structure and transitions that he uses in this essay. How do they enhance his arguments and organization?

About the Writer

A self-described "global village on two legs," Pico Iyer was born in England to East Indian parents on February 11, 1957. He was educated at Eton, Oxford, and Harvard. A constant globetrotter, Iyer has written travel books since 1988, and his writing has been published in *Time* magazine (where "Of Weirdos and Eccentrics" appeared) since 1982. His novels include *Video Night in Kathmandu*, *The Lady and the Monk*, *Cuba and the Night*, and, the most recent, *The Global Soul*.

When discussing the act and importance of writing, Pico Iyer has said, "Writing should be an act of communication more than of mere self-expression—a telling of a story rather than a flourishing of skills. The less conscious one is of being 'a writer,' the better the writing. And though reading is the best school of writing, school is the worst place for reading. Writing, in fact, should, ideally, be as spontaneous and urgent as a letter to a lover, or a message to a friend who has just lost a parent. And because of the ways a writer is obliged to tap in private the selves that even those closest to him never see, writing is, in the end, that oddest of anomalies: an intimate letter to a stranger."

C HARLES WATERTON WAS JUST another typical eccentric. In his 80s the eminent country squire was to be seen clambering around the upper branches of an oak tree with what was aptly described as the agility of an "adolescent gorilla." The beloved 27th lord of Walton Hall also devoted his distinguished old age to scratching the back part of his head with his right big toe. Such displays of animal high spirits were not, however, confined to the gentleman's later years. When young, Waterton made four separate trips to South America, where he sought the wourali poison (a cure, he was convinced, for hydrophobia), and once spent months on end with one foot dangling from his hammock in the quixotic hope of having his toe sucked by a vampire bat.

2   James Warren Jones, by contrast, was something of a weirdo. As a boy in the casket-making town of Lynn, Ind., he used to conduct elaborate funeral services for dead pets. Later, as a struggling preacher, he went from door to door, in bow tie and tweed jacket, selling imported monkeys. After briefly fleeing to South America (a shelter, he believed, from an imminent nuclear holocaust), the man who regarded himself as a reincarnation of Lenin settled in Northern California and opened some convalescent homes. Then, one humid day in the jungles of Guyana, he ordered his followers to drink a Kool-Aid-like punch soured with cyanide. By the time the world arrived at Jonestown, 911 people were dead.

3   The difference between the eccentric and the weirdo is, in its way, the difference between a man with a teddy bear in his hand and a man with a gun. We are also, of course, besieged by other kinds of deviants—crackpots, oddballs, fanatics, quacks and cranks. But the weirdo and the eccentric define between them that invisible line at which strangeness acquires an edge and oddness becomes menace.

4   The difference between the two starts with the words themselves: eccentric, after all, carries a distinguished Latin pedigree that refers, quite reasonably, to anything that departs from the center; weird, by comparison, has its mongrel origins in the Old English wyrd, meaning fate or destiny; and the larger, darker forces conjured up by the term—*Macbeth's* weird sisters and the like—are given an extra twist with the slangy, bastard suffix –o. Beneath the linguistic roots, however, we feel the difference on our pulses. The eccentric we generally regard as something of a donny, dotty, harmless type, like the British peer who threw over his Cambridge fellowship in order to live in a bath. The weirdo is an altogether more shadowy figure—Charles Manson acting out his messianic visions. The eccentric is a distinctive presence; the weirdo something of an absence, who casts no reflection in society's mirror. The eccentric raises a smile; the weirdo leaves a chill.

5   All too often, though, the two terms are not so easily distinguished. Many a criminal trial, after all, revolves around precisely that gray area

where the two begin to blur. Was Bernhard Goetz just a volatile Everyman, ourselves pushed to the limit, and then beyond? Or was he in fact an aberration? Often, besides, eccentrics may simply be weirdos in possession of a VIP pass, people rich enough or powerful enough to live above convention, amoral as Greek gods. Elvis Presley could afford to pump bullets into silhouettes of humans and never count the cost. Lesser mortals, however, must find another kind of victim.

To some extent too, we tend to think of eccentricity as the prerogative, even the hallmark, of genius. And genius is its own vindication. Who cared that Glenn Gould sang along with the piano while playing Bach, so long as he played so beautifully? Even the Herculean debauches of Babe Ruth did not undermine so much as confirm his status as a legend.   6

Indeed, the unorthodox inflections of the exceptional can lead to all kinds of dangerous assumptions. If geniuses are out of the ordinary and psychopaths are out of the ordinary, then geniuses are psychopaths and vice versa, or so at least runs the reasoning of many dramatists who set their plays in loony bins. If the successful are often strange, then being strange is a way of becoming successful, or so believe all those would-be artists who work on eccentric poses. And if celebrity is its own defense, then many a demagogue or criminal assures himself that he will ultimately be redeemed by the celebrity he covets.   7

All these distortions, however, ignore the most fundamental distinction of all: the eccentric is strange because he cares too little about society, the weirdo because he cares too much. The eccentric generally wants nothing more than his own attic-like space in which he can live by his own peculiar lights. The weirdo, however, resents his outcast status and constantly seeks to get back into society, or at least get back at it. His is the rage not of the bachelor but the divorced.   8

Thus the eccentric hardly cares if he is seen to be strange; that in a sense is what makes him strange. The weirdo, however, wants desperately to be taken as normal and struggles to keep his strangeness to himself. "He was always such a nice man," the neighbors ritually tell reporters after a sniper's rampage. "He always seemed so normal."   9

And because the two mark such different tangents to the norm, their incidence can, in its way, be an index of a society's health. The height of British eccentricity, for example, coincided with the height of British power, if only, perhaps, because Britain in its imperial heyday presented so strong a center from which to depart. Nowadays, with the empire   10 gone and the center vanishing, Britain is more often associated with the maladjusted weirdo—the orange-haired misfit or the soccer hooligan.

11   At the other extreme, the relentless and ritualized normalcy of a society like Japan's—there are only four psychiatrists in all of Tokyo—can, to Western eyes, itself seem almost abnormal. Too few eccentrics can be as dangerous as too many weirdos. For in the end, eccentricity is a mark of confidence, accommodated best by a confident society, whereas weirdness inspires fear because it is a symptom of fear and uncertainty and rage. A society needs the eccentric as much as it needs a decorated frame for the portrait it fashions of itself; it needs the weirdo as much as it needs a hole punched through the middle of the canvas.

After-Reading Activities

Analyzing the Content

1. Use an Internet search engine to research any proper name in this essay with which you are unfamiliar.

2. In your notebook, consider the following:
   • Identify the precise difference between an eccentric and a weirdo as the terms are defined by Pico Iyer in this essay.
   • According to Iyer, why is it difficult to classify Bernhard Goetz as either an eccentric or a weirdo? Do additional research on Goetz, if necessary, and explain which term you think best applies.
   • Explain why Iyer says that the strangeness of the eccentric is that he cares too little about society, and that of the weirdo is that he cares too much. Do you agree with his assessment?

Structure and Style

3. If you had to select one sentence from this essay to illustrate its thesis, which one would you choose? Explain your choice.

4. What do you think is Iyer's main purpose in this essay?

5. Assess the extent to which the use of etymology in paragraph 4 strengthens Iyer's main idea in this essay.

6. Explain how this essay also exemplifies the organizational patterns of definition and comparison and contrast.

7. Give an example of non-inclusive language in this essay. Would the essay be stronger if it used inclusive language? Would the essay be stronger if it used female examples in the development of its thesis? Why do you think Iyer did not refer to, or include examples of, women in this essay?

Some Notes on Parody

Dwight Macdonald

Elements of the Essay

In "Some Notes on Parody," Dwight Macdonald defines and explains travesty, burlesque, and parody. He draws upon examples and authorities to illustrate his points. His language is formal, yet accessible, providing his readers with a basic understanding of the differences and similarities between the three literary forms.

About the Writer

Essayist and political, social, and literary critic Dwight Macdonald was born in New York in 1906. He was educated at Yale University and worked as an editor at *Fortune* (1928–1936) and later at *The New Yorker* (1951–1971). His essays and criticisms, known for their ironic wit, appear in several collections, including *The Memoirs of a Revolutionist* (1957) and *Against the American Grain: Essays on the Effects of Mass Culture* (1962). A left-wing activist, Macdonald frequently debated political issues in public. He died in 1982.

1   THE FIRST QUESTION IS: What *is* parody? The dictionaries are not helpful. Dr. Johnson defines parody as "a kind of writing in which the words of an author or his thoughts are taken and by a slight change adapted to some new purpose," which is imprecise and incomplete. The Oxford dictionary comes closer: "a composition … in which characteristic turns of an author … are imitated in such a way as to make them appear ridiculous, especially by applying them to ludicrously inappropriate subjects." This at least brings in humor. But it does not distinguish parody from its poor relations, *travesty* ("a grotesque or debased imitation or likeness") and *burlesque* ("aims at exciting laughter by caricature of the manner or spirit of serious works, or by ludicrous treatment of their subjects"). Such definitions tend to run together, which is just what a definition shouldn't do, since *definire* means "to set limits." I therefore propose the following hierarchy:

TRAVESTY (literally "changing clothes," as in "transvestite") is the 2
most primitive form. It raises laughs, from the belly rather than the
head, by putting high, classic characters into prosaic situations, with a
corresponding stepping-down of the language. Achilles becomes a
football hero, Penelope a suburban housewife, Helen a beauty queen.
Scarron did it in the seventeenth century with his enormously popular
Virgile Travesti, John Erskine in the twentieth with his *The Private Life
of Helen of Troy*. Boileau was severe on Scarron:

> Au mépris du bon sens, le burlesque effronté
> Trompa les yeux d'abord, plut par sa nouveauté.…
> Cette contagion infecta les provinces,
> Du clerc et du bourgeois passa jusques aux princes.

It hardly bears thinking what his reaction would have been to Erskine's
book. Or to the contemporary imitation of Scarron by the English
poetaster, Charles Cotton, which begins:

> I sing the man (read it who list)
> A Trojan true as ever pist,
> Who from Troy-Town by wind and weather
> To Italy (and God knows whither)
> Was pack'd and rack'd and lost and tost
> And bounced from pillar unto post.

BURLESQUE (from Italian *burla*, "ridicule") is a more advanced 3
form since it at least imitates the style of the original. It differs from
parody in that the writer is concerned with the original not in itself but
merely as a device for topical humor. Hawthorne's charming *The
Celestial Railway*, for example, is not a parody of Bunyan but a satire on
materialistic progress that is hung on the peg of *Pilgrim's Progress*. The
instinct for filling a familiar form with a new content is old as history.
The *Iliad* was burlesqued a few generations after it was composed.
Sacred themes were popular in the Middle Ages, such as the Drunkards'
Mass *(Missa de Potatoribus)*, which began:

> *Va.* Introibo ad altare Bachi
> *R.* Ad eum qui letificat cor homins.
>   Confiteor reo Bacho omnepotanti, et reo vino coloris rubei, et
> omnibus ciphis eius, et vobis potatoribus, me nimis gulose potasse
> per nimian nauseam rei Bachi dei mei potatione, sternutatione,
> ocitatione maxima, mea crupa, mea maxima crupa.… Potemus.

Twenty-five years ago, when the eleven-year-old Gloria Vanderbilt was the subject of a famous custody suit between her mother and her aunt, the court's decision awarding her to the aunt except for week ends was summarized by an anonymous newspaper wit:

> Rockabye baby
> Up on a writ,
> Monday to Friday, mother's unfit.
> As the week ends, she rises in virtue;
> Saturday, Sunday,
> Mother won't hurt you.

And last year, the London *Economist* printed a political carol:

> On the tenth day of Cwthmas,[1] the Commonwealth
>   brought to me
> Ten Sovereign Nations
> Nine Governors General
> Eight Federations
> Seven Disputed Areas
> Six Trust Territories
> Five Old Realms
> Four Present or Prospective Republics
> Three High Commission Territories
> Two Ghana-Guinea Fowl
>
> > One Sterling Area
> > One Dollar Dominion
> > One Sun That Never Sets
> > One Maltese Cross
> > One Marylebone Cricket Club
> > One Trans-Arctic Expedition
>
> And a Mother Country up a Gum Tree.

4   Finally and at last, PARODY, from the Greek *parodia* ("a beside- or against-song"), concentrates on the style and thought of the original.[2] If burlesque is pouring new wine into old bottles, parody is making a new wine that tastes like the old but has a slightly lethal effect. At its best, it is a form of literary criticism. The beginning of Max Beerbohm's parody of a Shaw preface may give the general idea:

A STRAIGHT TALK

When a public man lays his hand on his heart and declares that his conduct needs no apology, the audience hastens to put up its umbrellas against the particularly severe downpour of apologies in store for it. I won't give the customary warning. My conduct shrieks aloud for apology, and you are in for a thorough drenching.

Flatly, I stole this play. The one valid excuse for the theft would be mental starvation. That excuse I shan't plead. I could have made a dozen better plays than this out of my own head. You don't suppose Shakespeare was so vacant in the upper storey that there was nothing for it but to rummage through cinquecento romances, Towneley mysteries, and such-like insanitary rubbishheaps in order that he might fish out enough scraps for his artistic fangs to fasten on. Depend on it, there were plenty of decent original notions seething behind yon marble brow. Why didn't our William use *them?* He was too lazy. And so am I.

Shaw's polemical style is unerringly reproduced—the short, punchy sentences; the familiarity ("yon marble brow … our William"), the Anglo-Saxon vigor, the calculated irreverences ("and such-like insanitary rubbishheaps"). But Beerbohm goes deeper, into the peculiar combination in Shaw of arrogance and self-depreciation, of aggressiveness and mateyness, so that the audience is at once bullied and flattered; shocking ideas are asserted but as if they were a matter of course between sensible people. Beerbohm's exposé of this strategy is true parody.

N o t e s

[The following are Macdonald's notes.]
1. Contraction of "Commonwealthmas."
2. Parody belongs to the family of para-words: parasite, parapsychology, paratyphoid, paranoia (against mind), paradox (against received opinion), paraphrase, paranymph (bridesmaid). It is not related to Paraguay, although that country is beside and against Uruguay.

After-Reading Activities

Analyzing the Content

1. In your own words, define "travesty," "burlesque," and "parody." Explain the elements that distinguish each of these forms from the others. Which do you think would be the most difficult to write? Why?

2. Examine the etymology of "travesty" (paragraph 2), "burlesque" (paragraph 3), and "parody" (paragraph 4). How does each word origin relate to each of the words as we now understand them?

3. Look up the following: Virgil's story of Helen of Troy, *Pilgrim's Progress*, biographical information about Gloria Vanderbilt, and information on the writing style of George Bernard Shaw. How does knowing some of this background information help with the understanding of this essay?

Structure and Style

4. The essay opens with two short sentences. How do the content and structure of these sentences encourage a reader to read on?

5. Considering the language and references in this essay, who is the intended audience?

6. a) Explain why this essay could be labelled either "classification" or "definition."
   b) Create an outline of this essay. Explain how Dwight Macdonald's organization helps make this difficult subject easier to understand.

7. Using Macdonald's definition of "burlesque," show how the verse starting "Rockabye baby" (paragraph 3) fits the "burlesque" classification.

Extending the Pattern

1. Choose two characters from fiction or history to illustrate the distinction between "weirdos" and "eccentrics," and describe them in two paragraphs that could be placed in the body of Pico Iyer's essay.

2. Using print or electronic sources, find examples of a parody that your classmates will understand and appreciate. Read some of the parodies aloud, and have classmates guess which work or writer is being parodied.

3. Choose a modern songwriter, and write a parody of one of his or her songs. Bring in the original along with your parody, and post both for the class to read.

4. Choose one of the following:
   • Using an analogy similar to that used in "It's Only a Paper World," write a humorous essay classifying the types of students who attend high school or the types of drivers on the road.
   • Imagine that office machines had human qualities. How would they classify themselves? What would they think about the jobs that each performs in the office? Consider everything from the manual pencil sharpener to the colour laser printer. Write an essay that uses classification as well as one other method of development to depict the various machines in the office.

   You may need to do additional research. After completing your first draft, work with a partner to revise and edit your essay, focusing on the organization and the strength of your arguments.

Elements of the Pattern

As humans, we have a natural drive to understand the world around us. We are continually looking for causal relationships. That is, we ask why things exist as they do. We look for the causes of certain actions, events, and occurrences. We also ask ourselves about their effects. The ability to do this type of analysis allows us to decide on a course of action based on the probable effects. A cause and effect essay explores causal relationships.

When writing a cause and effect essay, you may begin by describing a particular condition (effect) and then explore all of the forces or events that caused the condition. Alternatively, you may start the essay by first focusing on particular forces or events (causes), and then explore what probable effects these might have. Further, in your essay you may choose to discuss both cause and effect, or you may focus on just the causes or the effects.

Cause and effect essays can be interesting and challenging to read and write. They inherently challenge us to think; in so doing, they expand our knowledge and understanding. They are challenging also because they provide an element of uncertainty. A reader and writer of such an essay must be aware and be willing to accept that other explanations, different from those presented in the essay, are possible.

Introducing logical relationships in cause and effect essays may pose some difficulties for writers. When writing a cause and effect essay, you should carefully think through the relationships you are presenting. Ask yourself if the relationship between the objects or events truly exists. Rumours, falsehoods, and flawed conclusions are known to have resulted from assumptions of causal relationships where none existed. For example, consider the statement, "The team won both times when it rained." Such a statement suggests that the wins were a result of the rain, when it would be more logical to attribute them to other causes. Think of alternative explanations before moving ahead. The first explanation is not always the best one. The best that you, as a writer, can do is to carefully formulate your argument, ensuring that your facts are supportable and that the relationships you have drawn are logical.

Barbie and Her Playmates

Don Richard Cox

Elements of the Essay

Originally published in the *Journal of Popular Culture*, "Barbie and Her Playmates" examines the effects of the Barbie doll phenomenon on the behaviour and attitudes of young girls. Don Richard Cox provides a detailed analysis of its impact, presenting his ideas in a combination structure of cause and effect and comparison and contrast.

About the Writer

Don Richard Cox was born in Kansas in 1943. He has authored or co-authored and co-edited several books, including *Emblems of Reality: Discovering Experience in Language* (1973), *The Technical Reader: Readings in Technical, Business and Scientific Communication* (1980, 1984), *Crafting Prose* (1991), and *Charles Dickens' The Mystery of Edwin Drood: An Annotated Bibliography* (1998). He is currently the associate dean of the College of Arts and Sciences at the University of Tennessee, Knoxville, teaching Victorian literature and exposition writing.

THE MATTEL CORPORATION'S WONDER doll, Barbie, is undoubtedly one of the toy phenomena of the second half of the twentieth century. The first of her kind, Barbie helped create a whole new breed of dolls—the fashion dolls. These dolls, all of whom are about eleven or twelve inches tall, are intended to represent attractive, apparently teenaged girls, who, like most teenaged girls, require large wardrobes. These wardrobes are purchased separately from the dolls of course, and initially most of Barbie's appeal to young purchasers involved the seemingly endless supply of fashions that Barbie and her friends could wear.

One did not simply buy a Barbie doll and stop, for Barbie was not an end in herself but an avenue to a whole world of Barbie accessories. The concept of a doll being primarily a vehicle for the future sale of related merchandise rather than being a terminal product whose marketing success ends with its sale is a concept that has caused Barbie to have the tremendous impact upon the toy industry that she has had and allowed her to survive in a doll market where the average product remains popular only a few years. Barbie's primary and social importance as a toy stems from the fact that she is different from the dolls that preceded her; this difference has reshaped our culture's way of looking at dolls and the way children now define their relationship to these dolls that sell in the millions. The sales figures alone are proof of Barbie's attractiveness. There is no doubt that Barbie and her friends have been accepted; they seem to have become a permanent part of twentieth-century life. But now that we have welcomed Barbie into our homes and placed her in our children's bedrooms, we should stop and examine what her presence there means, and what effect it may have.

3   Barbie was first introduced to sell clothes, but her initial role as a vehicle for doll fashions was soon expanded. For example, Barbie's size made her either too large or too small for conventional doll furniture that had existed, so a new line of doll furniture tailored to her dimensions was created. Barbie's "Dream House" then became one of her first "non-fashion" accessories. Because Barbie was a young and presumably active young lady, her merchandise took on a distinctive character. Barbie was not a "baby" doll and she had no need for baby cribs, high chairs, or other "baby" furniture. So Barbie acquired recreational equipment—a dune buggy, a Volkswagen van, a swimming pool. She also acquired some friends—P.J. and Skipper—and most important of all Barbie found a boyfriend—Ken. With the addition of these friends to share her fun Barbie's need for equipment became as unlimited as the needs of any modern consumer. Barbie could ski, camp, swim, skate, cycle, perform gymnastics, boat, dance, shop, have her hair styled, or just entertain friends in her studio bedroom, her country home, or her penthouse apartment. Almost any activity open to today's teenagers became available to Barbie, and by extension became available to those who brought Barbie into their lives.

4   The success of the total Barbie market helped initiate several new series of dolls, all of whom parlayed the Barbie format to success. Many of these dolls, drawing upon the interest Barbie's Ken had aroused in young boys, turned to a relatively untapped doll market—dolls for the male population. Selling dolls to young boys, however, necessitated a basic change in terminology. Boys' dolls were not called *dolls*, because

that word has a distinctly feminine ring. Accordingly we find today that young males are interested in *action figures*, male dolls who are supposedly basically rugged individuals devoted to an outdoor life. "Big Jim," "Johnny West," and most notably "G.I. Joe," all belong to this exclusive club of adventurous spirits who demand enough dune buggies, jeeps, motorcycles, planes, boats, and helicopters to outfit a small mercenary force. Once again we can see that what is essentially being marketed here is a sophisticated type of doll "furniture," merchandise that surrounds and supports the original doll vehicles.

The major appeal of the action figures lies in the variety of accessories   5
that can be adapted to them; like Barbie they are not terminal products. The action figures for boys, however, although they represent a direct result of Barbie's impact upon the toy market, do not necessitate a redefinition of the male role in play situations in the same way that Barbie has redefined the female role in these situations. The action figures are distinctly male and they inhabit a world that is exclusively male. A young boy will have to borrow his sister's fashion doll if he wants any feminine intruders invading his all-male play world. In this respect the male action figures do not require an adjustment in the masculine play role. Although we can label a boy's action figures "dolls," we should understand that as a collection of adult male dolls they might also be seen as simply elaborate toy soldiers, a traditional plaything of boys for generations. Young girls, however, have had their feminine play roles changed significantly by Barbie. Because the consequences of that redefinition could alter a child's basic attitudes toward sex, marriage, or a career, let us examine more closely the value structure implicit in Barbie's world.

We should begin by noting that Barbie's age is not completely clear.   6
Ostensibly she is a teenager and therefore is no more than nineteen years old. Physically, however, as many people have pointed out, Barbie is a rather fully endowed and curvaceous woman possessing a figure few nineteen-year-olds have. Barbie is of course single so her friend Ken is just that—a boyfriend not a husband. Barbie's exact relationship with Ken is noticeably loose. She apparently is free to embark unescorted on all kinds of outings with Ken, including camping overnight (they each have their own sleeping bags, however). Barbie seemingly lives alone in all of her plushly furnished homes although there are certainly enough chairs, couches, and beds to accommodate overnight guests. Again, Ken is free to visit any time he wishes. The point here is not that Barbie is a doll of questionable morals, but we should note that her lifestyle is remarkably uncluttered and free

of such complications as nosey little brothers or nagging parents.

7   Barbie's life is that of the ultimate swinging single. Although she has no parents to cast shadows into her life of constant boating, skiing, and camping, she also does not seem to have a need for them. Total independence is a central characteristic of Barbie. Although she owns an extensive amount of sporting equipment, Barbie seemingly has no need for employment that allows her to purchase this merchandise. There is no such thing as a Barbie office in any of the Barbie equipment, nor are there accessories that remotely suggest a job situation for this carefree doll; although Barbie might be in high school or college there are no accessories that hint at her having to endure the boredom of education. Life for Barbie appears to be a kind of endless summer vacation, an extended tour of summer homes and resorts, free from school, family, and financial worries.

8   Barbie's influence upon the minds of the children who share their play hours with her and her expensive wardrobe and recreation equipment is potentially a very strong one. Barbie provides a means of vicarious escape to her young female playmates—a glittering jet trip into a world of leisure and luxury that very few of her young friends will ever actually know. We can see that Barbie is a symbolic escape vehicle, a vicarious toy that encourages fantasy rather than a toy that encourages behavior imitative of normal living patterns.

9   The dolls that survive outside of the category of fashion dolls are still basically the kind of dolls that existed before Barbie and the fashion dolls came on the scene. These dolls are mostly "baby" dolls, dolls that require young mothers to feed and diaper them. A child who owns such a doll usually assumes a play role that is imitative of her own mother's role. The babies can be loved and cuddled, or punished and put to bed at a young mother's whim. In this play role the child assumes an adult personality, dominating the inferior doll-child just as the youngster herself is dominated. Obviously the work and responsibility involved in being a mother receives a good share of the child's attention in this particular situation. And, although a certain amount of fantasy is involved, presumably these fantasies will one day become more or less true when the child experiences motherhood herself. She in essence is only rehearsing for a future real-life role.

10   The play role initiated in a child's relationship with Barbie differs considerably from the play role required by a conventional baby doll. First of all Barbie is obviously not a child. She is a teenager and therefore

is usually "older" than the child who owns her. The child's personality then is not necessarily a dominant one when she relates with Barbie. Barbie has the clothes, sporting equipment, and most important, freedom, to do as she pleases. The child only directs Barbie in activities that the child herself may not be able to experience. The mother-child relationship that is an inherent part of owning a baby doll is considerably altered. One does not necessarily cuddle or punish a Barbie doll any more than one allows her mother to sit on her lap, or sends her mother to bed without dinner. Barbie's stature in this psychological relationship is not so great that she dominates the child; she does not become a symbolic parent in spite of her independent superiority.

Barbie's independence in fact is just what prevents her from becoming a miniature parent to the child. There are no children in Barbie's life; children, after all, involve responsibility and Barbie is not one to be burdened by such responsibilities. Instead of assuming the duties and pressures of adulthood, Barbie retains the worry-free aura of childhood, becoming a kind of surrogate big sister to the child. This relationship, the interaction between sisters at play, is fundamentally different from the mother-child relationship, and the values inculcated by this interaction are plainly different also.   11

As a model sister, Barbie, who leads a life free from responsibility, is able to stimulate a similar desire for independence in her owners. The degree to which her influence has actually affected children in the sixties and seventies needs to be investigated more closely. Of interest also is Barbie's impact upon future families, the families formed by the young girls of the "Barbie generation." Will they, like Barbie, resist the responsibility of having children, or, following Barbie's lead even more completely, resist the responsibility of marriage and family altogether? There is also the question of the sexual mores of today's Barbie owners. Barbie is a physically attractive woman with no visible permanent attachments. Will she produce a generation of sexually liberated playmates intent on jetting from resort to resort? Will these same playmates become a group of frustrated cynics if their private Barbie fantasies do not come true? Older sisters often set social and marital patterns that their younger sisters attempt to emulate; Barbie is capable of being a dominant model for all her young sisters in this respect.   12

Certainly Barbie's dream world has already affected the sexual lives of her playmates in one way: she has caused girls as young as five or six to confront the problems of teenagers. Very young children, children who   13 might once have been content to feed bottles to their infant dolls, are now exposed to the dating experience. Girls who once spent the second grade believing that boys were generally unpleasant creatures now spend their days escorting Barbie and Ken through idyllic afternoons. Dating and the opposite sex—"those awful boys"—have now become familiar experiences to jaded nine-year-olds who have "accompanied" their "big sister" and her boyfriend on unchaperoned camping trips many times. The accelerating interest of big business in "pre-teenagers" (presumably those children between the ages of seven and twelve) as a potential market for cosmetics, magazines, and phonograph records, is a positive indication of a budding sexual awareness in this age group. The girls who screamed for Elvis in the fifties were seventeen; those who now swoon at Donny Osmond are eleven.

14   The total impact of Barbie should now begin to make itself visible in her playmates. As each generation finds its own particular fantasy of escape the values of that fantasy become imprinted in the generation itself. Motion pictures, the great escape of the forties and early fifties, provided Hollywood's vision of life for those who grew up munching popcorn in dark theaters. Similarly, it has been proposed that many of the youth protests of the late sixties reflected the desires of a generation that was used to seeing life neatly resolved in sixty-minute segments on a flickering tube. Barbie and her glittering accessories have now been purchased by a generation of children; her fantasy world becomes steadily more elaborate. If Barbie has indeed provided a behavioral model for a segment of the population, the values instilled in her miniature utopia will play an increasing role in the lives of those children who buy her version of the American Dream.

After-Reading Activities

Analyzing the Content

1. Identify the main elements that have made the Barbie doll one of the most successful toys of all time.

2. Explain the distinction between a "doll" and an "action figure." How important is this distinction?

3. Does this essay over-analyze toys? Is it worthwhile to study dolls as consumer products, moral models, and phenomena of popular culture?

Structure and Style

4. If you had to select one sentence from this essay to illustrate its thesis, which one would you choose? Explain your choice.

5. What is the writer's main purpose in this essay?

6. List the causes and the effects presented in this essay. Match the causes to the effects. Does one cause produce more than one effect? Do several causes contribute to a single effect?

7. Are the conclusions in the final paragraph supported by the rest of the essay?

8. Explain how the organizational pattern of comparison and contrast is also used in this essay.

Fast Food Nation: The Dark Side of the All-American Meal

Eric Schlosser

Elements of the Essay

"This year, Americans will spend more money on fast food than on higher education.... [Eric] Schlosser shows how the fast food industry conquered both appetite and landscape," wrote a critic from *The New Yorker* in his review of Eric Schlosser's recent book, *Fast Food Nation: The Dark Side of the All-American Meal* (2002). This selection has been excerpted from that book. Schlosser develops his ideas with examples, quotations, and statistics to show the effects of fast food on Americans and to support his position.

About the Writer
Award-winning journalist Eric Schlosser is a correspondent for *The Atlantic Monthly*. *Fast Food Nation* is his first book, and it has won rave reviews. Said one reviewer from *The Globe and Mail,* "All children who can read should be issued a copy of Eric Schlosser's *Fast Food Nation."*

1   CHEYENNE MOUNTAIN SITS ON the eastern slope of Colorado's Front Range, rising steeply from the prairie and overlooking the city of Colorado Springs. From a distance, the mountain appears beautiful and serene, dotted with rocky outcroppings, scrub oak, and ponderosa pine. It looks like the backdrop of an old Hollywood western, just another gorgeous Rocky Mountain vista. And yet Cheyenne Mountain is hardly pristine. One of the nation's most important military installations lies deep within it, housing units of the North American Aerospace Command, the Air Force Space Command, and the United States Space Command. During the mid-1950s, high-level officials at the Pentagon worried that America's air defenses had become vulnerable

to sabotage and attack. Cheyenne Mountain was chosen as the site for a top-secret, underground combat operations center. The mountain was hollowed out, and fifteen buildings, most of them three stories high, were erected amid a maze of tunnels and passageways extending for miles. The four-and-a-half-acre underground complex was designed to survive a direct hit by an atomic bomb. Now officially called the Cheyenne Mountain Air Force Station, the facility is entered through steel blast doors that are three feet thick and weigh twenty-five tons each; they automatically swing shut in less than twenty seconds. The base is closed to the public, and a heavily armed quick response team guards against intruders. Pressurized air within the complex prevents contamination by radioactive fallout and biological weapons. The buildings are mounted on gigantic steel springs to ride out an earthquake or the blast wave of a thermonuclear strike. The hallways and staircases are painted slate gray, the ceilings are low, and there are combination locks on many of the doors. A narrow escape tunnel, entered through a metal hatch, twists and turns its way out of the mountain through solid rock. The place feels like the set of an early James Bond movie, with men in jumpsuits driving little electric vans from one brightly lit cavern to another.

Fifteen hundred people work inside the mountain, maintaining the facility and collecting information from a worldwide network of radars, spy satellites, ground-based sensors, airplanes, and blimps. The Cheyenne Mountain Operations Center tracks every manmade object that enters North American airspace or that orbits the earth. It is the heart of the nation's early warning system. It can detect the firing of a long-range missile, anywhere in the world, before that missile has left the launch pad. 2

This futuristic military base inside a mountain has the capability to be self-sustaining for at least one month. Its generators can produce enough electricity to power a city the size of Tampa, Florida. Its underground reservoirs hold millions of gallons of water; workers sometimes traverse them in rowboats. The complex has its own underground fitness center, a medical clinic, a dentist's office, a barbershop, a chapel, and a cafeteria. When the men and women stationed at Cheyenne Mountain get tired of the food in the cafeteria, they often send somebody over to the Burger King at Fort Carson, a nearby army base. Or they call Domino's. 3

Almost every night, a Domino's deliveryman winds his way up the lonely Cheyenne Mountain Road, past the ominous DEADLY FORCE 4

AUTHORIZED signs, past the security checkpoint at the entrance of the base, driving toward the heavily guarded North Portal, tucked behind chain link and barbed wire. Near the spot where the road heads straight into the mountainside, the delivery man drops off his pizzas and collects his tip. And should Armageddon come, should a foreign enemy someday shower the United States with nuclear warheads, laying waste to the whole continent entombed within Cheyenne Mountain, along with the high-tech marvels, the pale blue jumpsuits, comic books, and Bibles, future archeologists may find other clues to the nature of our civilization—Big King wrappers, hardened crusts of Cheesy Bread, Barbeque Wing bones, and the red, white, and blue of a Domino's pizza box.

What We Eat

5   Over the last three decades, fast food has infiltrated every nook and cranny of American society. An industry that began with a handful of modest hot dog and hamburger stands in southern California has spread to every corner of the nation, selling a broad range of foods wherever paying customers may be found. Fast food is now served at restaurants and drive-throughs, at stadiums, airports, zoos, high schools, elementary schools, and universities, on cruise ships, trains, and airplanes, at K-Marts, Wal-Marts, gas stations, and even at hospital cafeterias. In 1970, Americans spent about $6 billion on fast food; in 2001 they spent more than $110 billion. Americans now spend more money on fast food than on higher education, personal computers, computer software, or new cars. They spend more on fast food than on movies, books, magazines, newspapers, videos, and recorded music—combined.

6   Pull open the glass door, feel the rush of cool air, walk in, get on line, study the backlit color photographs above the counter, place your order, hand over a few dollars, watch teenagers in uniforms pushing various buttons, and moments later take hold of a plastic tray full of food wrapped in colored paper and cardboard. The whole experience of buying fast food has become so routine, so thoroughly unexceptional and mundane, that it is now taken for granted, like brushing your teeth or stopping for a red light. It has become a social custom as American as a small, rectangular, hand-held, frozen, and reheated apple pie.

7   This is a book about fast food, the values it embodies, and the world it has made. Fast food has proven to be a revolutionary force in American life; I am interested in it both as a commodity and as a metaphor. What people eat (or don't eat) has always been determined by

a complex interplay of social, economic, and technological forces. The early Roman Republic was fed by its citizen-farmers; the Roman Empire, by its slaves. A nation's diet can be more revealing than its art or literature. On any given day in the United States about one-quarter of the adult population visits a fast food restaurant. During a relatively brief period of time, the fast food industry has helped to transform not only the American diet, but also our landscape, economy, workforce, and popular culture. Fast food and its consequences have become inescapable, regardless of whether you eat it twice a day, try to avoid it, or have never taken a single bite.

The extraordinary growth of the fast food industry has been driven by fundamental changes in American society. Adjusted for inflation, the hourly wage of the average U.S. worker peaked in 1973 and then steadily declined for the next twenty-five years. During that period, women entered the workforce in record numbers, often motivated less by a feminist perspective than by a need to pay the bills. In 1975, about one-third of American mothers with young children worked outside the home; today almost two-thirds of such mothers are employed. As the sociologists Cameron Lynne Macdonald and Carmen Sirianni have noted, the entry of so many women into the workforce has greatly increased demand for the types of services that housewives traditionally perform: cooking, cleaning, and child care. A generation ago, three-quarters of the money used to buy food in the United States was spent to prepare meals at home. Today about half of the money used to buy food is spent at restaurants—mainly at fast food restaurants.

The McDonald's Corporation has become a powerful symbol of America's service economy, which is now responsible for 90 percent of the country's new jobs. In 1968, McDonald's operated about one thousand restaurants. Today it has about thirty thousand restaurants worldwide and opens almost two thousand new ones each year. An estimated one out of every eight workers in the United States has at some point been employed by McDonald's. The company annually hires about one million people, more than any other American organization, public or private. McDonald's is the nation's largest purchaser of beef, pork, and potatoes—and the second largest purchaser of chicken. The McDonald's Corporation is the largest owner of retail property in the world. Indeed, the company earns the majority of its profits not from selling food but from collecting rent. McDonald's spends more money on advertising and marketing than any other brand. As a result it has replaced Coca-Cola as the world's most famous brand. McDonald's operates more playgrounds than any other private entity in the United States. It is one of the nation's largest distributors of toys. A survey of American schoolchildren found that 96 percent could identify Ronald McDonald. The only fictional character with a higher degree of recognition was Santa Claus. The impact of McDonald's on the way we live today is hard to overstate. The Golden Arches are now more widely recognized than the Christian cross.

10   In the early 1970s, the farm activist Jim Hightower warned of "the McDonaldization of America." He viewed the emerging fast food industry as a threat to independent businesses, as a step toward a food economy dominated by giant corporations, and as a homogenizing influence on American life. In *Eat Your Heart Out* (1975), he argued that "bigger is *not* better." Much of what Hightower feared has come to pass. The centralized purchasing decisions of the large restaurant chains and their demand for standardized products have given a handful of corporations an unprecedented degree of power over the nation's food supply. Moreover, the tremendous success of the fast food industry has encouraged other industries to adopt similar business methods. The basic thinking behind fast food has become the operating system of today's retail economy, wiping out small businesses, obliterating regional differences, and spreading identical stores throughout the country like a self-replicating code.

11   America's main streets and malls now boast the same Pizza Huts and Taco Bells, Gaps and Banana Republics, Starbucks and Jiffy-Lubes, Foot Lockers, Snip N' Clips, Sunglass Huts, and Hobbytown USAs. Almost every facet of American life has now been franchised or chained. From the maternity ward at a Columbia/HCA hospital to an embalming room owned by Service Corporation International—"the world's largest provider of death care services," based in Houston, Texas, which since 1968 has grown to include 3,823 funeral homes, 523 cemeteries, and 198 crematoriums, and which today handles the final remains of one out of every nine Americans—a person can now go from the cradle to the grave without spending a nickel at an independently owned business.

12   The key to a successful franchise, according to many texts on the subject, can be expressed in one word: "uniformity." Franchises and chain stores strive to offer exactly the same product or service at numerous locations. Customers are drawn to familiar brands by an instinct to avoid the unknown. A brand offers a feeling of reassurance

when its products are always and everywhere the same. "We have found out ... that we cannot trust some people who are nonconformists," declared Ray Kroc, one of the founders of McDonald's, angered by some of his franchisees. "We will make conformists out of them in a hurry ... The organization cannot trust the individual; the individual must trust the organization."

One of the ironies of America's fast food industry is that a business so   13
dedicated to conformity was founded by iconoclasts and self-made men, by entrepreneurs willing to defy conventional opinion. Few of the people who built fast food empires ever attended college, let alone business school. They worked hard, took risks, and followed their own paths. In many respects, the fast food industry embodies the best and the worst of American capitalism at the start of the twenty-first century—its constant stream of new products and innovations, its widening gulf between rich and poor. The industrialization of the restaurant kitchen has enabled the fast food chains to rely upon a low-paid and unskilled workforce. While a handful of workers manage to rise up the corporate ladder, the vast majority lack full-time employment, receive no benefits, learn few skills, exercise little control over their workplace, quit after a few months, and float from job to job. The restaurant industry is now America's largest private employer, and it pays some of the lowest wages. During the economic boom of the 1990s, when many American workers enjoyed their first pay raises in a generation, the real value of wages in the restaurant industry continued to fall. The roughly 3.5 million fast food workers are by far the largest group of minimum wage earners in the United States. The only Americans who consistently earn a lower hourly wage are migrant farm workers.

A hamburger and french fries became the quintessential American   14
meal in the 1950s, thanks to the promotional efforts of the fast food chains. The typical American now consumes approximately three hamburgers and four orders of french fries every week. But the steady barrage of fast food ads, full of thick juicy burgers and long golden fries, rarely mentions where these foods come from nowadays or what ingredients they contain. The birth of the fast food industry coincided with Eisenhower-era glorifications of technology, with optimistic slogans like "Better Living through Chemistry" and "Our Friend the Atom." The sort of technological wizardry that Walt Disney promoted on television and at Disneyland eventually reached its fulfillment in the kitchens of fast food restaurants. Indeed, the corporate culture of

McDonald's seems inextricably linked to that of the Disney empire, sharing a reverence for sleek machinery, electronics, and automation. The leading fast food chains still embrace a boundless faith in science— and as a result have changed not just what Americans eat, but also how their food is made.

15   The current methods for preparing fast food are less likely to be found in cookbooks than in trade journals such as *Food Technologist* and *Food Engineering*. Aside from the salad greens and tomatoes, most fast food is delivered to the restaurant already frozen, canned, dehydrated, or freeze-dried. A fast food kitchen is merely the final stage in a vast and highly complex system of mass production. Foods that may look familiar have in fact been completely reformulated. What we eat has changed more in the last forty years than in the previous forty thousand. Like Cheyenne Mountain, today's fast food conceals remarkable technological advances behind an ordinary-looking façade. Much of the taste and aroma of American fast food, for example, is now manufactured at a series of large chemical plants off the New Jersey Turnpike.

16   In the fast food restaurants of Colorado Springs, behind the counters, amid the plastic seats, in the changing landscape outside the window, you can see all the virtues and destructiveness of our fast food nation. I chose Colorado Springs as a focal point for this book because the changes that have recently swept through the city are emblematic of those that fast food—and the fast food mentality—have encouraged throughout the United States. Countless other suburban communities, in every part of the country, could have been used to illustrate the same points. The extraordinary growth of Colorado Springs neatly parallels that of the fast food industry: during the last few decades, the city's population has more than doubled. Subdivisions, shopping malls, and chain restaurants are appearing in the foothills of Cheyenne Mountain and the plains rolling to the east. The Rocky Mountain region as a whole has the fastest-growing economy in the United States, mixing high-tech and service industries in a way that may define America's workforce for years to come. And new restaurants are opening there at a faster pace than anywhere else in the nation.

17   Fast food is now so commonplace that it has acquired an air of inevitability, as though it were somehow unavoidable, a fact of modern life. And yet the dominance of the fast food giants was no more preordained than the march of colonial split-levels, golf courses, and manmade lakes across the deserts of the American West. The political

philosophy that now prevails in so much of the West—with its demand for lower taxes, smaller government, an unbridled free market—stands in total contradiction to the region's true economic underpinnings. No other region of the United States has been so dependent on government subsidies for so long, from the nineteenth-century construction of its railroads to the twentieth-century financing of its military bases and dams. One historian has described the federal government's 1950s highway-building binge as a case study in "interstate socialism"—a phrase that aptly describes how the West was really won. The fast food industry took root alongside that interstate highway system, as a new form of restaurant sprang up beside the new off-ramps. Moreover, the extraordinary growth of this industry over the past quarter-century did not occur in a political vacuum. It took place during a period when the inflation-adjusted value of the minimum wage declined by about 40 percent, when sophisticated mass marketing techniques were for the first time directed at small children, and when federal agencies created to protect workers and consumers too often behaved like branch offices of the companies that were supposed to be regulated. Ever since the administration of President Richard Nixon, the fast food industry has worked closely with its allies in Congress and the White House to oppose new worker safety, food safety, and minimum wage laws. While publicly espousing support for the free market, the fast food chains have quietly pursued and greatly benefited from a wide variety of government subsidies. Far from being inevitable, America's fast food industry in its present form is the logical outcome of certain political and economic choices.

In the potato fields and processing plants of Idaho, in the ranchlands east of Colorado Springs, in the feedlots and slaughterhouses of the High Plains, you can see the effects of fast food on the nation's rural life, its environment, its workers, and its health. The fast food chains now stand atop a huge food-industrial complex that has gained control of American agriculture. During the 1980s, large multinationals—such as Cargill, ConAgra, and IBP—were allowed to dominate one commodity market after another. Farmers and cattle ranchers are losing their independence, essentially becoming hired hands for the agribusiness giants or being forced off the land. Family farms are now being replaced by gigantic corporate farms with absentee owners. Rural communities are losing their middle class and becoming socially stratified, divided between a small, wealthy elite and large numbers of the working poor. Small towns that seemingly belong in a Norman Rockwell painting are being turned into rural ghettos. The hardy, independent farmers whom Thomas Jefferson considered the bedrock of American democracy are a truly vanishing breed. The United States now has more prison inmates than full-time farmers.

19   The fast food chains' vast purchasing power and their demand for a uniform product have encouraged fundamental changes in how cattle are raised, slaughtered, and processed into ground beef. These changes have made meatpacking—once a highly skilled, highly paid occupation—into the most dangerous job in the United States, performed by armies of poor, transient immigrants whose injuries often go unrecorded and uncompensated. And the same meat industry practices that endanger these workers have facilitated the introduction of deadly pathogens, such as *E. coli* 0157:H7, into America's hamburger meat, a food aggressively marketed to children. Again and again, efforts to prevent the sale of tainted ground beef have been thwarted by meat industry lobbyists and their allies in Congress. The federal government has the legal authority to recall a defective toaster oven or stuffed animal—but still lacks the power to recall tons of contaminated, potentially lethal meat.

20   I do not mean to suggest that fast food is solely responsible for every social problem now haunting the United States. In some cases (such as the malling and sprawling of the West) the fast food industry has been a catalyst and a symptom of larger economic trends. In other cases (such as the rise of franchising and the spread of obesity) fast food has played a more central role. By tracing the diverse influences of fast food I hope to shed light not only on the workings of an important industry, but also on a distinctively American way of viewing the world.

21   Elitists have always looked down at fast food, criticizing how it tastes and regarding it as another tacky manifestation of American popular culture. The aesthetics of fast food are of much less concern to me than its impact upon the lives of ordinary Americans, both as workers and consumers. Most of all, I am concerned about its impact on the nation's children. Fast food is heavily marketed to children and prepared by people who are barely older than children. This is an industry that both feeds and feeds off the young. During the two years spent researching this book, I ate an enormous amount of fast food. Most of it tasted pretty good. That is one of the main reasons people buy fast food; it has been carefully designed to taste good. It's also inexpensive and convenient. But the value meals, two-for-one deals, and free refills of soda give a distorted sense of how much fast food actually costs. The real

price never appears on the menu.

The sociologist George Ritzer has attacked the fast food industry for   22
celebrating a narrow measure of efficiency over every other human value,
calling the triumph of McDonald's "the irrationality of rationality."
Others consider the fast food industry proof of the nation's great
economic vitality, a beloved American institution that appeals overseas to
millions who admire our way of life. Indeed, the values, the culture, and
the industrial arrangements of our fast food nation are now being
exported to the rest of the world. Fast food has joined Hollywood
movies, blue jeans, and pop music as one of America's most prominent
cultural exports. Unlike other commodities, however, fast food isn't
viewed, read, played, or worn. It enters the body and becomes part of
the consumer. No other industry offers, both literally and figuratively, so
much insight into the nature of mass consumption.

Hundreds of millions of people buy fast food every day without   23
giving it much thought, unaware of the subtle and not so subtle
ramifications of their purchases. They rarely consider where this food
came from, how it was made, what it is doing to the community around
them. They just grab their tray off the counter, find a table, take a seat,
unwrap the paper, and dig in. The whole experience is transitory and
soon forgotten. I've written this book out of a belief that people should
know what lies behind the shiny, happy surface of every fast food
transaction. They should know what really lurks between those sesame-
seed buns. As the old saying goes: You are what you eat.

After-Reading Activities

Analyzing the Content

1. List the effects on society that Eric Schlosser attributes to the fast food
   industry.

2. Is Schlosser more for or against fast food?

3. Explain the irony described in paragraph 13 of this essay.

4. Do you think publication of the information in the first three paragraphs
   of this essay compromises the security of North America, which the
   Cheyenne Mountain Air Force Station was originally created to protect?
   Explain your position.

5. Does this essay over-analyze fast food outlets? Is it worthwhile to study fast food companies as symbols of our society, threats to traditional social and cultural values, and phenomena of popular culture?

Structure and Style

6. What is the main argument or thesis of this essay? Is the essay about more than fast food?

7. a) Make an outline of this essay that shows its cause and effect structure.
   b) Explain how this essay also exemplifies the organizational patterns of analogy and compare and contrast.

8. Does Schlosser develop his argument inductively (presenting specific examples that lead to his general point) or deductively (presenting a general point and showing how it can be seen in specific examples)?

9. Assess the unity and cohesiveness of this essay. What, if anything, would you cut to increase the unity and cohesiveness? Explain your decision(s).

10. Assess the effect of the use of quotations from other authors and authorities in this essay. Are they effective supports for Schlosser's arguments?

After the War Is Over

Renata Salecl

Elements of the Essay

Renata Salecl begins her essay, "After the War Is Over," with a specific incident, a poignant narrative that draws her readers' attention and identifies her topic of post-traumatic stress disorder. She then continues to examine the causes and the effects of the disorder, drawing on different sources. While her topic is scientific and technical, Salecl chooses vocabulary and a level of language that are easily understood by readers, and examples that affect their emotions.

About the Writer

Philosopher and sociologist Renata Salecl has published widely in the areas of feminism, psychoanalysis, and political theory. Two of her books are *The Spoils of Freedom: Psychoanalysis and Feminism After the Fall of Socialism* (1994) and *(Per)versions of Love and Hate* (1998). She is also a teacher at the London School of Economics and works as a researcher for the Department of Law and Criminology in Slovenia.

THERE WAS A LITTLE GIRL on the ground in purple rubber boots, not breathing. A crowd was forming around her, which was what drew Darryl King's attention in the first place. The corporal was on routine duty, closing up his peacekeeping tour in Kosovo, with Canadian Forces 15 Combat Engineers, when he saw civilians running towards a car that had stopped near his position in Priština. It was early December 1999. 1

What happened over the next few minutes eventually strained his family relationships, hindered his military career and, to this day, haunts his thoughts. The little girl, who had been struck by a speeding car, was actually known to King. She used to tease him when he did his daily exercise run in Priština. 2

But that day, he scooped her up in his arms and ran for her life towards a nearby medical unit. Later, with her blood still on his hands, 3

King found out the child had died. He worried then—and worries now—that his spur-of-the-moment rescue run might somehow have contributed to her death. "She was about seven or eight years old," he says quietly. "Her name was Hannah. She was born in war and survived it—for what? To get run over by a car?"

4   The incident was central to King's mental anguish on his return to Edmonton Garrison, and to his eventual diagnosis of Post-Traumatic Stress Disorder, the bane of the modern peacekeeping soldier. Those succumbing to PTSD face a classic military Catch 22: seek help and perhaps the nightmares, the chronic anxiety and the unchecked anger will be treated, but run the risk of arousing the suspicion of fellow soldiers that you are shirking your duty.

5   There are numerous reports dealing not only with the suffering of the victims of the most recent wars in the Balkans, but also of those who tried to stop those wars—the peacekeepers. And the debate on their suffering seems to continue the decades-long discussion on post-war trauma. In World War I, psychologists spoke about shell shock, seeking to link psychological breakdown to the horror of shelling. In the Vietnam War, however, the concept of "post-traumatic stress disorder" was introduced in an effort to remove guilt from the individual soldier: his condition is the result of external circumstances, not of his own psychological predisposition.

6   For decades, military psychiatrists tried to figure out what causes breakdown in the midst of combat; and why many veterans continue for years to have nightmares, depression or panic attacks, often leading to suicide. A soldier is usually able to carry on in combat for considerable time, under conditions of extreme danger and discomfort, until something happens that his defence mechanism cannot encompass.

7   As one psychiatrist explains: "The actual events varied tremendously, ranging from things as simple as a friendly gesture from the enemy or an unexpected change in orders to the death of a leader or a buddy." In all these cases, the soldiers suddenly changed their perception of the war and were unable to continue participating in the battle. These soldiers did not suddenly become cowards; rather, they experienced an acute state of anxiety, radically different from fear.

8   In general, we fear something we can see or hear, a tangible object or situation. Fear can be articulated: we can say, for example, "I fear the dark," or "I fear barking dogs." In contrast, we often perceive anxiety as a state of fear that is objectless: we cannot say what it is that is making

us anxious. Anxiety has a more powerful effect/affect than fear precisely because we cannot pin down the cause.

This definition of the difference between anxiety and fear corresponds to what we *think* we experience in our daily lives. Psychoanalysis, however, gives a more complex view of this difference. Freud, for instance, had two theories of anxiety: one that links it to an excess of libidinal energy that has not been discharged; another which takes anxiety as a feeling of an imminent danger to the ego, thus pushing the subject into a state of panic.

9

When French psychoanalyst Jacques Lacan speaks about anxiety, he introduces the problem of castration and the subject's relation with what he calls the Other—the term used to designate the social-symbolic structure in which we live: language, culture, institutions. However, it is not that the subject has some kind of a castration anxiety in regard to the Other, that he or she takes the Other to be someone who might take something precious from him or her. Lacan points out that the neurotic does not retreat from the castrating Other, but from making of his own castration what is lacking in the Other. What does this mean? When psychoanalysis claims that the subject undergoes symbolic castration by becoming a speaking being it is asserting that language marks the subject in a specific way, which makes the human being very different from other living beings. Language introduces a constitutive lack into the subject, because of which, the subject is able to desire, and constantly searches for objects of this desire that might fill the void or sense of lack and make it disappear.

10

However, the subject not only always fails in this attempt, the subject also faces the fact that he or she has no full identity which would grant him or her some stability and consistency. When we say that the subject is castrated, we mean primarily that the subject *per se* is empty, nothing by him/herself. All the subject's power comes from the symbolic insignia he/she temporarily takes on. Take, for instance, a policeman; a nobody, perhaps, until he puts on his uniform and becomes a person with power. The subject is castrated, that is to say, powerless by himself. Only by occupying a certain place in the symbolic order does he or she temporarily acquire some power or status.

11

On the one hand, the subject is concerned with his or her own inconsistency (the lack that marks him or her); on the other hand, the subject is also bothered by the fact that the society in which he or she lives is marked by antagonisms, that is to say, that the Other (the symbolic order) is inconsistent—divided, non-whole. The subject can

12

thus never get a full answer to what it is the Other wants or how the Other sees him or her. This creates a specific discomfort.

13   One of the ways the individual manages this unease is by creating a fantasy. Fantasy is a way of covering up the fundamental lack by creating a scenario, a story that gives his or her life a sense of consistency and stability, while he also perceives the social order as being coherent and not marked by antagonisms. Fantasy and anxiety present two different ways for the subject to deal with the lack that marks him as well as the Other, the symbolic order. If fantasy provides a certain comfort to the subject, anxiety incites the feeling of discomfort. However, anxiety does not simply have a paralysing effect. The power of anxiety is that it creates a state of preparedness so that the subject is less paralysed, less surprised by events that might radically shatter his or her fantasy and thus cause a breakdown or the emergence of trauma.

14   Fantasy, however, also helps prevent the emergence of anxiety. Take the case of the Israeli soldier Ami, as recorded in Zahava Solomon's *Combat Stress Reaction: The Enduring Toll of War*. Ami served in the Yom Kippur and Lebanon wars. He had been an avid filmgoer in his youth and during the Yom Kippur war he felt as if he was playing the part of a soldier in a war movie. This fantasy sustained him throughout the war: "I said to myself, it is not so terrible. It's like a war movie. They're actors, and I'm just some soldier. I don't have an important role. Naturally, there are all the weapons that are in a war movie. All sorts of helicopters, all sorts of tanks, and there's shooting ... [But] basically, I felt that I wasn't there. That is, all I had to do was finish the filming and go home." Later, in the Lebanon war, Ami felt like a tourist observing pretty villages, mountains, women, etc.

15   But at some point, the fantasy of being on tour or in a movie collapsed. This happened when Ami witnessed massive destruction in the Lebanon War and was involved in heavy face-to-face fighting. The scene that triggered his breakdown happened in Beirut when he saw stables piled with corpses of Arabian racehorses mingled with corpses of people. The sight filled him with a sense of apocalyptic destruction, and he collapsed: "I went into a state of apathy, and I was not functioning." Ami explains the process as follows: "In the Yom Kippur war, I put my defence mechanism into operation and it worked fantastically. I was able to push a button and start it up ... In Lebanon, the picture was clearer. In the Yom Kippur war, we didn't fight face-to-face or shoot from a short distance ... If I saw a corpse, it was a corpse in the field. But here [in

Lebanon] everything was right next to me ... And of all things, the thing with the horses broke me ... A pile of corpses ... and you see them along with people who were killed. That's a picture I'd never seen in any movie ... I began to sense the reality [that] it's not a movie any more."

Anxiety emerges when, at the place of the lack—the point of inconsistency that the fantasy covers up—the individual encounters a certain object that perturbs his fantasy framework. For the soldier Ami, this happened when he saw the pile of dead horses. His fantasy had enabled him to observe dead soldiers because he was an outsider watching a movie; horses were something else. The fantasy collapsed and Ami broke down. [16]

Today, there are similar problems with peacekeepers. Wendy Holden points out in *Shell Shock: The Psychological Impact of War* that peacekeepers suffer from the fact that they must observe atrocities but are helpless to fight back or defend those they have been sent to save. "Proud to become professional soldiers and keen to fight a war, they are, however, distanced from death and the reality of killing. They are members of a society that finds fatalities unimaginable. When presented with the unimaginable, they crack." British peacekeeper Gary Bohanna came to Bosnia with a belief that a peacekeeping role was better than a war in which colleagues got killed. [17]

But he was quickly disillusioned when he saw civilians killed, women raped and whole families slaughtered. The traumatic event which precipitated his breakdown was when he saw a young girl who had "shrapnel wounds in her head, half her head was blown away. Her eye was coming out of its socket and she was screaming. She was going to die, but I couldn't bear her pain. I put a blanket over her head and shot her in her head. That was all I could do." Here again is the soldier who comes to war with the protective shield of fantasy—this time that he is coming to do good deeds but is not fully engaged in war—only to have his fantasy undermined by events. [18]

Unlike the recent past, in which wars still involved at least minimal engagement between the soldier and the victims on the battlefield, the soldier today is often a distant actor who shoots from afar and has no knowledge of the consequences on the front. Contemporary wars are supposed to be aseptic, so that US soldiers can fly for a couple of hours to drop bombs over Kosovo, but return home in time for football on TV. For those soldiers who will still need to engage in direct battle, military psychiatrists anticipate anxiety will be so overwhelming, so [19] paralysing they will need a magic potion to alleviate anxiety and turn soldiers into robots with no emotional engagement with the atrocities they are committing. So far, all attempts to create such drugs have failed. The anti-anxiety drugs allegedly used on the front at the time of the Gulf War not only failed to alleviate anxiety, they produced numerous side effects that made soldiers zombie-like creatures, barely able to function or perform their duties.

20   The trend towards making war anxiety-free paradoxically goes hand in hand with today's attempts to make wars independent from political struggles. In the West's assessment of the situation in former Yugoslavia, the political dimensions of the conflicts were constantly overlooked or too quickly historicised. The problem with NATO interventions is that they were publicly presented as simple humanitarian missions that had nothing to do with the political situation in the region and never admitted the West's strong economic interests in the Balkans. This humanitarian ideology goes hand in hand with the media's depiction of the war. On the one hand, we are shown war as a simple computer game in which the soldiers dropping the bombs from the air are completely detached from the reality of the situation on the ground. On the other, we see images of suffering victims—the destruction of villages, people being killed, wounded and dead bodies exposed on the screen, and so on. This over-visibility of one side, and complete invisibility of the other, are linked to the fact that the economic and political logic of intervention in the war zones remained unravelled.

21   Advances in science and the vast cyberworld of new technologies foster the impression that life is like a computer game; that we live in a world of simulacra in which bodies and identities are something we can change and play with. The boundary between life and death also seems to be changed. In cyberspace, one can enjoy playing with numerous imaginary personas; in the near future, it will be possible to create new body parts out of existing genetic material; easy, eventually, to imagine the laboratory production of the entire human body. Given this scientific background, we can assess breakdowns in war rather differently. Freud pointed out that war forces people to deal with the question of death in a new way: they usually avoid thinking about the possibility of their own death and it even seems as if the unconscious has no image of it at all.

22   Today, with the proper genetic code and the intervention of new drugs, people hope that matters of life and death will be more predictable and

controllable in the future. In the same way, military psychiatry hopes it will be able to master the soldier's traumas in regard to death with the help of new drugs. The ideal soldier of the future will be completely detached from the situation (an outsider not really present in the war) and will neutrally observe the atrocities going on in the war. However, the problem with the military's attempts to find a cure for anxiety, for example with the help of drugs, is that rather than preventing the soldier's anxieties, such drugs actually help to provoke new ones. While it is unclear how much the military has actually tested such drugs on the battlefield (for example, at the time of the Gulf War), soldiers have indulged in numerous conspiracy theories. A whole set of new anxieties is emerging as soldiers speculate on the nature of the dangerous new drugs scientists are allegedly testing on them and the paralysing side effects these have. The ultimate trauma for soldiers becomes a fight against the hidden enemy within: against those who sent him to war in the first place.

After-Reading Activities

Analyzing the Content

1. Identify other names given to post-traumatic stress disorder in this essay. Assess whether they help or hinder the reader's understanding of the condition.

2. Explain the role of fantasy in protecting someone from post-traumatic stress disorder.

3. Explain the differences the writer mentions between the cyberworld and world of Freudian psychology.

4. Debate one or both of the following resolutions:
   • Be It Resolved That Canadian Soldiers Should Continue to Serve as Peacekeepers and Combatants in Troubled Areas of the World
   • Be It Resolved That the Canadian Government Should Provide Complete Financial Support for Canadian Soldiers Suffering from Post-Traumatic Stress Disorder Resulting from Service in the Canadian Armed Forces

   Additional research may be necessary.

Structure and Style

5. If you had to select one sentence from this essay to illustrate its thesis, which one would you choose? Explain your choice.

6. What do you think is Renata Salecl's main purpose in this essay?

7. The introductory paragraph to this essay could be the introduction to a short story. At which point does it become clear to the reader that this is a non-fiction essay? Assess the effectiveness of the introduction to this essay.

8. Show how this essay follows a cause and effect structure.

9. Is the final paragraph of this essay as effective as it could be? Suggest one change that would enable the paragraph to give the essay more unity and cohesiveness.

Extending the Pattern

Using one of the three essays in this section as a model, write your own cause and effect essay. Consider topics such as the following:

- a toy or consumer product other than those discussed in "Barbie and Her Playmates"
- fast food outlets and their effect on individual lifestyles and society in general
- post-traumatic stress disorder based on information raised in the debates in activity 4 of "After the War Is Over"
- the importance of a good education
- the value of travel
- how growing up in Canada shapes a person's character

You may need to do additional research. After completing your first draft, work with a partner to revise and edit your essay, focusing on the organization and the strength of your arguments.

Elements of the Pattern

Narration is simply storytelling. Although we most immediately associate storytelling with entertainment, this may not be its primary objective in an essay. Narration in an essay is meant to make or support a point. It supports the essay's thesis.

Since the objective of the narration essay is to make a point, it is important to strive for clarity and conciseness. When writing a narration essay, ensure that your readers are not distracted from the intended point of the story. Here are a few strategies that will help you achieve this:

1. **Focus on the point you are making, not on the story.** If you lose sight of your point, you may go off on tangents or start introducing unrelated details. Before writing your narration essay, list the details that you would like to include, and then review each one to ensure that it helps achieve your objective. If it doesn't, delete it.

2. **Limit the number of details.** Too much detail can cause difficulties for both the writer and the reader. As a writer, if you put too much detail in a short narration essay, it can become unnecessarily dense. From the reader's point of view, too much detail can be tedious and confusing, distracting the reader's attention from the main point.

3. **Follow a chronological order.** Generally, a story that follows a chronological order is easier to grasp. In cases where a chronological order is not appropriate, you should still use a logical order to help your readers understand your point. Before writing, take the time to put the list of details into a logical order.

4. **Establish the primary characters and details early.** You should try to introduce the main characters and the situation in the first paragraph. This enables the reader to gain an immediate understanding of the situation and will help alleviate any confusion. The *Who, What, Where, When, Why,* and *How* of the story should be achieved as quickly and clearly as possible.

A Home at the End of the Journey

Allen Abel

Elements of the Essay

What does it mean to become and be a Canadian citizen? This question is the focal point of Allen Abel's essay, "A Home at the End of the Journey." His tone is light, but his message is serious. Based on his own experience, Abel builds a reflective narration, taking his readers through the citizenship ceremony.

About the Writer

Journalist Allen Abel was born in Brooklyn, New York, and moved to Canada in the late 1970s, settling in Toronto. He started his career as a sports reporter, writing for *The Globe and Mail* for several years before becoming the newspaper's Beijing correspondent in 1983 and then the producer of CBC television's *The Journal* in 1986. His published books include *Scaring Myself: Far Flung Adventures of a TV Journalist* (1993), *Flatbush Odyssey: A Journey Through the Heart of Brooklyn* (1995), and the most recent, *Abel's Outback: Explanations and Misadventures on Six Continents, 1990–2000* (2001), all based on his personal experiences.

O N AN EARLY WINTER EVENING in the bottomlands of Toronto's untamed River Don, 70 would-be Canadians file into a blinding bright conference room and take their seats in the alphabetical order of their mutually incomprehensible names. Outside, a first frosting has rendered this quadrant of the city even more picturesque than usual. The coatracks are crammed like Tokyo commuters; overshoes slump limply on the floor.

The 70 are to take the Oath of Citizenship, pledging allegiance to the woman in England—and her lovelorn son and *his* son and so forth forever—who still embodies the vast, infant Canadian state. In front of

1

2

the oath-takers, a speaker's podium has been set up, and there is a small desk on which are piled the certifying documents, emblazoned with Lion and Unicorn, that each new citizen will receive. I'm a little nervous, my throat a bit dry. I am one of the 70.

3   Now the clerk of the court comes out, a tall, energetic woman in billowing robes, dashing around like a refugee claimant from the cast of *Sister Act 2*. The ceremony will begin soon, she announces. When the oath has been sworn, she instructs, we new Canadians are to proceed from our seats in a seamless serpentine to shake the hand of the presiding judge and then, doing a single axel in front of the podium, we are to return immediately to our assigned chairs. All of this is to be accomplished swiftly, to leave more time for speeches.

4   Photography is permitted, the clerk says, but not during the swearing of the oath itself. This act, it seems, is as sacred as the fox dance of the British Columbia Musqueam, and snapshots would defile the affair. But Beta cameramen from local television stations are here, and they will roll right over the taboo, and no one will complain or try to halt them.

5   It is International Human Rights Week, so the ceremony is to include more ceremony than usual. Decorated dignitaries from various ethnic communities of Metro Toronto have been invited to witness the swearing-in and then—it is a lovely touch—they are to reaffirm their own loyalty to Crown and Canada by taking the oath themselves. A red-coat Mountie stands at crisp attention, and officers of the Canadian Jewish Congress warmly greet each immigrant family. It is they who are hosting this group naturalization, here at their modern headquarters in this snowbound suburban vale.

6   I study my fellow foreigners as they arrive, and I try to guess which ones are war orphans and day laborers and entrepreneurs, and which ones are gangsters and welfare cheats. Tonight's new Canadians, we are informed, have come from 27 countries, borne by the strange and sweeping currents of life to reunite, for this brief instant, in the saying of 43 words. Then, we will scatter into the infinite city, to meet again in fear or fellowship only at bus shelters, and some other less Toronto-centric place. But around me now, as the presiding judge arrives and the crowded room falls to a hush, I see the faces I have faced as a foreign correspondent in the refugee camps of Kurdistan, the back alleys of Havana, the cages of Hong Kong that hold escaped Vietnamese. It is a swirling sensation—that I have been sent from this city to their worlds and now their worlds have joined with mine.

(An hour earlier, I had thought: this is the night I finally leave   7
Brooklyn, my home town, behind me. But then, my wife and I had
jumped into a taxi to make the ceremony on time and it had been
outfitted with a bullet-proof partition between driver and passenger, an
emblem of the new urban Canada. No one spoke; I stared glumly at the
snow. Brooklyn had followed me north.)

The presiding judge greets us. An immigrant herself from some   8
European duchy, I cannot locate her accent—Latvia? Luxembourg?—she
has performed this procedure manifold times but her voice still swells
with proud anticipation. We are gaining a new country, she tells us. The
gifts of this land will be limited only by the capacity of our hearts.

We stand at the clerk's command and begin the affirmation, some of   9
us mumbling, some nearly shouting, others utterly lost in the antiquated
Anglophile creed ("I will be faithful and bear true allegiance…"). The
cameras are on us. We will observe the laws of Canada, we utter. We will
fulfil our duties. We will remain standing and do it all over again, says
the presiding judge—in French.

The slow parade to the podium begins. I clasp the judge's hand,   10
receive my Commemoration of Canadian Citizenship. Now, the
Canadians who have been citizens for longer than six minutes are invited
to restate their vows. In the peanut gallery to my right, I see my
Canadian wife with her right hand raised, serenely chanting along. But I
am already contemplating the fruits of my neonate heritage: seats on
royal commissions; diplomatic postings to warm, benign republics;
poets' allowances; jury duty. Shaking me from this reverie, *O Canada*
begins, sung by two young stars of *Miss Saigon*.

The ceremony is over. We take our coats and re-enter the intemperate   11
night. Shivering, our teeth playing marimba melodies, we give up on the
bus after a couple of minutes and hail another cab. I slide in, expecting
more anticrime plastic, more mistrust, more silence.

Instead there is a slim, blushing Arab in the driver's seat and a   12
giggling Chinese woman right beside him. They both are in their 20s,
lost in laughter. Turning east on Sheppard, skating sideways on the
pond, the pilot turns around to shake my hand and to introduce his
companion.

"Don't be afraid," the driver says. "This is my girlfriend."   13

"Congratulations!" I tell him. I'm thinking: Maybe this place *can* work.   14

After-Reading Activities

Analyzing the Content

1. Discuss the following:
   - Allen Abel says of the 70 new Canadians, "... we will scatter into the infinite city, to meet again in fear or fellowship only at bus shelters, and some other less Toronto-centric place" (paragraph 6). What does he mean by this?
   - The writer says, "Brooklyn had followed me north" (paragraph 7). Why does he say this? How does the tone of this paragraph differ from the tone of paragraphs 12 to 14?

Structure and Style

2. What is the thesis of this essay?

3. Abel uses a narration or storytelling approach for his essay. Why is this an effective way of getting his message across to his audience?

4. Find examples of the following devices in the essay, analyzing how each adds liveliness to the writing: alliteration, allusion, simile, personification, imagery.

5. Find places where Abel uses humour to contrast the seriousness of the message of his essay. Explain why these moments work so well.

6. Paragraph 9 contains three sentences that begin with "We will." The third sentence provides a rhetorical twist. What is it, and what is the effect this sentence is trying to achieve?

7. Why does Abel leave the fact that he is going to be part of this ceremony until the end of the second paragraph?

8. Abel takes a taxi twice: once to get to the ceremony and once to return home. Although the anecdote about the ride to the ceremony is not at the beginning of the essay, it, along with the final ride, still acts as a frame around the story. Why is this a particularly strong structural device?

Anecdotes of Racism: A View Across the Aisle

Miguna Miguna

Elements of the Essay

The events related in "Anecdotes of Racism" are based on African-Canadian Miguna Miguna's own experiences with systemic racism. He develops the anecdotes in a storytelling style, relating them in the present tense to give the events immediacy and to convey the anger and frustration he feels about the ill treatment he received at the hands of government employees.

About the Writer

Miguna Miguna is a defence lawyer living in Toronto. He was a member of the African Canadian Legal Clinic, a non-profit organization that provides legal representation for African-Canadians, especially for "race-based test case litigation." He is currently a faculty member of the newly formed Nelson Mandela Academy of Applied Legal Studies (Canada), an organization that offers education on Canadian law to immigrants, refugees, and minorities to help them start their own legal practices.

Part I: Racist Thorns at the Gates of Injustice: A Biased Reflection

I SLOWLY CLIMB THE STAIRS leading into the August House, the House so revered by most Canadians that one often will witness fright, genuine fright, and wobbly legs in many a soul so unfortunate as to be brought to it by members of the all powerful Metropolitan Toronto Police force and duly christened "an accused." As I reach the top of the first set of stairs, I turn right and take the elevators. The climbing feels good for my legs. But this is enough exercise for today. As the elevator chimes and comes to a brief halt, the doors open wide and I emerge, with a brief case in hand and a stern face, I enter the tenth-floor Registry of the Superior Court of Justice (formerly the Ontario Court,

1

General Division). I can hear my heart pounding, my chest moving up and down and small strings of sweat crawling lazily down my cheeks. I momentarily observe my protruding pouch and swear at myself for allowing my weight to become this bothersome. "It's either because I am overeating or it is due to lack of exercise," I say silently to myself. I try to rationalize by adding that the private practice of law requires too much reading and sitting down and I actually do not have time to exercise.

2   Still smiling at my thoughts, I approach the Court Clerk, seated on a high stool looking important. I quickly retrieve the nicely bound Motion Record. I then immediately produce a cheque for $75.00 that I had written to the order of the Minister of Finance, Mr. Paul Martin, as required, and wait for service. The Clerk looks briefly at me over her thickly rimmed glasses and sighs deeply. "She must be tired already," I think to myself, but say nothing. She suddenly turns and begins what appears to be an endless tap on her computer keyboard. "Hi." With my voice slightly quivering, I manage an embarrassing greeting. She ignores it and continues her laborious tapping. I continue to wait.

3   Occasionally, the Clerk answers the incessantly ringing telephone and engages in small talk. However, as soon as her conversations end, she continues her endless tapping on the keyboard without any discernible sign that she is aware of my presence right here in front of her. Finally, after thirty minutes (time that seems to me like a decade), I hear a growl:

4   "Yes! What can I help you with?"

5   Having resigned myself to what appeared as a long wait, I quickly stand at attention and stammer out my words ...

6   "Ooh ... I ... I ... I ... I would like to file an ex parte motion, returnable on ..."

7   "Wait, wait a minute!"

8   She cuts me in mid sentence, strongly waving me to stop what I am trying to say. Then she props her chin on her clenched fists, her knuckles reddish, and strained. She inquires:

9   "Do you have a LAWYER SIR?"

10   "I AM THE LAWYER," I answer back, firmly and deliberately. Repressed anger begins to show on my face. I am slowly gaining my composure, my confidence. I am beginning to show my displeasure at this unnecessary discourtesy.

11   She quickly grabs the package I had placed on the counter before her and scans through it.

12   "Hmm ... Hmmm ... Hmm ... Yah ... ya ..." she hams her way

through the document.

I can swear that she is planning to pull some trick, blame me for a missing comma, maybe a full stop. But I am sure there are no mistakes. Not even minor typographical ones. I had taken the trouble to spell-check and I literally read through every single word, line, sentence and paragraph three times. I stand proudly and wait. 13

"Where is your affidavit of service sir?" she asks firmly but does not bother to wait for my answer before she continues. 14

"If you are really a lawyer then you must know that we can't accept any motion materials without proof of service …" 15

"But it is an ex parte motion madam. We are not required to serve ex parte motions," I manage a response and hope that my explanation will put this fishing expedition to an end. I am sure she has read the Rules of Civil Procedure and is aware that ex parte motions are a unique breed, allowing parties to bring an urgent motion on short notice without the necessity of notifying the responding parties since the granting of such motions would not result in any injustice or serious prejudice to the other side. "She has to know that," I say silently, in a rage. 16

"Says who?" she shoots back, unabated. 17

"Well, if you must know, says the Rules of Civil Procedure," I reply. 18

We are clearly at a standstill. We have reached a point of no return. "She does not want to accept my argument, not because it is illogical or baseless; she simply does not want to lose face," I think to myself once more. 19

"Show me which Rule says that SIR?" she is determined to push me to the wire. 20

"Subrule 37.01 of the Ontario Rules of Civil Procedure states that 'A motion shall be made by a notice of motion (Form 37A) unless the nature of the motion or the circumstances make a notice of motion unnecessary,'" I read aloud, exasperated. 21

"Clearly this Rule was intended for precisely the same set of circumstances as this one. The nature of this motion and the circumstances make service entirely unnecessary. Please take your time and read under our 'Grounds for the Motion' and you will see that we have been unable to contact the respondent. All our registered letters to him, sent pursuant to Subrule 16.06(1), have been returned by Canada Post unclaimed. Please read the affidavit in support of our motion and see the attached exhibits. In any event, we are also seeking relief under Rule 16.04(1), for an order dispensing with service. This is plain and 22 clear. I honestly don't see what you find so difficult to understand ..."

23   I am beginning to get agitated.

24   She sternly fixes me with her gaze and calls out "Next?" without pomp or ceremony. She then motions to the person behind me to move forward to be served and pushes my documents to the side of the counter. The white process server behind me eagerly rushes to take my spot. I have been dismissed.

25   "You can stand aside as you look for a better Rule to persuade me that what you are attempting to do is valid. Meanwhile, I have to serve the next person on line. We have a lot of people waiting." As she says this, she reaches out and takes the process server's motion materials and proceeds to file them without even a brief examination as to whether or not the documents were in good order.

26   I momentarily reach for my briefcase and retrieve my 1998 Ontario Civil Practice text. I want to make sure that my rendition of the Rules has been accurate, that I have not made any mistakes. I quickly confirm that all my citations were accurate. By this time, some people seem to have noticed our protracted "discussion" and are watching it with obvious delight.

27   "Well Mr. Lawyer, I set the RULES here! At this counter! If I say that you need an affidavit of service, then that's what you must produce before I can file any of your documents. Case closed." Whatever reservations I might have had about her, this last statement completely changed my mind. I immediately conclude that it would be a waste of time to continue talking to her and I ask to speak to her supervisor.

28   "Be my guest," she says, walking slowly away from the counter after serving the process server.

29   Thirty minutes later, a young man emerges and inquires about my problem. I briefly explain it to him, and without apologizing for the discourtesy and unprofessional behaviour of the Clerk, this man, expressionless, simply takes my motion record, quickly taps on the computer, takes my cheque and issues a receipt.

30   "Done," he announces.

31   I hurriedly pick up my bags and leave, exhausted and wishing that I had never become a lawyer. However, as soon as I reach the subway stop, my mind rapidly moves to my next case and the incident at the court registry recedes to the back of my mind, only to be retrieved later as part of my literary effort to chase after John Grisham. I intend to make it a heated pursuit.

Part II: The Courtroom

I arrive early at the Brampton Court and dutifully approach the notice   32
board to determine which courtroom my case has been assigned today.
As soon as I locate the room, I proceed to the Court Clerk's office in
order to find out the particulars of the judge assigned that courtroom. It
is considered a good practice for a lawyer to know the temperaments of
the presiding judges. Sometimes it helps one avoid embarrassment. Most
of the time, however, it simply assists one to be psychologically prepared
for any sudden idiosyncratic outburst that many judges are known for.
This is expected when one deals with a large population of senile
individuals with huge egos, massive power, and lots of discretion. As a
young Afrikan lawyer in Canada, I have not been able to conclusively
assess or determine the benefits, if any, of this bizarre practice among
lawyers. But, as with everything else in this tightly controlled profession,
I unquestioningly end up doing some things just because other
individuals do them. Or simply because it has always been done.

When I approach the Court Clerk and plead for his assistance, he   33
quickly tells me that he is not in a position to help. He explains to me that
without a list of judges provided by the Court Administrator's office and
posted on the board at the Registry, he himself is unable to say, precisely,
which judge would be in which court at any given time or day. I
reluctantly accept his explanation and file my body into Courtroom 11A.

"Oye, Oye. The Court is now in process. Judge Tomlinson presiding.   34
God Save the Queen," the clerk announces after we have been waiting
for one hour.

An old man in ancient regalia enters and waves us to be seated. He   35
then turns to the Clerk, who takes a pile of documents to his desk.

"We are first going to purge the list," the judge announces.   36

He then calls out each number and asks whether the matter will proceed   37
by way of consent or by argument. He then reaches my case and says:

"Yes, Mr. Maunda, I see that something has fallen on your head."   38
There was a deliberate emphasis on what was meant to be my name.

I quickly look around, thinking that perhaps the judge has confused   39
me for someone else who may have a name that may have looked to him
as closely resembling my own. Seeing no one, I nervously touch my
head but cannot understand what the judge is trying to say to me.

"I'm sorry Your Honour, but my name is M-I-G-U-N-A, initial M, for   40
the record." I obviously leave out the part about something having fallen

on my head, hoping that the judge would move on, but I am mistaken.

41   "Yes, there is something on your head Mr. Maunda!" He persists, not acknowledging my polite correction.

42   "Oh! Your Honour, the kofia I am wearing is for religious purposes," I manage a coherent response after realizing that the judge is indeed referring to my kofia. I stress "religious purposes" with the hope that he will understand.

43   "May I ask what religion that is?" he insists, with a unique emphasis on "religion."

44   "I am a Moslem sir," I reply in utter disappointment. My heart starts racing. I begin to doubt whether this is a genuine inquiry or merely intended as an embarrassment for me.

45   "Is it a recognized religion? Say, like the Jewish religion?" The judge inches forward ridiculously. Everyone around him looks satisfied by this line of questioning but I am not impressed. The problem is that I am totally powerless. I cannot do anything but participate "respectfully" in this judicial cultural homicide.

46   "I am sure that Your Honour is not trying to limit the application of the Charter and restrict what is legitimate from some so-called illegitimate religion. Of course Islam is a recognized religion!"

47   Judge Tomlinson then briefly confers with the Clerk, they both rapidly nod their heads and he moves on to the next item on the list. Mine has been seriously purged. I turn around to look at my client's reaction and can tell from the expression on his face that he thinks he has lost the case.

48   As the judge proceeds with his deliberate partial purge, I recall other similar instances when the so-called Captains of Justice have demonstrated their naked insensitivity, bias and plain racism. For example, I easily remember the time when I, as an articling student-at-law with Roach, Schwartz & Associates, had attended a court session during the trial of the Black activist, Dudley Laws. The courtroom was packed with supporters of Mr. Laws. I was seated next to the counsel table, assisting Mr. Laws's lead counsel at the time, Mr. Peter Rosenthal. However, before the trial could proceed, the judge loudly announced that everyone who was wearing what he termed "head gears" must take them off or else they would have to leave the courtroom.

49   Confusion immediately descended upon the courtroom, with some people quickly obeying the order and occupying themselves with the removal of their hats, kofias, whatever. Some others, however, refused to

obey the order and simply remained seated. They engaged in loud arguments with the guards and a few police officers, trying to explain to them that their "head gears" were not atomic missiles but religious and/or cultural items that could not be removed. Eventually, Mr. Laws's lawyer stood up and presented an argument to the judge, imploring him not to evict Laws's supporters from the courtroom. He also explained why the spectators ought to be allowed to remain with their kofias on. He cited several Supreme Court of Canada cases where the Court had ruled that religious items like kofias are constitutionally protected and that to compel any individual to conform to the majority's will by not allowing people to wear them in public places, including inside courtrooms, constitutes a denial of that individual's constitutionally protected right.

Despite the confusion and counsel's arguments, the presiding judge   50
ruled that that was his Court and he, not the Supreme Court of Canada, made the rules in his courtroom. I then decided to leave the courtroom quietly instead of accepting this arbitrary exercise of power and unfettered discretion. But I resolved to put up a spirited fight once I had been called to the bar and given a license to practice law.

"And this is what I am doing now. Whether Judge Tomlinson likes it or   51
not, I am not removing my kofia," I silently resolve as my client's eyes try to communicate some inscrutable message. "I may well lose both this case and the client, but I shall not allow them to uproot my conscience and self-worth in the process. Nothing can justify this cultural onslaught …"

When our matter is finally called for adjudication, our opponents   52
stand up and request a thirty-minute adjournment to confer with us on possible disposition. This is very surprising to us since I had tried to have them discuss settlement to no avail in the past few weeks. But perhaps our opponents have reconsidered after seeing my resolve.

I eventually walk out of Courtroom 11A with a signed Minutes of   53
Settlement, mostly in favour of my client. "Perseverance, courage and focus are sometimes better than a thousand bullets," I say to myself as I prepare for another encounter with the so-called justice system.

TINDA! May I grow as tall as my uncle's pine tree.   54

After-Reading Activities

Analyzing the Content

1. Explain the meaning of the essay's title.

2. By alluding to John Grisham in paragraph 31, what does Miguna suggest he is going to do with his experiences?

3. Write the following expressions in your own words:
   • "… she hams her way through the document." (paragraph 12)
   • "… and hope that my explanation will put this fishing expedition to an end." (paragraph 16)
   • "I cannot do anything but participate 'respectfully' in this judicial cultural homicide." (paragraph 45)

Structure and Style

4. The writer not only has to tell his story, but he has to explain some intricate aspects of the law in order for non-lawyers to understand his essay. Examine each of the passages where he does this, and assess their effectiveness.

5. In paragraph 32, Miguna makes many generalizations about judges. Are his statements fair in the context of this essay? Why or why not?

6. Miguna often appeals to the reader's senses. Choose two examples, and explain how the writer has achieved these sensory appeals.

7. Describe the tone of this essay. Give specific examples of words and phrases used to create the tone.

8. The writer places some of his thoughts in quotation marks, similar to direct speech. What is the purpose of this technique? Should it be used more, or less? Explain your opinion.

9. How does the ending add to or detract from the essay?

Double Vision in a New Old World

Naomi Shihab Nye

Elements of the Essay

"Double Vision in a New Old World" is based on Naomi Shihab Nye's own experience as a child of parents from two different races—Palestinian and German-American—seeing the world through a kind of "double vision." On her visit to the Middle East with her American-born son, she experiences this double vision even more acutely, particularly with regard to her young son, who is American and yet also belongs to "this new old world" of the Middle East. Nye's essay weaves the present with the past, creating a reflective and heartfelt narrative style.

About the Writer

Poet and essayist Naomi Shihab Nye was born on March 12, 1952, in St. Louis, Missouri, to an American mother and a Palestinian father. She was educated at Trinity University in San Antonio, Texas. Nye has published collections of poetry, which include *Juke Box* (1982), *Red Suitcase* (1994), and *Fuel* (1998). She has also written an autobiographical novel, *Habibi* (1996), about a teenaged Arab-American who goes to live in Jerusalem.

BECAUSE MY SIX-YEAR-OLD SON has never held the hands of his great-grandmother, tattooed seventy years ago by a gypsy who said she could turn hands into birds about to fly away, I want him to hold them. Before they fly, far, and the knowing of great-grandmothers is denied him forever.

My father, Aziz, travels with us to my grandmother's home in the Middle East, upon my urging, to make the generational ladder complete. Also, he comes to translate; my Arabic remains limited to the zone of "What's the story?" and "salt." Besides, it's good to have my father along for general moral support; to take a child into the turbulent

West Bank involves a kind of courage I can't depend on alone.

3   On the airplane, my son, Madison, chatters peacefully, and sleeps. He's told his friends he can't come to their birthday parties this month because he "has to go to the Middle East." He says it as if he has business there, as if he knows where it is.

4   I know where we are when we drive the pristine, stony slopes toward Jerusalem. The air smells crisp and cool. I think of the term my old uncles used to favor when they would leave the house for a walk—they were going out to "smell the air." My father hasn't heard anyone say this for a long time now. Now they say they're going out to "measure the streets."

5   We sleep heavily in an old stone hotel with high arched windows in east Jerusalem, on the Arab side of town. Twenty-five years ago I went to high school here for one year, at an Armenian school tucked into the Armenian convent sector of the Old City. Worlds within worlds. My family lived north of Jerusalem, in an upstairs flat of a wide stone house with balconies and a spectacular, craggy view. Shepherds would stand in the fields around our house all day, leaning against their curved canes. Their sheep drifted hungrily about them, poking for slim spokes of green. I liked to imagine what shepherds thought about as the light shifted slowly on the stones. I liked to wonder what the history of this land would have been had it all been left to shepherds.

6   The next morning a hard rain pounds the streets. We will take a taxi to the town of Ramallah, through a rolling countryside dotted with white stone houses and small grocery stores called "Garden of Eden," then switch to another car to take us deeper into the West Bank to my grandmother's village. License plates bear heightened implications here. Only certain colored plates are allowed to go certain places. Palestinians have been under curfew so often during the last few years, meaning they can't be out of their houses or traveling on the roads, that one must find out daily whether passage is even possible. Evening curfews—after 5:30—have been in effect for many months now. We call an American consul friend to find out today's regulation and he tells us the roads are open but iffy—they could close any moment.

7   Our bags stuffed with the usual assortment of oddball gifts—Ben-Gay in a tube for my grandmother's aching wrists, long scarves stitched with shiny threads, packets for making instant hot cocoa—we travel north, crowded in a car. Blacked-out graffiti on every wall shouts a muffled story.

8   In Ramallah, we huddle under a dripping awning while my father

looks for a taxi driver he recognizes. The name of my grandmother's village, spelled variously Sinjil and Singel, comes from St. Giles, who is said to have drunk from a well there about 1,200 years ago. I notice how time immediately stretches its dimension in this part of the world. To say something happened hundreds or thousands of years ago near a certain spot feels reasonable, unlike America, where houses built in the 1920s are considered old. I have tried to give a sense of this to my son, for whom "the old days" were two years ago.

"You are going to meet Sitti, my grandma, who is probably the oldest   9 person you have ever met. She is definitely more than ninety-five years old. Everyone says she is more than a hundred."

"Can she talk?" he asks. "Can she walk?" Reports fluctuate as to her   10 well-being. Some days she is weak and other days she feels more vigorous than the sixty-three-year-old widowed aunt she lives with.

West of Ramallah, the staunch hills grow larger, more rolling. I keep   11 pressing my son down in the taxi seat, suggesting he take a nap, which insults him. Really I'm just trying to keep his head lower than the windows. My father has lapsed into his solemn, West Bank personality. He stares silently out at terraces of dusky gray-green olive trees rising on either side. Sometimes I try to imagine what it's like for him—the youngest, beloved son—to come back here. His family lost their home in Jerusalem in 1948. My grandfather, who worked variously as a builder of roads and a neighborhood mediator, moved with his family up to this village where they'd had relatives for a long time. My grandmother bore ten children; three survived to adulthood. And then my father left. Forty years ago, he had a scholarship for university study in America. Since he'd never been there before, he asked to be sent "to the middle," and ended up in Kansas. That's where my American mother—art school graduate, liberal thinker, and working woman—met him.

He became a naturalized citizen in St. Louis, city of my birth, when I   12 was five. "The old country" sent him thin, blue air-letters that always made him grow very quiet. After reading them, he would stare through the window at our American trees. Sometimes he talked about "home," meaning a place other than the one we shared.

As a child, I felt secret pleasure in belonging to a world I had never   13 seen, where women wore long embroidered dresses and dinners crackled with pine nuts, sprigs of mint. In our house we ate hummus spread lavishly on little plates, drizzled with olive oil. My friends took small, curious bites. My father perfected his English while my mother memorized his recipes. On the school playground at recess, I'd squint and see my world as a far-off one, too. If those distant relatives were with me, what would they make of monkey bars and Hula-Hoops? Having parents from two worlds gave me a kind of double-vision.

14   The road to the village curves abruptly up onto the side of a hill between houses and almond trees. We pull to a stop at the oldest-looking stone house with a door painted in linked blue and pink squares, leading to a courtyard. Once I was here in the spring, and white almond blossoms floated around our heads like snow. A few old men stare curiously at our car. Everyone knows everyone else's business in a village like this—who received a letter, who hosted a guest. The two times I visited during the 1980s, people came to see us whom I'd never met before, proclaimed themselves relatives, and asked why I'd forgotten them all this time.

15   A female cousin runs out, insists on carrying my father's bags. We stumble through the arched doorway calling out greetings. I've forgotten to prepare my son for the double kisses, one on each cheek. My grandmother is seated inside the high, vaulted main room of her 200-year-old house, warming her hands over some white-hot coals in a charcoal brazier. It's always amazed me how cold it gets here. Most people picture the Middle East as a stretch of hot desert, but this is neither desert, flat, nor warm. Weeping, I fling my arms around her. We are hugging hard not only for now, but for all the days of six years since we saw each other last. My tears spring out of great relief. *She is still here.*

16   She gazes at Madison with a kind of intimate knowing. I've tucked his pictures into envelopes and sent them here. On my last visit she predicted, "You'll have a son, soon—wait and see." We've told him she talks a little like a Munchkin in *The Wizard of Oz.* Her voice curves and lilts, dipping deeply into the lower registers, then rising up into girlish giggles. Madison hugs her tenderly. He's lived with her picture, too. The cousins swoop around him, removing his coat, offering oranges to moisten our throats after the drive. "Oranges from Jericho," they say, meaning the sweetest ones in the world. I've eaten ten oranges in a day here before.

17   Madison is fascinated with the charcoal heater and immediately wants to find a stick to poke the whitened coals around. Everyone complies with his wishes. In a minute he has five sticks. My aunt, my female cousins, and my grandmother are dressed in their most beautiful long dresses, with their large white scarves draped snugly around their

heads. It makes sense in this chilly weather. Before I leave I'll have my Nepalese muffler wrapped around my head, too.

My father plunges into the usual litany of questions, greetings from relatives in the States, special messages. "Everyone says hello, everyone misses you, everyone wishes they were here, too." I've carried an extra suitcase of gifts—pastel cardigans and shoes—from cousins transplanted to San Antonio. Before I forget, I urge a cousin to take the four-generation portrait I've been dreaming of—mother, son, mother, son—spanning a hundred years. We congregate around Sitti, who suddenly acts shy and won't lift her face. What might have been the best picture will have our heads cut off entirely.   18

Everyone wants to know what we'd like for lunch so someone can run out to the little store and buy the ingredients. I love that immediacy here. As usual, they're disappointed when we request the most humble dishes: hummus, rice with eggplant, yogurt, bread, and cheese. It must seem dull to them. We never ask for meat or chicken, which they'd rather prepare to celebrate our coming. Madison says he'd like something *he* can cook on the fire. They bring him a wide pan and a giant spoon. They begin shelling almonds ("from their own trees," I whisper to him) and give him all the shells to cook.   19

My eyes rove around the room, noting how little has changed between visits: familiar pictures of family members, slightly more mottled around the edges; the same couch and round of chairs; our own old beds from when we lived in Jerusalem, sagging a bit more toward the middles; thick comforters and cupboards of extra comforters along the walls; and on them also, prayer rugs with scenes of Mecca. My aunt will rise up regularly at prayer times when the amplified voice of the muezzin calls to her from the nearby village mosque, and bow down repeatedly in the corner of the room. I love how Arabs do that. It's such a dependable part of a day. Madison accepts it naturally. I love how five-year-olds accept things without finding them odd.   20

My grandmother's lemon tree—she speaks of it as if it were a person—stands bare in the center of the patio, encased in January chill. About fifteen years ago, she started refusing to go anywhere, even to the doctor in Ramallah, because she needed to stay home to "take care of her tree." I point it out to Madison and she tells him, "Wait, it's dreaming of lemons right now."   21

Food is served on a big woven head-carried tray. Madison is too excited to eat. He doesn't want to leave his invented kitchenette at the   22 brazier, growing more elaborate by the moment. Now he's cooking peanuts he brought from the plane. He offers them, one by one, to each person. He revels in their enthusiasm. Even my grandmother with scarcely any teeth is eating peanuts. She pats his head each time he stands near enough. He keeps stroking her cheek and hand. I grab my camera to photograph their two hands together, the small, plump, smooth hand next to the graceful, tattooed one. Where will this scene be lodged in his memory?

23   Of course, as the excitement of arrival wears off, there are the usual small arguments. My grandmother wants my father to build a house here in the village and stay. It's her endless hope, the undertone of every conversation. Also she wants him to participate in a ritual he finds ridiculous: "sponsor a meal" for his older brother, who died two years ago, to be offered to any strangers who pass by. The only problem is that few strangers pass here. The effect isn't the same if the meal's eaten by friends. Besides, my father already did this on last year's visit, and it didn't work. No strangers appeared, and all the food sat around a whole day. My grandmother acts glum for ten minutes after he refuses.

24   Then Madison offers Sitti a wrapped chocolate kiss he's found in his backpack. She pops it into her mouth, shiny paper, tag, and all. He shouts, "No! Stop! She's eating the paper!" I can't tell if she did it to tease him or because she didn't see. They're laughing together, laughing hard in a land hungry for laughter. The most humble items evoke the most response—thick slipper-socks with non-skid patches on the bottom. I always wish I had brought ten times more gifts.

25   We blow up balloons from Madison's pocket. Now even a formal elderly cousin wearing a suit rises to punch the happy red, yellow, and blue planets skyward—and a little six-year-old, Muhammad, grinning in the cowboy hat we've just balanced on his head, pokes a tentative finger out. Beyond the window, a crowd of shaggy sheep scuttles past on the way home from pasture. They're followed by their faithful shepherd with his cane and we run outside to watch. I climb the stairs to the roof to look out over the exquisite patchwork of winter grays and greens—so many far-flung rolling hills and fields. These families have lived on them hundreds of years. One year an old man in this village introduced me to his garden practically by inches, naming every plant and every coming sprout.

26   I feel I grew up somehow in the seam between this old, rooted world and my American one. Whenever I come here, a deep ease overtakes me, as if these simple images and colors, this scent of bubbling lentil and

damp sheep wool and water on stone permeated my blood and bones from the beginning. What must it feel like for my father? What will it feel like for my son?

Soon my cousins speak their Arabic questions and comments directly to Madison, without waiting for translation. Madison seems to catch their meanings, but asks me, "If I'm part Arab, why can't I speak Arabic?" It's the question I've always asked, too. I wear it as regret, as shame. When I studied Arabic in school here, I never seemed to learn any words people would really want to *say*. Muhammad and Madison read a bilingual Arabic/English storybook together—Spot, the famous dog, with lift-up flaps and grinning animals. Animals, at least, speak every language.   27

Later we'll play peekaboo with giant rounds of flat bread to make my cousin's new baby smile. We'll tuck ourselves under the weighty woolen comforters that my aunt lifts out of the cupboard. Once I climbed to the top of the stack and made someone take a picture of me, in *Princess and the Pea* fashion. Madison startles me by asking my aunt if he can do the very same thing.   28

When we're almost asleep, we hear a loud boom in the distance that worries me, considering where we are and how many booms there have been through history both ancient and modern. I sit up in bed. My aunt sits up in her bed on the other side of the room. "What's that?" I ask. "It's airplanes," she says calmly. Sonic booms. Of course.   29

They've locked the giant lock in the door to their patio with a giant iron key. My grandmother sleeps in her bed in the next room, beside a kerosene lamp and an ancient comb. Round straw trays hang on the wall above her head. How many meals did they carry?   30

And a little boy sleeps soundly, troubled by nothing, in this new old world which belongs to him, too.   31

After-Reading Activities

Analyzing the Content

1. The title is taken from a combination of words used in the essay. What is its meaning? Reread the essay and choose other words that could have been used just as effectively as a title.

2. Analyze the following:
   - What does the writer mean when she says "to take a child ... involves a kind of courage I can't depend on alone" (paragraph 2)?
   - The writer's uncles used to leave the house and say they were going to "smell the air"; now they say they are going to "measure the streets" (paragraph 4). What is the meaning of the latter expression? Why have they stopped using the former?
   - The writer says, "I liked to wonder what the history of this land would have been had it all been left to shepherds" (paragraph 5). Reread the paragraph and explain what she is suggesting with this statement.

Structure and Style

3. This essay is written in a narration style. Why is this a good choice for the subject and theme of this essay?

4. "Double Vision in a New Old World" starts with a periodic sentence. What is a periodic sentence? Why is this an effective sentence with which to start this essay?

5. Choose two strong images from the essay. For each, explain its effect on the reader.

6. Locate and clarify an example of paradox within this essay.

7. Create a chart like the one below, and fill it in for paragraph 6.

Sentence	# Words	Sentence Order	Sentence Type	Special Punctuation
1				
2				

After completing the chart, write your observations about Nye's writing style.

Extending the Pattern

1. How do the visions of Toronto compare and contrast in the two essays "Anecdotes of Racism" and "A Home at the End of the Journey"?

2. Examine the order used within each of the three narration essays in this section. For one of them, think of alternative ways the writer could have structured the essay to increase or reduce tension, build suspense, introduce more interest, etc.

3. Choose one of the following:

   • Write a personal essay (see pages 171 to 182) using a narration structure. Remember that you are writing for an audience and that personal experiences must be told in such a manner as to interest the general reading public.

   • Write a narration essay in which you describe a time you were treated unfairly. When brainstorming your ideas and creating your outline, think carefully about how you will lead your reader through the event (order of the narration).

   • Write a narration essay of a childhood memory that, on looking back, you realize taught you something important about life. Focus on how you recount the event and the way you allow the reader to learn what you learned.

   • Write a humorous narration essay. Use figurative language and strong imagery to help your reader sense your experience.

   After completing your first draft, work with a partner to revise and edit your essay, focusing on the organization and the use of stylistic devices.

Unit II

PURPOSE

Elements of the Persuasive and Argument Essay

A persuasive or argument essay attempts to persuade the reader to accept, and perhaps even adopt, the writer's viewpoint on a topic. Following are some guidelines for writing effective persuasive and argument essays.

1. **Be clear about your thesis**. Before writing your essay, you should be clear in your own mind about the position you hold on a topic. If there is doubt in your mind, there will be doubt in the reader's.

2. **Recognize and refute alternative viewpoints**. Recognize that there are other perspectives on your topic. You can strengthen your message by considering the alternative viewpoints and addressing them in your essay. This not only shows that you have thought the topic through, but it answers your critics even before they offer their counterarguments.

3. **Place your thesis strategically.** Consider the nature of your argument and how your audience will react to it. Generally, readers stop reading after they are presented with a point of view with which they disagree. Therefore, if you think that your audience will hotly contest your thesis, you may want to place it later in the essay, after presenting your supporting points. On the other hand, if you feel that your thesis will not be too contentious, present it at the beginning of the essay.

4. **Support your argument with concrete evidence.** Use examples that are relevant, concrete, and verifiable. Avoid the "They say ..." trap. Cite authorities that are credible and verifiable. If the legitimacy of your sources can be challenged, your argument will suffer.

5. **Point out the probable outcome of accepting or not accepting your argument.** You should illustrate how accepting your viewpoint will lead to a more favourable situation than if an alternative viewpoint is accepted. You can't be sure that your readers will reach the conclusion you are hoping for, so provide it for them!

A Vindication of the Rights of Woman

Mary Wollstonecraft

Elements of the Essay

Controversial at the time of its publication in 1792, *A Vindication of the Rights of Woman* strongly argues for equality for women. Persuasive, in turns argumentative, Mary Wollstonecraft anticipates the objections she might receive as she outlines the purpose of her book in her introduction, which appears below.

About the Writer

One of the most important figures of the early feminist movement, Mary Wollstonecraft was born in 1759 in London. In 1784, with a friend and a sister, Wollstonecraft established a school, in which she became schoolteacher and headmistress. The school did not last long, however, closing down just two years after it was opened. But Wollstonecraft's interest in education and women's issues did not wane, and she published her first book, *Thoughts on the Education of Daughters*, in 1787. *A Vindication of the Rights of Woman* (1792), which was published several years later, on the heels of her other publications, came to be known as one of the most important documents in the feminist movement. Wollstonecraft died at the age of 38 in 1797, a few days after giving birth to daughter Mary, who would later become Mary Shelley, author of *Frankenstein*.

AFTER CONSIDERING THE HISTORIC page, and viewing the living world with anxious solicitude, the most melancholy emotions of sorrowful indignation have depressed my spirits, and I have sighed when obliged to confess, that either nature has made a great difference between man and man, or that the civilization which has hitherto taken place in the world has been very partial. I have turned over various books written on the subject of education, and patiently observed the

1

conduct of parents and the management of schools; but what has been the result?—a profound conviction that the neglected education of my fellow-creatures is the grand source of the misery I deplore; and that women, in particular, are rendered weak and wretched by a variety of concurring causes, originating from one hasty conclusion. The conduct and manners of women, in fact, evidently prove that their minds are not in a healthy state; for, like the flowers which are planted in too rich a soil, strength and usefulness are sacrificed to beauty; and the flaunting leaves, after having pleased a fastidious eye, fade, disregarded on the stalk, long before the season when they ought to have arrived at maturity.—One cause of this barren blooming I attribute to a false system of education, gathered from the books written on this subject by men who, considering females rather as women than human creatures, have been more anxious to make them alluring mistresses than affectionate wives and rational mothers; and the understanding of the sex has been so bubbled by this specious homage, that the civilized women of the present century, with a few exceptions, are only anxious to inspire love, when they ought to cherish a nobler ambition, and by their abilities and virtues exact respect.

2   In a treatise, therefore, on female rights and manners, the works which have been particularly written for their improvement must not be overlooked; especially when it is asserted, in direct terms, that the minds of women are enfeebled by false refinement; that the books of instruction, written by men of genius, have had the same tendency as more frivolous productions; and that, in the true style of Mahometanism,[1] they are treated as a kind of subordinate beings, and not as a part of the human species, when improveable reason is allowed to be the dignified distinction which raises men above the brute creation, and puts a natural sceptre in a feeble hand.

3   Yet, because I am a woman, I would not lead my readers to suppose that I mean violently to agitate the contested question respecting the equality or inferiority of the sex; but as the subject lies in my way, and I cannot pass it over without subjecting the main tendency of my reasoning to misconstruction, I shall stop a moment to deliver, in a few words, my opinion.—In the government of the physical world it is observable that the female in point of strength is, in general, inferior to the male. This is the law of nature; and it does not appear to be suspended or abrogated in favour of woman. A degree of physical superiority cannot, therefore, be denied—and it is a noble prerogative! But not content with this natural pre-eminence, men endeavour to sink us still lower, merely to render us

alluring objects for a moment; and women, intoxicated by the adoration
which men, under the influence of their senses, pay them, do not seek to
obtain a durable interest in their hearts, or to become the friends of the
fellow creatures who find amusement in their society.

I am aware of an obvious inference:—from every quarter have I heard   4
exclamations against masculine women; but where are they to be found?
If by this appellation men mean to inveigh against their ardour in
hunting, shooting, and gaming, I shall most cordially join in the cry; but
if it be against the imitation of manly virtues, or, more properly speaking,
the attainment of those talents and virtues, the exercise of which
ennobles the human character, and which raise females in the scale of
animal being, when they are comprehensively termed mankind;—all
those who view them with a philosophic eye must, I should think, wish
with me, that they may every day grow more and more masculine.

This discussion naturally divides the subject. I shall first consider   5
women in the grand light of human creatures, who, in common with
men, are placed on this earth to unfold their faculties; and afterwards I
shall more particularly point out their peculiar designation.

I wish also to steer clear of an error which many respectable writers   6
have fallen into; for the instruction which has hitherto been addressed to
women, has rather been applicable to *ladies*, if the little indirect advice,
that is scattered through Sandford and Merton,[2] be excepted; but,
addressing my sex in a firmer tone, I pay particular attention to those in
the middle class, because they appear to be in the most natural state.
Perhaps the seeds of false-refinement, immorality, and vanity have ever
been shed by the great. Weak, artificial beings, raised above the common
wants and affections of their race, in a premature unnatural manner,
undermine the very foundation of virtue, and spread corruption through
the whole mass of society! As a class of mankind they have the strongest
claim to pity; the education of the rich tends to render them vain and
helpless, and the unfolding mind is not strengthened by the practice of
those duties which dignify the human character.—They live only to
amuse themselves, and by the same law which in nature invariably
produces certain effects, they soon only afford barren amusement.

But as I purpose taking a separate view of the different ranks of   7
society, and the moral character of women, in each, this hint is, for the
present, sufficient; and I have only alluded to the subject, because it
appears to me to be the very essence of an introduction to give a cursory
account of the contents of the work it introduces.

8   My own sex, I hope, will excuse me, if I treat them like rational creatures, instead of flattering their *fascinating* graces, and viewing them as if they were in a state of perpetual childhood, unable to stand alone. I earnestly wish to point out in what true dignity and human happiness consists—I wish to persuade women to endeavour to acquire strength, both of mind and body, and to convince them that the soft phrases, susceptibility of heart, delicacy of sentiment, and refinement of taste are almost synonymous with epithets of weakness, and that those beings who are only the objects of pity and that kind of love, which has been termed its sister, will soon become objects of contempt.

9   Dismissing then those pretty feminine phrases, which the men condescendingly use to soften our slavish dependence, and despising that weak elegancy of mind, exquisite sensibility, and sweet docility of manners, supposed to be the sexual characteristics of the weaker vessel, I wish to show that elegance is inferior to virtue, that the first object of laudable ambition is to obtain a character as a human being, regardless of the distinction of sex; and that secondary views should be brought to this simple touchstone.

10   This is a rough sketch of my plan; and should I express my conviction with the energetic emotions that I feel whenever I think of the subject, the dictates of experience and reflection will be felt by some of my readers. Animated by this important object, I shall disdain to cull my phrases or polish my style;—I aim at being useful, and sincerity will render me unaffected; for, wishing rather to persuade by the force of my arguments, than dazzle by the elegance of my language, I shall not waste my time in rounding periods, or in fabricating the turgid bombast of artificial feelings, which, coming from the head, never reach the heart.— I shall be employed about things, not words!—and anxious to render my sex more respectable members of society, I shall try to avoid that flowery diction which has slided from essays into novels, and from novels into familiar letters and conversation.

11   These pretty superlatives, dropping glibly from the tongue, vitiate the taste, and create a kind of sickly delicacy that turns away from simple unadorned truth; and a deluge of false sentiments and over-stretched feelings, stifling the natural emotions of the heart, render the domestic pleasures insipid, that ought to sweeten the exercise of those severe duties, which educate a rational and immortal being for a nobler field of action.

12   The education of women has, of late, been more attended to than formerly; yet they are still reckoned a frivolous sex, and ridiculed or pitied

by the writers who endeavour by satire or instruction to improve them. It is acknowledged that they spend many of the first years of their lives in acquiring a smattering of accomplishments; meanwhile strength of body and mind are sacrificed to libertine notions of beauty, to the desire of establishing themselves,—the only way women can rise in the world,—by marriage. And this desire making mere animals of them, when they marry they act as such children may be expected to act:—they dress; they paint, and nickname God's creatures.—Surely these weak beings are only fit for a seraglio!³—Can they be expected to govern a family with judgment, or take care of the poor babes whom they bring into the world?

If then it can be fairly deduced from the present conduct of the sex, from the prevalent fondness for pleasure which takes place of ambition and those nobler passions that open and enlarge the soul; that the instruction which women have hitherto received has only tended, with the constitution of civil society, to render them insignificant objects of desire—mere propagators of fools!—if it can be proved that in aiming to accomplish them, without cultivating their understandings, they are taken out of their sphere of duties, and made ridiculous and useless when the short-lived bloom of beauty is over,⁴ I presume that *rational* men will excuse me for endeavouring to persuade them to become more masculine and respectable. 13

Indeed the word masculine is only a bugbear: there is little reason to fear that women will acquire too much courage or fortitude; for their apparent inferiority with respect to bodily strength must render them, in some degree, dependent on men in the various relations of life; but why should it be increased by prejudices that give a sex to virtue, and confound simple truths with sensual reveries? 14

Women are, in fact, so much degraded by mistaken notions of female excellence, that I do not mean to add a paradox when I assert, that this artificial weakness produces a propensity to tyrannize, and gives birth to cunning, the natural opponent of strength, which leads them to play off those contemptible infantine airs that undermine esteem even whilst they excite desire. Let men become more chaste and modest, and if women do not grow wiser in the same ratio, it will be clear that they have weaker understandings. It seems scarcely necessary to say, that I now speak of the sex in general. Many individuals have more sense than their male relatives; and, as nothing preponderates where there is a constant struggle for an equilibrium, without it has naturally more gravity, some women govern their husbands without degrading themselves, because intellect will always govern. 15

Notes

1. Islam.
2. Wollstonecraft is referring to Thomas Day (1748–89), *The History of Sandford and Merton*, 3 vols. (1783–89).
3. Shakespeare, *Hamlet*, III, i, 142–46. Seraglio: harem.
4. A lively writer, I cannot recollect his name, asks what business women turned of forty have to do in the world? [Wollstonecraft's note.] It has been suggested that Wollstonecraft may be thinking of a character in Frances Burney (1752–1840), *Evelina; or, The History of a Young Lady's Entrance into the World* (1778).

After-Reading Activities

Analyzing the Content

1. What is the main idea or thesis of this essay?

2. Make an outline of this essay. Highlight the issues in the outline that are most important to Wollstonecraft.

3. Create a chart showing which ideas presented by Mary Wollstonecraft in this eighteenth-century essay today's feminists would most strongly agree and disagree with.

Structure and Style

4. On what is the central position in this essay based—fact or opinion? Give reasons for your choice.

5. Describe the tone of this essay. How does Wollstonecraft create this tone? Assess whether the tone is appropriate for the subject matter of the essay. Is it appropriate for the main argument of the essay? Would any other tone be appropriate?

6. Is the final paragraph of this essay as effective as it could be? Suggest one change that would enable the paragraph to give the essay more unity and cohesiveness.

7. Identify the qualities of this essay that characterize it as written in the eighteenth century. Do the diction and style make the ideas presented more, or less, relevant to the modern reader?

If Black English Isn't a Language, Then Tell Me, What Is?

James Baldwin

Elements of the Essay

In this essay, James Baldwin argues that Black English *is* a language. It is a language grown out of necessity, and it reflects the history and the situation of African-Americans. Baldwin's purpose is to argue the legitimacy of Black English, to define it, and to compel readers to accept his position. Using strong language and a first-person point of view, Baldwin conveys his indignation toward, and criticisms of, racist attitudes.

About the Writer

James Baldwin was born on August 2, 1924, in Harlem, New York, to an impoverished mother. His love for reading led him to a literary career, which started during the 1940s. In 1948, he moved to France to escape the racist climate of the United States at the time. He spent 10 years living in Paris and Istanbul, occasionally returning to the U.S. to lecture. As his writing career progressed, he became an important voice during the civil rights movement. So great was his influence that he came under the investigation of the FBI. His large body of work includes essay collections, notably the bestseller *The Fire Next Time* (1963), novels, and plays. Baldwin died on November 30, 1987.

T HE ARGUMENT CONCERNING THE use, or the status, or the reality, of black English is rooted in American history and has absolutely nothing to do with the question the argument supposes itself to be posing. The argument has nothing to do with language itself but with the *role* of language. Language, incontestably, reveals the speaker. Language, also, far more dubiously, is meant to define the other—and, in this case, the other is refusing to be defined by a language that has never been able to recognize him.

2   People evolve a language in order to describe and thus control their circumstances, or in order not to be submerged by a reality that they cannot articulate. (And, if they cannot articulate it, they *are* submerged.) A Frenchman living in Paris speaks a subtly and crucially different language from that of the man living in Marseilles; neither sounds very much like a man living in Quebec; and they would all have great difficulty in apprehending what the man from Guadeloupe, or Martinique, is saying, to say nothing of the man from Senegal—although the "common" language of all these areas is French. But each has paid, and is paying, a different price for this "common" language, in which, as it turns out, they are not saying, and cannot be saying, the same things: They each have very different realities to articulate, or control.

3   What joins all languages, and all men, is the necessity to confront life, in order, not inconceivably, to outwit death: The price for this is the acceptance, and achievement, of one's temporal identity. So that, for example, though it is not taught in the schools (and this has the potential of becoming a political issue) the south of France still clings to its ancient and musical Provençal, which resists being described as a "dialect." And much of the tension in the Basque countries, and in Wales, is due to the Basque and Welsh determination not to allow their languages to be destroyed. This determination also feeds the flames in Ireland, for among the many indignities the Irish have been forced to undergo at English hands is the English contempt for their language.

4   It goes without saying, then, that language is also a political instrument, means, and proof of power. It is the most vivid and crucial key to identity: It reveals the private identity, and connects one with, or divorces one from, the larger, public, or communal identity. There have been, and are, times, and places, when to speak a certain language could be dangerous, even fatal. Or, one may speak the same language, but in such a way that one's antecedents are revealed, or (one hopes) hidden. This is true in France, and is absolutely true in England: The range (and reign) of accents on that damp little island makes England coherent for the English and totally incomprehensible for everyone else. To open your mouth in England is (if I may use black English) to "put your business in the street": You have confessed your parents, your youth, your school, your salary, your self-esteem, and, alas, your future.

5   Now, I do not know what white Americans would sound like if there had never been any black people in the United States, but they would

not sound the way they sound. *Jazz,* for example, is a very specific sexual term, as in *jazz me, baby,* but white people purified it into the Jazz Age. *Sock it to me,* which means, roughly, the same thing, has been adopted by Nathaniel Hawthorne's descendants with no qualms or hesitations at all, along with *let it all hang out* and *right on! Beat to his socks,* which was once the black's most total and despairing image of poverty, was transformed into a thing called the Beat Generation, which phenomenon was, largely, composed of *uptight,* middle-class white people, imitating poverty, trying to *get down,* to get *with it,* doing their *thing,* doing their despairing best to be *funky,* which we, the blacks, never dreamed of doing—we *were* funky, baby, like *funk* was going out of style.

Now, no one can eat his cake, and have it, too, and it is late in the   6
day to attempt to penalize black people for having created a language that permits the nation its only glimpse of reality, a language without which the nation would be even more *whipped* than it is.

I say that the present skirmish is rooted in American history, and it   7
is. Black English is the creation of the black diaspora. Blacks came to the United States chained to each other, but from different tribes: Neither could speak the other's language. If two black people, at that bitter hour of the world's history, had been able to speak to each other, the institution of chattel slavery could never have lasted as long as it did. Subsequently, the slave was given, under the eye, and the gun, of his master, Congo Square, and the Bible—or in other words, and under these conditions, the slave began the formation of the black church, and it is within this unprecedented tabernacle that black English began to be formed. This was not, merely, as in the European example, the adoption of a foreign tongue, but an alchemy that transformed ancient elements into a new language: *A language comes into existence by means of brutal necessity, and the rules of the language are dictated by what the language must convey.*

There was a moment, in time, and in this place, when my brother, or   8
my mother, or my father, or my sister, had to convey to me, for example, the danger in which I was standing from the white man standing just behind me, and to convey this with a speed, and in a language, that the white man could not possibly understand, and that, indeed, he cannot understand, until today. He cannot afford to understand it. This understanding would reveal to him too much about himself, and smash that mirror before which he has been frozen for so long.

Now, if this passion, this skill, this (to quote Toni Morrison) "sheer   9
intelligence," this incredible music, the mighty achievement of having

brought a people utterly unknown to, or despised by "history"—to have brought this people to their present, troubled, troubling, and unassailable and unanswerable place—if this absolutely unprecedented journey does not indicate that black English is a language, I am curious to know what definition of language is to be trusted.

10   A people at the center of the Western world, and in the midst of so hostile a population, has not endured and transcended by means of what is patronizingly called a "dialect." We, the blacks, are in trouble, certainly, but we are not doomed, and we are not inarticulate because we are not compelled to defend a morality that we know to be a lie.

11   The brutal truth is that the bulk of white people in America never had any interest in educating black people, except as this could serve white purposes. It is not the black child's language that is in question, it is not his language that is despised: It is his experience. A child cannot be taught by anyone who despises him, and a child cannot afford to be fooled. A child cannot be taught by anyone whose demand, essentially, is that the child repudiate his experience, and all that gives him sustenance, and enter a limbo in which he will no longer be black, and in which he knows that he can never become white. Black people have lost too many black children that way.

12   And, after all, finally, in a country with standards so untrustworthy, a country that makes heroes of so many criminal mediocrities, a country unable to face why so many of the nonwhite are in prison, or on the needle, or standing, futureless, in the streets—it may very well be that both the child, and his elder, have concluded that they have nothing whatever to learn from the people of a country that has managed to learn so little.

After-Reading Activities

Analyzing the Content

1. With a partner, make a list of the purposes of language according to James Baldwin. Add other purposes of language to the list based on your own ideas.

2. Explain the origins of Black English in America as presented in this essay.

3. In light of the information in this essay, debate the following resolution: Be It Resolved That Human Beings Would Be Better Off If Everyone Spoke English. Additional research may be necessary.

Structure and Style

4. What is the main argument or thesis of this essay?

5. Is the central argument in this essay based on fact or opinion? Explain.

6. Explain the relationship of the French, Basque, and Welsh examples in paragraphs 2 and 3 to the main idea about Black English presented in this essay. Assess their contribution to the impact of Baldwin's argument.

7. What is the tone of this essay? How does Baldwin create this tone? Assess its appropriateness for the subject matter of the essay. Is it appropriate for the main argument of the essay you identified in activity 4? Would any other tone be appropriate?

8. Who are the intended readers of this essay? Give reasons for your answer.

Jurassic Conservation?

Malcolm Tait

Elements of the Essay

Calling cloning a "scientific gimmick" and "a classic case of lazy science that will spare us all the bother of preventing extinction," Malcolm Tait challenges the scientific community's argument that cloning could serve as a form of conservation, particularly of endangered species. The purpose of his essay is clear—to point out the dangers of cloning for conservation and to make readers question it, not just accept it blindly.

About the Writer

Malcolm Tait is managing editor of *The Ecologist,* a British magazine based in London.

1   RECENTLY, A COW IN IOWA named Bessie gave birth to a gaur, an endangered oxlike animal native to Asia. This miracle was achieved by injecting gaur cells, complete with their DNA, into hollowed-out cow eggs, then electrically fusing the eggs and DNA together.

2   Already there are plans afoot for more cross-species surrogate motherhood. The bucardo, a Pyrenean mountain goat, became extinct in January 2000, when the last of its kind was put out of its lonely misery by a falling tree. Cells were taken from the corpse, and the Massachusetts-based company Advanced Cell Technology is planning to clone the creature back to life. The panda is next on the list for rejuvenation, and there's talk of trying to bring back the Tasmanian tiger, a wolflike animal that lost its last grip on survival in the 1930s. Even the prehistoric mammoth is being considered for a possible comeback. It's a fascinating scientific gimmick, a perfect example of doing something because we can. We should leave it at that.

3   But we won't. There's excited talk of cloning and genetic engineering offering a marvelous boost to wildlife conservation, a high-tech solution to our tendency to drive plant and animal species to extinction. This is

tripe, for the cloning of endangered species completely contradicts the spirit and practice of conservation. Conservation isn't just about saving a particular species, it's about reducing our destructive impact on natural systems that are in increasing danger of being unable to sustain themselves, and ultimately, of sustaining us.

Wildlife conservation is a precarious affair, because failure is forever. It has, quite literally, a deadline. Sometimes that deadline is easy to see, other times it's not. In the 1980s, it became clear that whales were struggling to survive and new laws were put into place. In the early 1990s, the plight of the elephant came to the world's attention and was reasonably successfully dealt with. We've recently discovered that the tiger is in even more danger than we'd previously thought, and wheels are beginning to turn to keep them going. Yet for every headline species that captures our heart, there are many more that don't make it. — 4

But conservation takes time and money. It requires careful management and planning, and it involves sacrifices. It demands that the long-term view take precedence over, or is at least built into, the short term. — 5

Which brings us back to Bessie. Suddenly, for the first time ever, we've got an alternative to conservation. It's only a tiny crack at present, but science will work to widen it. What's the point in putting all that effort into looking after ecosystems if we've got the ability to clone extinct species back into existence? Just think of what this makes possible—we can keep on crashing our way across the planet, doing what we want, and whenever some species starts to disappear as a result, we've got the technology to keep the species going. — 6

Cloning endangered species is a classic case of lazy science that will spare us all the bother of preventing extinction. However much its supporters may protest that cloning will only be used to complement conservation, to step in when conservation has failed, the day will come when the financial benefits of, say, clearing a rainforest will outweigh the costs of cloning the endangered species within. Someone will be prepared to pay for it, and the rot will have begun. — 7

And what will we do with these phoenixlike creatures? If their habitat is no more, where will we put them? Perhaps we will create reservations for them—but to save space, we'll need to make sure we only hang on to the species that benefit ourselves. We'll need to recreate habitats that suit them, and if the new cloned versions of once-wild animals require special diets, or develop viruses or illnesses that their originals never encountered, then we can genetically modify their surroundings to suit. — 8

9   None of this is to say that genetic scientists and those who fund them are power-mad seekers who want to remake the whole world according to their whims. Science is the discipline of discovery, of finding out, of increasing knowledge. And so it is that, generally, each new step forward is taken with the honest and sincere desire to benefit humankind. Yet it's curious how often genetic scientists, nudging the process onward, tend to see their own work in isolation from the overall results of these new technologies.

10   "The prospect of human cloning causes us grave misgivings," writes Ian Wilmut, co-cloner with Keith Campbell in 1996 of the famous sheep, Dolly, in his book *The Second Creation: Dolly and the Age of Biological Control.* "It is physically too risky, it could have untoward effects on the psychology of the cloned child, and in the end we see no medical justification for it. For us, the technology that produced Dolly has far wider significance."

11   Wilmut is fully convinced of the benefits of his own work; he knows that he has paved the way for future cloning, yet is distancing himself from any responsibility for it. It's rather like the work of atomic scientists in the 1930s—everyone involved spoke of the possible positive benefits in their own specific research, but never mentioned the obvious potential for the destruction of the entire planet.

12   Which is why, ultimately, we should not be fooled by the arguments about cloning as boon to endangered species. Let's honestly admit to ourselves what we're getting into. Cloning is a brand-new chapter in the history of humankind, but it has nothing, absolutely nothing, to do with conservation.

After-Reading Activities

Analyzing the Content

1. Clearly explain the following:
   - the specific scientific activity the writer is describing in this essay
   - the stated motives of the scientific projects described
   - the reasons the writer is against this use of science

2. Explain the relationship between the title of this essay and the film *Jurassic Park*.

3. In light of the information in this essay, debate the following resolution: Be It Resolved That the United Nations Should Establish International Rules Governing Biological Research. You may need to do additional research.

Structure and Style

4. What is the writer's main argument or thesis in this essay?

5. Is the main argument that you identified in activity 4 based on fact or opinion? Give reasons for your position.

6. Does the writer have strong feelings about the argument he is making in this essay? How do you know? Does the personal tone strengthen or weaken the writer's argument?

7. Who are the intended readers of this essay? Give reasons for your answer.

8. How has the writer used the introductory paragraph, the concluding paragraph, connecting words and phrases, and the repetition of keywords and examples to increase the unity of the essay?

Fragile Freedoms

Thomas Berger

Elements of the Essay

In these excerpts from Thomas Berger's book, *Fragile Freedoms: Human Rights and Dissent in Canada* (1982), the writer develops his ideas persuasively, defining what it means to be Canadian and describing the founding principles that have made Canada the country that it is.

About the Writer
Thomas Berger was born on March 23, 1933, in Victoria, British Columbia. A British Columbia Supreme Court judge, as well as a humanitarian, Berger came under the national spotlight when he was appointed to head the Mackenzie Valley Pipeline Inquiry. The inquiry was conducted to study the impact that the construction of a pipeline would have on the communities of northern Yukon and the Northwest Territories, particularly the Native communities.

1   FREEDOM IS A FRAGILE COMMODITY in the world today. Everywhere human rights are beset by ideology and orthodoxy, diversity is rejected, and dissent is stifled.

2   Alexander Solzhenitsyn, Steve Biko, Lech Walesa, Jacobo Timerman—their names have made human rights one of the great issues of our time. They have given form and substance to the contest between freedom and repression. They and other brave men and women have been imprisoned and tortured, and some have been executed, for wanting to be free, and for believing that their countrymen should be free. They have claimed the right to question—and to challenge—the political ideas under-girding the regimes in their own countries. They speak for all mankind.

3   Mass deportations, terror and torture, racial prejudice, political and religious persecution, and the destruction of institutions from which people derive their sense of identity are assaults upon human dignity and the human condition that are odious to men and women everywhere.

In the Western democracies, we especially cherish representative institutions and the rule of law, democracy and due process. These traditions affirm the right to dissent: in politics, in religion, in science and in the arts. We conceive of these rights as individual rights, but they are much more than that. They are the means whereby diversity is maintained, and whereby minorities can thrive.

Questions of human rights and dissent in Canada are linked to questions of human rights and dissent around the world. Our own successes and failures, our own attempts to accommodate minorities, are important not only to ourselves. If people of differing races, religions, cultures, and languages can live together harmoniously within a great federal state, perhaps they may learn to live together harmoniously in the wider world.

And what of the Canadian experience? What does our history say to us and to the world? Canada has adopted a new Constitution and a Charter of Rights and Freedoms. In doing so, we have severed the last formal link to colonial dependency. Far more important, however, is the fact that this exercise in constitution-making has forced us to articulate our idea of Canada. For a Constitution does not merely provide the means of settling present disputes, it is a legal garment that reveals the values that we hold. It is a document expressing that decent respect which the present owes to the past; it is, at the same time, a document addressed to future generations.

A Constitution is not intended simply to divide up revenue and resources between the federal government and the provinces. Canada's new Constitution, like the British North America Act before it, divides legislative powers between Parliament and the provinces. This division is precisely that, a division of powers, powers exercised by a majority within each of the provincial governments. But every thoughtful person realizes that limits must be set to these powers: there must be guarantees for the rights of minorities and dissenters; there must be protection for those who would otherwise be powerless.

Although our notions of democracy and due process evolved in the ethnically defined nation-states of Europe, Canada is not such a nation-state. We have two founding peoples, English and French, within a single state; we have aboriginal peoples with an historic claim to special status; and we have a variety of ethnic groups and races who have immigrated to Canada. Thus, we have many linguistic, racial, cultural, and ethnic minorities. Each of them has a claim to collective as well as to individual guarantees under the new Constitution and the Charter of Rights and Freedoms, and each of them has a claim on the goodwill of the majority. For all of these minorities the right to dissent is the mainstay of their freedom.

8   In Canada, we have two great societies, one English-speaking, one French-speaking, joined by history and circumstance. When we look to our past, we can see that the central issue of our history has been the working out of relations between these two societies. No discussion of Canadian institutions can proceed except as a discussion of the evolution of relations between the English and the French on this continent. The dominant theme of the constitutional discussions that led to Confederation in 1867 was the accommodation of these two communities in Canada. This theme, though sometimes it recedes, still overshadows the continuing constitutional debate of our own time.

9   These two societies, today, have much in common. Both are urban, industrial and bureaucratic. Although their linguistic and cultural differences are still significant, and they are responsible for the creative tension that is the distinctive characteristic of the Canadian political scene, these differences no longer threaten either side. As Pierre Trudeau has remarked, "The die is cast in Canada. Neither of our two language groups can force assimilation on the other."

10   It was not always so. The conquest of New France by the British in 1759 led to a series of attempts to assimilate the people of Quebec. These attempts were stoutly resisted by Quebecers, and their population of 60,000 has grown to some six million, and their culture flourishes as never before. The history of the French Canadians of Quebec epitomizes the struggle of minorities everywhere.

11   Today, in every Canadian province, there is a minority that speaks either English or French, and this fundamental duality places the condition of minorities at the very centre of our institutional arrangements. At the same time, the diversity of our huge nation has given rise to many forms of dissent.

12   The Canadian Constitution has always recognized that we are a plural, not a monolithic, nation. This is one of the finest Canadian traditions. Refugees from every continent, immigrants of every race, peoples of all faiths, and persons seeking political asylum have all found their place in Canadian life. It is our good fortune not to be of one common descent, not to speak one language only. We are not cursed with a triumphant ideology; we are not given to mindless patriotism. For these reasons Canada is a difficult nation to govern; there is never an easy consensus. Yet, our

diversity shouldn't terrify us: it should be our strength, not our weakness.

Along every seam in the Canadian mosaic unravelled by conflict, a   13
binding thread of tolerance can be seen. I speak of tolerance not as mere
indifference, but in its most positive aspect, as the expression of a
profound belief in the virtues of diversity and in the right to dissent.

Many Canadians have championed the ideal of tolerance throughout   14
our history. Who can forget the tortured figure of Louis Riel, who died
insisting upon the rights of his people? Or the great Laurier, pleading
the cause of the Franco-Ontarians during the First World War? Or
Angus MacInnis, who insisted upon the rights of Japanese Canadians
during the Second World War when the whole of British Columbia—in
fact, the whole nation—stood against them? Or John Diefenbaker,
calling for an end to the persecution of Jehovah's Witnesses during the
Second World War; Pierre Trudeau, defender of civil liberties in Quebec
during the 1950s under the Duplessis regime; Ivan Rand, a great judge
and legal philosopher, who affirmed the rights of political and religious
dissenters during the 1950s; and Emmett Hall, whose humane
judgement in the Nishga Indians' case in 1973 opened up the whole
question of Native claims in Canada?

I am not urging that we set up a national waxworks. But the   15
Canadian imagination is still peopled almost exclusively by the heroes
and heroines of other nations, and our knowledge of who we are has
suffered as a result. The crises of times past have thrown into
prominence many men and women who have articulated and defended
an idea of Canada that has illuminated the Canadian journey.

These Canadians—men and women of courage and compassion—   16
were committed to an idea of Canada that we can all share today, an
idea that goes deeper than the division of powers, an idea more eloquent
than any set of constitutional proposals, an idea that took root long
before the present crisis and which will endure beyond it—a faith in
fundamental freedoms and in tolerance for all peoples. This idea of
Canada represents the highest aspiration of any nation, and it evokes the
best in our Canadian traditions.

After-Reading Activities

Analyzing the Content

1. "Human rights" is a broad term. Create a list of freedoms and rights mentioned in this essay that Thomas Berger identifies as human rights. Write a brief description of any term that is new or unfamiliar to you.

2. As a class, conduct research on Alexander Solzhenitsyn, Steve Biko, Lech Walesa, Jacobo Timerman, Louis Riel, Wilfrid Laurier, Angus MacInnis, John Diefenbaker, Pierre Trudeau, Ivan Rand, and Emmett Hall. For each name, write a paragraph explaining what and how the person contributed to the fight for human rights. Create a Human Rights Hall of Fame booklet or bulletin board display to present your paragraphs for others to read.

3. Why is Canada recognized as a world leader on the issue of human rights? What conditions have led to Canada taking this role?

Structure and Style

4. Identify the thesis of this essay.

5. What is the main means the writer uses to make the reader agree with his position?

6. Describe the tone of this essay. How effective is it?

Extending the Purpose

Using one of the four essays in this section as a model, write your own persuasive and argument essay. You may choose one of the following:

- Praise and agree with the ideas expressed by Mary Wollstonecraft in her introduction to *A Vindication of the Rights of Woman*, or challenge and disagree with her ideas.
- Argue for or against the use of non-standard English (for example, dialects, slang, colloquialisms) in academic or business writing.
- Research recent advances in an aspect of biotechnology (for example, cloning, the human genome project, stem cell research, organ transplants or replacements). Argue for or against the continuation of the research.
- Research an endangered species. Argue for a plan of action to save, or to abandon attempts to save, the species.
- Conduct research on a human rights activist not mentioned in Thomas Berger's "Fragile Freedoms." Write an essay arguing that the person you have researched has made a significant contribution to the fight for human rights.
- Explain why you do or do not agree with the following statement: Diversity is Canada's strength, not its weakness.
  After completing your first draft, work with a partner to revise and edit your essay, focusing on the organization, the use of supporting evidence, and the strength of your arguments.

If time allows, organize a class debate in which you present the arguments in your essays.

Elements of the Explanation/Information Essay

The purpose of an explanation or information essay is to educate the reader. Assuming the role of an authority on the topic, the writer presents the information in a way that will give the reader a deeper understanding of a concept or process. The tone of the presentation is one of efficiency and confidence. Since the essay does not attempt to persuade the reader or defend a position, its points do not need to be argued. The information is presented in a clear, concise, straightforward manner, as if the information is unquestioned in its authority.

In explanation/information essays, writers often choose to write on a topic that they are interested in or that they know a lot about. Therefore one of the greatest challenges of writing this type of essay is limiting the scope of the discussion. Your first task, then, as a writer, is to decide which aspect of the topic your essay will focus on. When doing this, it is best to consider what will most interest your audience. Even though entertainment isn't necessarily an objective of explanation/information essays, an essay that fails to engage its reader may go unread.

Once you have clearly defined a concept on which you will focus, you need to decide on your approach to the topic. Teaching is not an easy undertaking; it takes a great deal of planning. If your audience is unfamiliar with your topic, you are basically "unfolding a new topic" in front of them. Be sure that you present the information in a logical order, in language that they can understand. Avoid using jargon the audience won't understand. Unfolding a topic also demands that you be particularly careful about the placement of topic sentences and the use of effective transitions. You should attempt to lead your reader gently through the topic, avoiding abrupt leaps in your discussion, which can confuse your reader.

We're Mesmerized by the Flickering Tube

Philip Marchand

Elements of the Essay

Why are we mesmerized by television? With the help of scientific theories and studies, Philip Marchand explains to readers in simple language the reasons for our attraction to the flickering tube. How does this essay compare with Marie Winn's "Television Addiction" (pages 37 to 40)?

About the Writer

Philip Marchand is a literary reviewer for *The Toronto Star* newspaper. While an undergraduate at the University of Toronto in 1969, he was taught by Marshall McLuhan. Marchand later wrote McLuhan's biography, *The Medium and the Message* (1989). He has also written a novel, *Deadly Spirits* (1995), and a collection of essays, *Ripostes: Reflections on Canadian Literature* (1998).

T HERE'S SOMETHING DEPRESSING ABOUT watching the Super Bowl, as opposed to a Stanley Cup final or a World Series game. I'm not sure why this is.

It's true that the actual game played at the Super Bowl, which takes place tomorrow, is usually boring, and that the dullness is tolerated because half the audience doesn't know much about the game anyway and the other half is only interested because bets have been laid on the outcome—any genuine football fan is driven crazy by the constant interruption of play by commercials.

Then there's the spectacle at halftime, which itself is depressing. What do howling musical performers, flashing lights and billows of coloured smoke have to do with anything?

But I think the most depressing thing about the Super Bowl is the fact that, for a dogged viewer, the better part of an entire Sunday is lost to television.

5   This is not an attack on TV. I'm as handy with a remote as anybody. But there seems to be a law of TV viewing. You can watch, say, four hours of movies on the big screen without getting depressed. You can read for four hours without getting depressed. You can even listen to the radio for four hours without getting depressed. But you can't watch four hours of TV without feeling awful afterward.

6   It doesn't matter whether you've been watching PBS or four straight episodes of *Who Wants To Be A Millionaire?* You just feel depleted and less alive than when you first switched on the set, four hours earlier.

7   For a long time, people have tried to figure out TV—how it works on the human brain and nervous system. The medium seems to have tricky properties, which puzzle and engage observers of all political and philosophical leanings.

8   In his recent book, *Them: Adventures With Extremists*, British journalist Jon Ronson quotes a right-wing conspiracy theorist who was baffled by how the U.S. government is able to get away with its nefarious plots. He had a hunch it had something to do with TV. "Then I found out one day that television is not a steady light, it's a rapidly flashing light," this man maintains. "As soon as I got that little bit of information, I realized what had happened. One of the ways you hypnotize people is with a rapidly flashing light. Everybody is hypnotized."

9   Where this man got his information, I do not know. Perhaps he got it from Marshall McLuhan. In McLuhan's posthumously published 1989 book, *The Global Village*, co-authored with Bruce Powers, there is a reference to people's brains being "lulled by the dots flashing sequentially across the screen at 1/30 of a second."

10   Sounds an awful lot like hypnotism to me.

11   McLuhan himself first caught the attention of the media in the early '60s when he went against the prevailing intellectual tide of bemoaning TV as a "great wasteland." At that time, intellectuals thought the big problem with TV was getting people to watch good stuff instead of *I Love Lucy*. McLuhan, of course, scoffed at that and said the problem was understanding the effect of the medium itself. Some of his pronouncements sounded almost enthusiastic—he thought TV, along with other electronic means of communication, created a "total field of instant awareness."

12   That sure sounded more hopeful than the great wasteland rhetoric. In private, however, McLuhan could be very acerbic about the effects of TV, as when he advised his son Eric to limit the time his children spent watching the tube. Television, he counselled, was a "vile drug which

permeates the nervous system, especially in the young."

Social scientists have long studied TV watching, but mostly in an attempt to determine whether violence on air causes violence in real life. (On the whole, it doesn't seem to.) Now in the latest issue of *Scientific American* comes an article, entitled "Television Addiction," which attempts a clinical view of the more general effects of the medium. 13

The authors, media specialist Robert Kubey and psychologist Mihaly Csikszentmihalyi, begin by stating the obvious: TV watching is "the world's most popular leisure pastime." They further state that "on average, individuals in the industrialized world devote three hours a day to the pursuit—fully half of their leisure time, and more than on any single activity save work and sleep." 14

The strange thing, however, is that these same people feel guilty about the amount of time they spend watching the tube. They'd like to spend less time but feel "strangely unable to reduce their viewing." 15

The set seems to have an almost occult power of seizing the attention of a viewer and not letting go. The authors quote a university professor who laments that, whenever a set is on in a room where he happens to be, he can't stop himself from periodically glancing at the screen. He could be engaged in the most fascinating conversation in the world, and every five minutes or so he'll still be turning his eyes away from the real-life speaker to that damned screen. 16

I know the feeling. It drives me nuts whenever there's a TV set on during a social gathering. In the midst of a lively conversation, I'll keep glancing at the screen in my line of vision, even if it's showing a soccer match or something equally boring, like car racing. 17

The authors then reported the results of a study they had undertaken on the response of TV viewers. As long ago as 1970, a research scientist named Herbert Krugman tested McLuhan's thesis that TV watching created a different head space, if you will, than other media, by measuring the brainwaves of viewers. Lo and behold, Krugman discovered that TV viewers responded with alpha brainwaves while glued to the set—that is to say, they were much more laid back and passive than they were when they were reading or doing other things. 18

Kubey and Csikszentmihalyi used a different method, too complicated to get into here, but their results were the same as Krugman's—TV viewers, no matter what the content of the programs they watched, were relaxed and passive and less mentally stimulated than they were during other activities. 19

20   What was even more interesting was their finding that the sense of relaxation ended as soon as the set was switched off—but the feeling of passivity and lowered alertness continued. "Survey participants commonly reflect that television has somehow absorbed or sucked out their energy, leaving them depleted," the authors report.

21   Play tennis or work on your model railroad in the basement, and you feel better afterward. Watch lots of TV and you feel worse afterward.

22   That, paradoxically, is the source of "television addiction." TV addicts know they're going to feel relaxed watching TV, so they turn it on. But they know that as soon as they turn it off, they're going to feel depressed, so they end up watching more than they intended.

23   Kubey and Csikszentmihalyi offer a theory as to why viewers feel so hypnotized—it has to do with what psychologists call "orienting response," or human sensitivity to certain kinds of movement. The gist of their hypothesis is that formal qualities of TV—perhaps those "dots flashing sequentially across the screen at 1/30 of a second," perhaps the peculiar cuts, edits, zooms, pans, sudden noises of TV—create the hypnotic effect.

24   They quote another media researcher: "It is the form, not the content, of television that is unique." What McLuhan intuited 50 years ago is now being verified in the laboratory. The medium is the message.

25   The authors do not urge us to junk our TV sets. Light viewing, which the authors define as less than two hours a day, presents no problems, like light drinking. But more than four hours a day is a sign of trouble.

26   That's why the Super Bowl is such an ominous occasion to a TV addict, like a New Year's Eve party to an alcoholic. To do a Super Bowl right means at least four hours of TV watching, and probably more.

27   No wonder so many people call it the Stupor Bowl.

After-Reading Activities

Analyzing the Content

1. In your own words, summarize one scientific theory about the way television affects the humans who watch it.

2. At the beginning of the essay, Philip Marchand compares a Stanley Cup and a World Series game to the Super Bowl. He never goes back to the former two. Discuss whether or not there is a need to return to his initial thought.

Structure and Style

3. State the effect of Marchand's use of the first-person point of view in this essay.

4. Explain the paradox that is described in paragraphs 11 and 12.

5. a) Many of Marchand's paragraphs are one or two sentences long. Examine and explain the differences between paragraphs of different lengths.

   b) Much of Marchand's writing appears in a newspaper. Defend his use of short paragraphs for a newspaper-reading audience.

Thunderstrokes and Firebolts

Janice McEwen

Elements of the Essay

What causes lightning? Janice McEwen's essay explains this natural phenomenon. To make this rather scientific explanation as easy to understand as possible, McEwen draws on humour and chooses accessible vocabulary and a second-person point of view. Along with her explanation, McEwen also provides some pointers on how to avoid being struck by lightning during an electrical storm.

1   IMAGINE THE CHAGRIN OF A Renfrew, Ontario, farmer who pulled on the handle of a recently repaired barn door one morning following a thunderstorm only to have the door crumble into a heap of individual boards at his feet.

2   The man was left sheepishly wondering about his carpentry skills until a local lightning protection contractor examined the door and explained that, unknown to the farmer, a bolt of lightning had hit the barn during the storm. Leapfrogging from nail-to-nail along the Z-shaped bracing boards that supported the door, the lightning made its way to the ground. In the process the heat produced by the bolt reduced the nails to dust.

3   For the 118 passengers aboard an Air Canada DC-8 jetliner, lightning had much more serious consequences: the ill-fated plane crashed in a swampy field shortly after take-off from Montreal in November, 1963. When investigators finished sifting through the rubble of what is still Canada's worst airplane disaster, lightning was high on the list of probable causes.

4   Lightning is the most awesome of nature's weather phenomena—a single stroke of lightning produces more electricity than the combined output of all electrical power plants in the United States. The average cloud-to-ground lightning bolt averages only six inches in diameter, but

attains a core temperature of about 50,000 degrees Fahrenheit—five times the temperature at the surface of the sun.

Each day some 44,000 thunderstorms break out around the globe, the greatest concentration of them within the belt extending 30 degrees north and south of the equator. As you read this there are 1,800 electrical storms raging throughout the world, and by the time you finish this sentence, lightning will have struck earth 100 times.

Too frequently, lightning strikes spell disaster. Each year several hundred North Americans are killed by lightning, and others die in the fires that follow in the wake of electrical storms. Ten thousand forest fires and more than 30,000 building blazes are caused by lightning. Damages to property and loss of timber are estimated at more than 50 million dollars annually.

Yet the scientific study of lightning is still in pioneering stages, leaving unexplained many aspects of the complicated series of events that take place in the five thousandths of a second required for the average lightning bolt to strike.

Scientists are, for example, at a loss to explain "ball" lightning, a rare occurrence in which an orb about 20 centimetres in diameter forms at the lightning impact point. This blinding ball of energy is able to move around at a speed of several metres per second and is said to be accompanied by a hissing sound. Ball lightning is able to pass through closed windowpanes and often disappears with an explosion.

Little wonder that this astounding natural force has always aroused man's curiosity and fear.

For our ancient forefathers, there was no doubt about what caused lightning: various gods were flamboyantly expressing their disapproval of somebody's actions.

Zeus, as legend would have it, was particularly keen to use a handy supply of lightning bolts to express his frequent outbursts of rage. Unfortunate were the troops that attacked friends of this surly deity— Zeus would often step in when his side was losing and tip the tides of battle with a few well-placed bolts among the enemy ranks.

But recent findings by Nobel Prize winner Dr. Harold Urey suggest that the ancients may not have underestimated the nearly divine role lightning plays in terrestrial life.

Through laboratory reconstruction of the atmosphere of the young, lifeless earth—an atmosphere composed of ammonia, methane, hydrogen and water—students of Urey found that when electrical sparks, much like lightning, were passed through this medium, amino acids were created—the first building blocks in the evolution of life.

14   Recent findings also suggest that we can thank lightning (at least partially) for giving the world plants. Although nitrogen makes up 80 per cent of the earth's atmosphere, in its pure state it is useless to plants.

15   It has been found that lightning causes atmospheric nitrogen to combine with oxygen, forming nitric-oxide gas. This gas dissolves in rain and falls to earth as usable nitrates. Some scientists estimate that hundreds of millions of tons of these nitrates are produced by lightning each year. It's enough to make a purveyor of bagged 20-20-20 weep.

16   Benjamin Franklin, that portly Renaissance man of the eighteenth century, made the first real breakthrough in man's understanding of lightning by determining that it was, indeed, a huge electrical spark. But it is ironic (in light of his factual discoveries) that one of the most prevalent schoolboy myths still surrounding lightning features Mr. Franklin as its main character.

17   Everyone has heard about Franklin's kite flying antics. What few people realize is that his kite was never struck by lightning. Had it been, either the string would have burned and Mr. Franklin would have lost his kite, or the experimenter himself would have been struck, and the world would have lost an able scholar and statesman.

18   What happened during this famous flight was that there was enough difference in the electrical charge between the earth and the air at the level of the kite to create a small finger-tingling flow of electrical current through Mr. Franklin's string.

19   Today we know that conditions leading to electrical storms begin when a strong negative charge builds in rain (cumulo-nimbus) clouds. How this charge develops is still a matter of scientific debate, but an accepted theory is that air turbulence in the clouds creates a build-up of negatively charged electrons.

20   Free electrons on the earth directly below the cloud are repelled by the huge numbers of electrons above, and therefore the charge of the earth becomes more positive.

21   Because opposing charges are attracted to each other, the electrons in the cloud yearn to get to the positive earth.

22   Air, however, is a poor conductor of electricity. As the cloud matures, the charge continues to build until pressure becomes great enough to permit the electrons to leap through the insulative layer of air.

23   The first tentative electrons probe toward the earth in a series of steps

that gives a lightning bolt its irregular shape. These first electrons clear a path for those in the cloud, and as soon as the first electrons connect with the ground, an avalanche of electricity surges from the sky.

Lightning has struck.   24

Lightning bolts range from 1,000 to 9,000 feet long, and can attain   25
speeds over 60,000 miles per second.

A lightning bolt seeks the route offering the least electrical resistance   26
in its journey from cloud to ground. Almost any solid object offers an easier path for electricity than air: it could be a tree, a utility pole, a high patch of ground; it could also be your barn, one of your outbuildings— or your house.

Lightning is a hazard deserving special attention from rural dwellers.   27
Grim statistics show that nine out of ten lightning-caused deaths occur outside city limits. Fire authorities estimate that lightning causes up to 37 per cent of all rural building fires.

G.A. Pelletier, chief of technical services in the Ontario Fire Marshall's   28
Office and one of Canada's foremost authorities on lightning, attributes part of this phenomenal loss of life and property in rural areas to people being misinformed about this frightening natural force.

"Most people are totally unaware of what lightning is, how it behaves   29
and what it can do," he said. "Take the old wives' tale about lightning never hitting the same place twice—a common enough belief. It's totally false. As a matter of fact, if a place has been hit once, it shows that it is a prime site for future strikes."

Pelletier also says that many people believe their homes to be safe   30
from lightning because of the proximity of tall trees or a high television aerial. Neither is necessarily true.

We can thank Ben Franklin's inquisitive (and financially long-sighted)   31
mind for the protection we now have against destruction of property caused by lightning.

"It has pleased God in His goodness to mankind, at length to   32
discover to them the means of securing their habitations and other buildings from mischief by thunder and lightning," wrote Franklin in the 1753 edition of *Poor Richard's Almanack*. He went on to outline a system that not only worked, but which remains, almost unchanged, as the most efficient form of lightning protection.

The heart of a lightning protection system is a series of rods extending   33
at least 12 inches above a structure at lightning vulnerable places: peaks, gable ends, chimneys, etc.

34   These lightning rods (or "air terminals" in the jargon of lightning experts) are connected to each other by a woven copper cable roughly one-half inch thick. The cable, in turn, is grounded on at least two sides of the building to rods driven 10 feet into the earth, although the depth will vary somewhat in accordance with soil conditions. It is often said that a lightning rod gives protection within a circle whose radius is the height of the tip of the rod from the ground. Unfortunately, lightning does not always adhere to this rule, but the Canadian Standards Association says that "a properly installed lightning rod system, if not 100 per cent effective, will ensure that in nearly all cases of lightning strikes to buildings, little or no damage will result."

35   Fire statistics support these claims: in 1975, the most recent year for which figures are available, only 91 of the 2,559 structural fires started by lightning in Ontario occurred in buildings protected by lightning rod systems.

36   Pelletier explains that a properly working lightning rod system creates an easy route for the electrical charges to follow, diverting them away from the building and allowing them to dissipate harmlessly in the ground.

37   This, of course, is preferable to the unprotected alternative—where the bolt strikes the roof of the building and passes through the structure itself, leaping through walls, appliances, plumbing fixtures, radiators (and in some cases human beings) en route to the earth....

38   Your chances of being killed by lightning this summer are roughly one in a million—certainly no reason to cancel plans for boating, picnics and hiking during the warm season, but reason enough to implement precautions.

39   An electrical storm that swept the New York City area took a typical toll of human victims. A golfer whose foursome had sought refuge from the rain beneath a tree (a common mistake that accounts for one-third of thunderstorm fatalities) died when lightning slammed into the tree. His companions were unharmed. The storm's next victim was a fisherman holding a metal casting rod. Lightning leapt from the rod to his jacket zipper. His single companion was injured but recovered. The final victim, a young man, died while standing near a beachhouse.

40   All of these deaths could have been prevented had the victims followed commonsense safety measures.

41   A car is perhaps the safest place to be during an electrical storm. There have been few, if any, substantiated cases of lightning striking an automobile, but laboratory experiments show that the charge would pass

harmlessly over the metal shell of the car and then leap from the undercarriage to the pavement.

Second only to a car (and virtually 100 per cent safe) is a dry building protected by lightning rods. When the first signs of thunder make themselves manifest, the sensible thing to do is go straight to the shelter of a protected building. Two-thirds of lightning-caused deaths occur outdoors.   42

When you are caught by a storm in an open area, do not, under any circumstances, take shelter under an isolated tree. If you cannot reach a protected building, seek a low-lying area of open land.   43

Trees are favourite targets for lightning, and electrical charges that surge from the base of a struck tree can kill for a considerable distance. In one instance, a single bolt of lightning struck a tree in a Utah pasture and killed 500 sheep. There are recorded cases of cattle being killed while standing 100 yards from a struck tree.   44

Few people are killed by direct lightning strikes. If someone were directly hit, he would be severely burned. In most cases, the lightning victim is not burned but dies because currents cast off from a nearby lightning strike pass through his body, stopping his breathing and heartbeat.   45

Lightning frequently strikes water and electrical charges travel freely through this medium. Boats are high on the list of undesirable places to be when there is an approaching electrical storm. If you are in a boat, get to shore immediately and move some distance inland; shoreline trees are prime candidates for lightning strikes.   46

Swimmers, too, are in danger of being injured or killed by electrical charges that surge through water as a result of lightning.   47

If you find yourself in a protected house at the outbreak of a thunderstorm, take heart; you are safe.   48

Still, it is wise to stay away from sinks and bathtubs—your plumbing system is connected to a metal vent pipe protruding through the roof and is a potential lightning target.   49

Avoid touching refrigerators, stoves and other large metal objects. Do not use telephones or other electrical appliances, and stay away from stovepipes, chimneys and fireplaces. Windows and doors should be closed.   50

If your home or one of your outbuildings is struck by lightning, an immediate check-over is due to insure that no hidden fires have started. (Old-timers often referred to hot and cold lightning—the former causing fires and the latter merely hitting with one explosive bolt.)   51

When lightning fells a human, it is often possible to revive him with prolonged artificial respiration. Many victims have recovered fully, while others were left with sight or hearing impairments.

52   But even when nestled in the security of a snug, lightning-protected house, there are still some people who find themselves quivering under the bed with the dog at the faintest rumble of thunder. This unfortunate segment of the population might consider moving to the Arctic or Antarctic—areas which see only one thunderstorm per decade.

53   If relocation does not fit your plans, we can only offer the slim comfort of words spoken by one lightning protection expert: "If you heard the thunder, the lightning did not strike you. If you saw the lightning, it missed you; and if it did strike you, you would not have known it."

After-Reading Activities

Analyzing the Content

1. Explain in your own words what causes electrical storms.

2. Make a list of astounding facts that Janice McEwen includes in her essay.

Structure and Style

3. Assess the effectiveness of the opening paragraph in encouraging the reader to read on. Why does McEwen separate the first two paragraphs, even though the second one is on the same topic as the first?

4. What is the effect of the juxtaposition of the two stories (paragraphs 2 and 3) about the effect of lightning?

5. Humour is one method McEwen uses to make her information appeal to a broad audience. Choose three incidents of humour (sarcasm, understatement, irony, or hyperbole) and explain how they have been used in this essay.

6. Describe the tone of the essay and the attitude of the writer. For each, use examples to support your description.

7. Why does the writer quote other people in her essay?

Food for Sloth

Carol Krenz

Elements of the Essay

Carol Krenz defines comfort foods and provides reasons why we choose certain types of foods. While parts of the explanation are scientific, the essay is understandable even to readers who may not be familiar with scientific vocabulary. Krenz's humour facilitates this accessibility, and the topic itself, comfort foods, is close to the experiences of most people.

About the Writer
Carol Krenz was born in Montreal and has been writing about fashion, popular culture, health, and beauty for numerous magazines and newspapers since 1987. She contributes to such publications as the *National Post*, *The Montreal Gazette*, *Nuvo*, and *Flare*, and is currently at work on her first novel, *The Scarf Dance*.

Controlling idea

COMFORT FOODS ARE HUMANKIND'S way of fighting back against the cruel realities of cold temperatures and blah days. 1

Justification for our need for comfort foods—our own type of hibernation (paragraphs 2 to 4)

Although anthropologists might disagree about humans' relationship to bears, physicians and psychologists attest to the fact that we are all prone to hibernation activities from the first November slushfests to May's crocuses. We tend to grow sluggish and stupid. We grumble and growl a lot. A large majority of *homo erectus urbanus* views with mock horror the folds of loose fat that begin to dangle from our midriffs around March. 2

Our greatest winter pleasure appears to be eating, then heavy sleeping followed by more eating. (Unlike bears, however, we have masochistic tendencies that occasionally take over in this period, forcing us to sit in front of the television, awash in winter pounds and 3 lethargy, watching finely honed bodies leap after a football or execute *grand jetés*.)

4   Instinctively we reach for foods loaded with simple sugars and complex carbohydrates—something we've been doing for centuries without question—only now we have medical science confirming that hearty bowls of bean and barley soup or mounds of pasta will actually make us feel sedated, fuzzy about the edges and blissfully sleepy.

5   There are no distinct separations between hibernation foods and comfort foods, but you could regard comfort foods as year-round pacifiers while hibernation edibles are great in cold weather. Case in point: a hot chocolate fudge sundae. It's adaptable. You could eat it anytime. (Mind you, chocolate anything needs no *raison d'être*.) However, Irish stew, shepherd's pie and homemade macaroni and cheese seem more appropriate in winter. Same for apple dumplings, blinis, cabbage rolls, tandoori chicken and nan, roasted or baked potatoes, strudel, peas and rice with curried goat, or baked beans and molasses.

Differences between comfort foods and hibernation foods

6   But one person's comfort food might be another's poison, at least psychologically speaking. The aim of comfort foods is to soothe, to make us retreat into childhood memories of warmth and security. If you look back, no matter how trauma-filled your early life might have been, there were times when you looked to food for solace. As Rhoda Morgenstern observed in the seventies, "The first thing I remember liking that liked me back was *food*." Ergo, you may long for baked custard sprinkled with nutmeg, I might hanker for blancmange or junket. A friend with a remarkable long-term memory reaches for Pablum when the going gets rough, and one chap I know thinks that toasted rye with peanut butter, sweet gherkins and mayonnaise is the answer. One might ask, how could his mother have allowed this? Which is the whole point. Comfort foods don't have to make nutritional sense (or be politically correct)!

How comfort foods came to be

How comfort
foods do not
have to be
nutritional

Sandra P., a mother of three grown daughters, can be   7
spotted at the Atwater Steinberg checking out low-fat
milk, alfalfa sprouts, tofu and seven-grain bread. As she
nears the cashier with her healthy selections, she steals a
furtive glance around, then quickly reaches under her
coat to produce five Tootsie Rolls, one box of Kraft
dinner, and a Monarch chocolate sponge pudding cake.
She explodes with a sigh of relief when the items are
finally secreted in (non-biodegradable) white plastic
bags. But Sandra P. has it all wrong. Comfort foods are
in. They should be flaunted. They should not be a
source of guilt.

Comment on
North American
society

The instinctive desire to hibernate through winter   8
with loads of comfort foods is understandable. Most of
us are not descended from Norse gods who lounged
naked around frigid fjords, ice fishing after their saunas,
drinking steaming bowls of cinnamon-laced grog. We're
a bunch of wimps, and we'll take our grog indoors,
thank you very much.

Explanation of
how comfort
foods work
(paragraphs 9 to 10)

The carbohydrate component to our food choices   9
offers new evidence of chemical alteration of the body's
brain. Rather than giving us energy, carbohydrates slow
people down, and can even decrease reaction time and
alertness. According to *Psychology Today*, unbalanced
carbohydrates—high amounts of sugars and starches
without accompanying protein—accomplish this
quickly, but are blocked somewhat when even the
smallest amount of protein is added. Armed with this
information, you may want to avoid eating pure carbs
during a mentally taxing business day. On the other
hand, try reaching for the Sugar Pops when you have to
visit the dentist. What better time to feel spaced out
and dopey?

Medical research into unbalanced carbohydrates   10
began in the early seventies. Experiments on rats at the
Massachusetts Institute of Technology proved that higher
levels of serotonin, a brain chemical that affects sleep,
pain perception and motor activity, are the end result of
carbohydrate consumption. According to neuroscientist

Richard Wurtman, chemicals in the bloodstream compete for access to the brain. Tryptophan, an amino acid, is converted into serotonin once inside the brain. By eating carbohydrates we make tryptophan the odds-on favourite among its competitors for brain entry. But it's not because carbs contain tryptophan. Rather, carbohydrates distract the competition by stimulating the release of insulin, which moves the other chemicals into muscles. The tryptophans, like conquering heroes, march unchallenged into the brain, change into serotonin and mellow us out.

11   So when Mom gave us a bowl of warm milk with wisps of white bread drenched in sugar, she may have insisted it was easy to digest, but we now know it was loaded with both tryptophan (in the milk) and carbohydrates or insulin releasers.

Links back to paragraph 6

12   It is therefore not surprising that most comfort foods are riddled with complex and simple carbohydrates. Physically and psychologically, they soothe us. So if it's February and you have this mad urge to consume mashed potatoes and turnips, take comfort. Get thee to a den and hibernate.

Conclusion

After-Reading Activities

Analyzing the Content

1. Explain the physical effects carbohydrates have on our systems.

2. How do the margin annotations help you with your understanding of the information in the essay?

Structure and Style

3. Record several ways Carol Krenz makes reading the information in this essay enjoyable.

4. Several times in the essay Krenz uses parentheses. Examine each use, and explain why she uses them and how they add to or detract from the essay.

5. Paragraphs 9, 10, and 11 are different from the rest of the essay. Describe the differences, and decide whether or not the writer is justified in clustering these differences into these three paragraphs.

6. The title and the final sentence of the essay are clichés with a twist. For each, state the original cliché, and discuss the effectiveness of the writer's twist.

Extending the Purpose

1. Choose one of the following:
   - Research a natural phenomenon, and, using Janice McEwen's essay as a model, write an explanation/information essay on that topic. Use some of her techniques to make the essay readable and interesting.
   - Write an explanation/information essay about some idiosyncratic behaviour that you have noticed in human beings. You may need to do additional research.
   - Using the information from Philip Marchand's essay, record what you know about Marshall McLuhan. Choose one of these pieces of information and research it further, using print or electronic sources. Write an explanation/information essay on McLuhan.
   - Read the essay "Television Addiction" by Marie Winn (pages 37 to 40). Combine information from both this essay and Marchand's to write an information essay of your own. Choose a style different from the styles of Marchand and Winn.

   After completing your first draft, work with a partner to revise and edit your essay, focusing on the organization and the clarity of your information and explanation.

2. Using a variety of persuasive techniques, argue for or against banning television viewing for children. (See pages 130 to 151 for examples of persuasive and argument essays.) You may need to do additional research to develop your arguments.

Elements of the Personal Essay

As its name suggests, a personal essay is just that—personal. It is based on one's personal experiences. Although a personal essay *may* project a sense of authority, it does not make any claim to objectivity. This type of essay presents the writer's perspective on a topic and is usually written in an informal style. It generally uses a first-person point of view, but other points of view may be used for effect. The objectives of personal essays vary widely. Some personal essays are written to argue a point, others to provide information, and others to entertain. As a result of these wide-ranging objectives, there is no set rule about the tone of these essays, either. They may be humorous, serious, nostalgic, confrontational, inspirational—whatever best suits the writer's purpose.

The following personal essays vary in topic, tone, and style, but they are all heartfelt, close to each writer's heart. What do you think is the purpose of each?

Thanks for Not Killing My Son

Rita Schindler

Elements of the Essay

This powerful letter appeared in *The Toronto Star* newspaper on December 30, 1990, and came to the attention of a student, who brought it to class to share with his classmates. It was written by a mother to the "strangers" who attacked her son and left him for dead. Though written as a letter, it has the elements of an essay, forceful in its ironic tone and eloquent in its point of view.

About the Writer
At the time she wrote this letter, Rita Schindler was a mother living in Scarborough, Ontario.

1   I HOPE YOU WILL PRINT my letter of gratitude to the strangers who have affected our lives.

2   Sometime between 1:30 P.M., Dec. 8, and 1 A.M., Dec. 9, a young man was viciously attacked—beaten and kicked unconscious for no apparent reason other than walking by you on a public sidewalk.

3   He was left lying in a pool of blood from an open head wound—in the Victoria Park–Terraview area. He was found around 1 A.M. and taken to Scarborough General Hospital where ironically his mother spent 48 hours in labor before giving him birth, 23 years earlier.

4   His mother is angry of course, but thankful for the following reasons.

5   First of all—his eye socket was shattered and hemorrhaging but his eyesight will not be affected. Thank you.

6   His ear canal was lacerated internally from a tremendous blow to the side of his head. The cut could not be stitched and the bleeding was difficult to stop. But his eardrum seems to be undamaged—thank you.

7   He required numerous stitches to his forehead, temple and face but your boots didn't knock one tooth out—thank you. His head was

swollen almost twice its size—but Mom knew that his brain was intact—for he held her hand for six hours as he lay on a gurney, by the nurses station, I.V. in his arm—his head covered and crusted with dried blood—waiting for x-ray results and the surgeon to stitch him up.

So, thank you for his eyesight, his hearing and his hands which you could have easily crushed. 8

His hands—human hands—the most intricately beautiful and complex instruments of incredible mechanism—the result of billions of years of evolution—and you people used yours to beat another human being. Five guys and two girls to beat one person. Who do I thank? Did you know he was a talented young musician with a budding career—and that playing his keyboards and piano mean more to him than any words can say. 9

And when his friends were talking about revenge, I heard him say, "No, I don't want someone else's mother to go through what mine has." That's who you were kicking in the head. And so—I thank you for not causing the most horrible and devastating thing that can happen to any parent—that is—the untimely tragic loss of a child—at any age. 10

You could have kicked him to death but you only left him to die, thank you. A person found him and called for help. 11

I am his mother—and I have been given a second chance—thanks to you. 12

I hope that someday you'll have children and love them as much as I love mine—but I wouldn't wish on your child what you did to mine. 13

Rita Schindler
Scarborough

After-Reading Activities

Analyzing the Content

1. Why would a mother whose son has been beaten write a letter to a newspaper?

Structure and Style

2. At the beginning of this letter, the writer talks about herself in the third person ("His mother is ..."). At the end she says, "I am his mother." State the effect of this conceit on the reader.

3. Instead of using invective, the writer uses a combination of irony, sarcasm, and hyperbole. Are these effective tools for the purpose of the letter? Explain your answer.

4. This letter is developed by example. Explain why the number and type of examples make the essay so powerful.

5. The repeated use of "thank you" builds a rhythm in the writing. What effect does this have on the reader and the message of the letter?

Life After Smoking

Peter Gzowski

Elements of the Essay

"Life After Smoking" appeared in *50+ Magazine* in June 2001, and also in *A Peter Gzowski Reader* (2001), just before the death of Peter Gzowski from chronic obstructive pulmonary disease (emphysema), caused by years of smoking. Although the essay topic is serious, it takes a positive approach. With lighthearted humour, this self-reflective essay takes a look at life after smoking. What do you think is the purpose of this essay?

About the Writer

Broadcaster and writer Peter Gzowski was born on July 13, 1934. His love for the written word began when he was editor of *The Varsity* at the University of Toronto. In 1962, he became the managing editor of *Maclean's* before moving on to *Star Weekly* (owned by *The Toronto Star*). Nine years later, he was the host of the CBC Radio show *This Country in the Morning* (1971–1974), followed by *90 Minutes Live* (1976–1978). However, it wasn't until he hosted CBC's *Morningside* (1982–1997) that Gzowski became the most highly recognized voice in the country and gained a wide following. During his lifetime, he published 11 books, including *The Sacrament* (1980), *The Game of Our Lives* (1981), and *A Peter Gzowski Reader* (2001). He also earned numerous honours and awards, notably the Governor General's Award for the Performing Arts (1995). Gzowski died on January 24, 2002.

NEARLY ALL THE LESSONS OF your early life, from tying your shoes to parallel parking to knowing which wine to order with dinner (not just before you take your parking class, I hope) are about things you're figuring out how to do as you grow up. Not only how to do but that you can do them, sometimes well, occasionally with some profit, and often just because you love doing them. From knowing your skills and dreaming of where they can take you, you begin to figure out not so much who you are, as they used to say in the 60s, but who   1 and what you'd like to be when, if ever, you grow up.

2 But there's another part of the process too: learning—and accepting—what you *can't* do, or sometimes what you used to do but can't do any longer. Some of that's just aging, accelerated, in my own case, by fifty years of smoking cigarettes—a tyranny I've been free of for well over a year now (thank God, the patch, Zyban and some wonderful professional help) but for which I am still paying a heavy price. But some of it's been going on for a long time too, and I realize now, hell-bent for seventy, and still with some growing up left to do, I'm beginning to understand that the limitations I'm facing up to now really aren't that different from those I've had to deal with all my life.

3 I was only about twelve, for instance, when it became clear that Elizabeth Taylor wasn't going to marry me, and not much older when I saw from the expression on the choirmaster's face as he listened to me run through some scales that I should probably give up my dream of succeeding Bing Crosby.

4 I held on a bit longer to the idea that I'd play in the National Hockey League some day. I had, after all, scored dozens of goals in the Stanley Cup finals, many of them in overtime—you could hear Foster Hewitt yelling my name as I broke down the wing of the outdoor rink in Dickson Park. "The Kid from Galt has done it again," Foster would shout over the roar of the crowd, even though he and I—or his voice and I—were all by ourselves in the winter morning.

5 Actually, I never stopped thinking there'd be a place for me in the NHL. Playing big-time hockey is the one ambition that draws all Canadian males together, and though I couldn't prove it I'd be willing to bet that if Chris Hadfield had been a better skater he might never have walked in space or if James Orbinski of Montreal had had a harder slap shot he might never have become the president of Medicins Sans Frontieres, which won the Nobel Peace Prize last year.

6 About thirty years after everyone else had given up on my hockey career, I spent a season hanging out with the Edmonton Oilers. Ostensibly I was writing a book about them, but in my heart I was just looking for a chance to show my stuff. It came one day at practice. The team had been playing well, and Glen Sather, their coach and general manager, set up a game of old-fashioned shinny. I borrowed some gear, joined in, and managed for a shift or two to become a winger on Wayne Gretzky's line. At one point I wobbled to a place in front of the opposition goal. Wayne set up behind the net—in his office, as we

reporters liked to say. He dug out the puck, feinted once, and flipped it right onto my stick. I took dead aim at the empty corner, cocked my wrist and …

Oh, well, maybe I wasn't cut out for the NHL after all—though I almost hit the net.   7

Hockey, crooning, or marrying movie stars aside—not to mention   8
breaking a quarter horse, flying my own jet or swimming the Strait of Juan de Fuca and other dreams that have faded as I've aged—I've had a pretty full life. On radio or television or with a pencil in my hand, I've got to meet the Queen, eight prime ministers (nine if you count Margaret Thatcher, who had a cold and couldn't hear my questions but kept on answering what she'd have liked me to ask anyway), four governors general, two chief justices, two Nobel Prize winners, the world yodelling, whistling and bagpipe champions (all Canadians) and every winner and most of the runners-up of the Giller Prize for Literature. I've danced with Karen Kain (well, I made a lifting motion and Karen sprang into the air, light as dandelion fluff), sang with Leonard Cohen (well, Leonard sang and I chanted along to "Tower of Song"), played chess with Boris Spassky (I moved, he moved, I asked if he wanted to resign, he grinned, said sure and we shook hands), golf with George Knudsen, cribbage with Gordon Sinclair and—well, sort of, as we've seen—hockey with Wayne Gretzky.

And I'm a long way from finished. I need oxygen most of the time now,   9
and without my walker—a kind of baby carriage without the baby—I'm pretty well confined to barracks. On radio, which I still love, I sometimes sound a little breathier than I'd like to, and if I'm asked to make a speech, I need to know there aren't too many stairs to the platform.

But, I've learned, once you accept your limitations you can deal with   10
them. Travel is hard for me now, but if I plan every move as carefully as I can, ask for rooms near elevators and make sure the airlines know I need oxygen, I can get to most of the places I want to go. Even around the city where I live, I've learned to call restaurants in advance to make sure washrooms are on the main floor. I've taken to—and hugely enjoy—having friends in for lunch rather than going out. I'm way ahead on my reading, and writing more than I have for years. I've bought a treadmill to keep myself as active as I can. I'd like to learn some Inuktitut—there are lessons, believe it or not, on the Internet—and I'm wondering if I could try a little watercolour sketching.

Elizabeth Taylor? I'd probably still be standing in line.   11

After-Reading Activities

Analyzing the Content

1. Explain whether or not the title of this essay is effective. Think of a different title for the essay.

2. What is the writer saying about a person's limitations? Do you agree? Why or why not?

Structure and Style

3. What is the thesis of this essay? Where is it found?

4. Create an outline for this essay, dividing the body into three distinct parts.

5. How does the structure of the recollection part (paragraphs 3 to 7) of the essay reflect its content?

6. This essay was written for *50+ Magazine*, geared to readers aged 50 and over. Does it have any appeal for readers under 50? Why or why not?

7. Peter Gzowski suffered from chronic obstructive pulmonary disease, which causes breathing difficulties, as a result of years of smoking. Despite this, the tone of his essay is upbeat and positive. How did he accomplish this?

Take Me Out of Their Ball Game

Maria Guhde Keri

Elements of the Essay

Should parents simply stay home and become less involved in their children's ball games? Maria Guhde Keri provides a unique perspective in her essay, stating that parents need not be as involved in their children's sports activities as most seem to be. Writing in a personal voice, she develops her arguments inductively, beginning with her son's last baseball game of the season, and ending with a general conclusion.

About the Writer
Maria Guhde Keri is a mother of four. She lives with her husband and children in Cincinnati, Ohio.

MY SON'S BASEBALL TEAM had just lost their last game of the season—they were out of the tournament. We losing parents tried our best to look glum, while the winning parents attempted to hide their jealousy. By the time we arrived at our cars, the lucky losers were excitedly discussing vacations we could take, projects we could begin, and friends we could finally see. Baseball season was over! We were free! 1

"At least until soccer season," one mom reminded us. "We're playing football this year," another added, rolling her eyes, and I couldn't block an image of parents and children all suited up in matching football uniforms, complete with pads. As a veteran sports mom, I knew exactly why she had used the plural *we*. 2

When one child in the family plays a sport, it is indeed a family affair. I think maybe the team photos should include us parents, derrieres parked in lawn chairs, arms laden with water bottles, diaper bags, and Barbie carry-alls. 3

We want to be there for our kids, to take an interest in what's 4 important to them. This is what good parents do, right? Maybe. When I was young, kids rode their bikes or were dropped off for their games and practices. Only later would Mom or Dad ask how it went. My father was a coach, but I don't remember being dragged along to my brother's games. In fact, the kids on my dad's teams would converge on our house to be driven to the games in our 12-seater station wagon. No parents required.

5   Sometimes I think that by being so involved in our kids' sports, we dilute their experience. After all, it's not *their* win, it's *our* win. Do all the valuable lessons—losing, striking out, missing the winning shot—have the same impact when Mom and Dad are there to immediately say it's OK?

6   Of course we need to make sure Michael is listening to the coach and the coach is listening to Michael, and to ensure that Lauren is getting off the bench but not being pushed too hard. And psycho sports parents are obviously a problem: the dad who screams at his son for every fumble, the mom who reacts to the 14-year-old umpire's bad call as if it were a threat to world peace. We know they are wacko.

7   But then there are the rest of us, the good parents. Are we cramping our kids' style? Maybe they just want to get together and play a game.

8   Did you ever walk into a room where kids are playing, say, a board game? They're animated, excited, totally focused on what they're doing. When you appear, they stiffen, grow quiet, and appear confused. An adult is watching, and suddenly the game and rules are changed—maybe even ruined. Now imagine 40 of us adults descending on a ball game. Do we really believe we make it more fun for our children?

9   I'm essentially a non-athlete: my only "sport" was cheerleading. I don't remember my mother ever coming to my games, much less shouting from the stands "Good, honey, but smile more!" or "Doing great, but you were late on that last turn." I think I would have told her to either shut up or stay home.

10   And don't the siblings deserve a well-balanced, un-rushed dinner once in a while? To play in their own neighborhood, their own yard? What are they learning when life revolves around Lauren's soccer games, and family harmony ranks a distant second?

11   Maybe we parents should be doing more constructive things: cutting the lawn, painting the dining room, volunteering, writing a book—in short, getting a life instead of just driving our children to theirs. Our time is important, too: we need to show our children that moms and dads can and need to do more than watch. Certainly, our involvement depends on our children's ages and personalities. My 5-year-old T-ball

player will surely not be so enthusiastic about my seeing his every hit when he is 15. My 8-year-old daughter, on the other hand, already seems relieved when we miss one of her soccer games. Somewhere there is a perfect balance between not caring at all and caring too much. As parents, we know that at some point we need to make it *their* game, *their* recital, *their* grades. If we share every element of their lives, we're cheating them out of part of it.

We need to shut up. And sometimes—not always—we need to stay home. As hard as it is to risk missing her first home run, or not being there to comfort him after the missed foul shot, at some point we need to take ourselves out of their ball game. Because this is what good parents do.

12

After-Reading Activities

Analyzing the Content

1. Does the reference to "Barbie carry-alls" in paragraph 3 of this essay support or contradict the position on Barbie dolls presented in "Barbie and Her Playmates" (pages 79 to 85)? Give reasons for your answer.

2. In light of the information in this essay, debate the following resolution: Be It Resolved That Parents Should Be Banned from Their Children's Competitive Sporting Events. You may need to do additional research to prepare your arguments.

Structure and Style

3. What is the main argument or thesis of this essay?

4. Is the central argument that you identified in activity 3 based on fact or opinion? Give reasons for your position.

5. Describe the tone of this essay. How does Maria Guhde Keri create this tone? Assess whether the tone is appropriate for the subject matter of the essay. Is it appropriate for the main argument of the essay you identified in activity 3? Would any other tone be appropriate?

6. Keri uses a number of questions in this essay. What effect do they have on her argument?

Extending the Purpose

1. The message in each of the essays in this section is serious. Still, each writer is able to convey the message in a readable style. Find some examples of other essays in which confusion, anger, sadness, or horror are made palatable for the reader. Investigate ways the writers have been able to achieve this fine balance.

2. Write the letter of apology that the mother of "Thanks for Not Killing My Son" would have loved to have received from the attackers. In this letter, try to explain the actions taken and what the attackers were thinking. Make it as convincing and as powerful as the original. You may want to use examples to develop your ideas, or you can use other methods.

3. Choose one of the following:
    *   Write a personal essay in which you present two points of view, arguing persuasively about each, but still supporting one over the other.
    *   Write a personal essay about "fitting in." Use a third-person perspective.
    *   Write a personal essay about the generation gap that exists between parents and teenagers.
    *   Write a personal essay in which you discuss an interesting fact you found out about yourself. Focus on one type of organizational pattern.
    *   Using Peter Gzowski's essay as a model, write a personal essay about a life lesson you have learned.
    *   Write your own opinions or personal essay about the behaviour of parents at competitive sporting events in which their children are playing.

    After completing your first draft, work with a partner to revise and edit your essay, focusing on the organization and the use of stylistic devices.

Elements of the Literary Essay

The literary essay is critical, interpretive writing—it is not meant to simply retell what happens in the literature being analyzed. This type of essay explores the meaning and construction of a piece of literature, trying to explain why, how, or if it works. To do so, it focuses on one or more of the literary elements such as structure, character, theme, style, tone, and subtext. The essayist supports his or her thesis by making direct reference to the work, or by making reference to literary criticisms of the work.

One aspect of interpretation that some students are uncomfortable with is that there is no "correct" interpretation. Literary analysis is like detective work where the reader tries to "get inside the artist's mind" by looking at the evidence on the page. This does not, however, mean that *any* position an essayist takes is correct or appropriate. The evidence that supports one interpretation may be better or more effective than evidence that supports others. Nonetheless, when you write this type of essay, trust your own interpretive abilities. Look first to the work of literature for supporting evidence, and then possibly look to the criticism that others have provided for support. Be careful, however, to not let others' points of view unduly influence your own. As well, ensure that you acknowledge all outside sources that form your support material.

The following literary essays offer interpretations of two poems and a chapter from a novel. Consider your own interpretations of these works. How would your interpretations be similar to or different from these? Why?

Dylan Thomas' "Do Not Go Gentle into That Good Night"

Elements of the Essay

The following explication has been excerpted from Richard Abcarian and Marvin Klotz's *Literature: The Human Experience* (Fifth Edition, 1990). This literary explication provides a detailed analysis of Dylan Thomas' famous poem "Do Not Go Gentle into That Good Night," moving from each line, stanza, and scene of the poem.

About the Writers

Dylan Marlais Thomas was born in Wales on October 27, 1914. At the age of 20, he had his first collection of poems, *Eighteen Poems* (1934), published. Besides writing poetry, he wrote scripts and worked as a journalist for the BBC. He often gave readings of his poetry and frequently travelled to the United States to do so. Other published works include *Twenty-Five Poems* (1936), *Portrait of the Artist as a Young Dog* (1940), and *In Country Sleep* (1952). Thomas died at the age of 39 in New York City on November 9, 1953.

Richard Abcarian and Marvin Klotz are both retired English professors from California State University, Northridge. They are co-editors of *Literature: Reading and Writing the Human Experience* (now in its seventh edition; the title has changed since its fifth edition).

Do Not Go Gentle into That Good Night

Dylan Thomas

Do not go gentle into that good night,   1
Old age should burn and rave at close of day;
Rage, rage against the dying of the light.

Though wise men at their end know dark is right,
Because their words had forked no lightning they   5
Do not go gentle into that good night.

Good men, the last wave by, crying how bright
Their frail deeds might have danced in a green bay,
Rage, rage against the dying of the light.

Wild men who caught and sang the sun in flight,   10
And learn, too late, they grieved it on its way,
Do not go gentle into that good night.

Grave men, near death, who see with blinding sight
Blind eyes could blaze like meteors and be gay,
Rage, rage against the dying of the light.   15

And you, my father, there on the sad height,
Curse, bless, me now with your fierce tears, I pray.
Do not go gentle into that good night.
Rage, rage against the dying of the light.

An Explication of Dylan Thomas' "Do Not Go Gentle into That Good Night"

Richard Abcarian and Marvin Klotz

1   DYLAN THOMAS'S VILLANELLE "Do Not Go Gentle into That Good Night" is addressed to his aged father. The poem is remarkable in a number of ways, most notably in that contrary to the most common poetic treatments of the inevitability of death, which argue for serenity or celebrate the peace that death provides, this poem urges resistance and rage in the face of death. It justifies that unusual attitude by describing the rage and resistance to death of four kinds of men, all of whom can summon up the image of a complete and satisfying life that is denied to them by death.

2   The first tercet of the intricately rhymed villanelle opens with an arresting line. The adjective "gentle" appears where we would expect the adverb "gently." The strange diction suggests that "gentle" may describe both the going (i.e., gently dying) and the person (i.e., gentleman) who confronts death. Further, the speaker characterizes "night," here clearly a figure for death, as "good." Yet in the next line, the speaker urges that the aged should violently resist death, characterized as the "close of day" and "the dying of the light." In effect, the first three lines argue that however good death may be, the aged should refuse to die gently, should passionately rave and rage against death.

3   In the second tercet, the speaker turns to a description of the way the first of four types of men confronts death (which is figuratively defined throughout the poem as "that good night" and "the dying of the light"). These are the "wise men," the scholars, the philosophers, those who understand the inevitability of death, men who "know dark is right." But they do not acquiesce in death "because their words had forked no lightning," because their published wisdom failed to bring them to that

sense of completeness and fulfillment that can accept death. Therefore, wise as they are, they reject the theoretical "rightness" of death and refuse to "go gentle."

The second sort of men—"good men," the moralists, the social reformers, those who attempt to better the world through action as the wise men attempt to better it through "words"—also rage against death. Their deeds are, after all, "frail." With sea imagery, the speaker suggests that these men might have accomplished fine and fertile things—their deeds "might have danced in a green bay." But, with the "last wave" gone, they see only the frailty, the impermanence of their acts, and so they, too, rage against the death that deprives them of the opportunity to leave a meaningful legacy.

So, too, the "wild men," the poets who "sang" the loveliness and vitality of nature, learn, as they approach death, that the sensuous joys of human existence wane. As the life-giving sun moves toward dusk, as death approaches, their singing turns to grieving, and they refuse to surrender gently, to leave willingly the warmth and pleasure and beauty that life can give.

And finally, with a pun suggestive of death, the "grave men," those who go through life with such high seriousness as never to experience gaiety and pleasure, see, as death approaches, all the joyous possibilities that they were blind to in life. And they, too, rage against the dying of a light that they had never properly seen before.

The speaker then calls upon his aged father to join these men raging against death. Only in this final stanza do we discover that the entire poem is addressed to the speaker's father and that, despite the generalized statements about old age and the focus upon types of men, the poem is a personal lyric. The edge of death becomes a "sad height," the summit of wisdom and experience old age attains includes the sad knowledge of life's failure to satisfy the vision we all pursue. The depth and complexity of the speaker's sadness is startlingly given in the second line when he calls upon his father to both curse and bless him. These opposites richly suggest several related possibilities. Curse me for not living up to your expectations. Curse me for remaining alive as you die. Bless me with forgiveness for my failings. Bless me for teaching you to rage against death. And the curses and blessings are contained in the "fierce tears"— fierce because you will burn and rave and rage against death. As the poem closes by bringing together the two powerful refrains, we may reasonably feel that the speaker himself, while not facing imminent death, rages because his father's death will cut off a relationship that is incomplete.

After-Reading Activities

Analyzing the Content

1. a) Discuss the meaning of "Do Not Go Gentle into That Good Night" with a partner.

   b) Assess this essay as a useful secondary source for a student researching the poetry of Dylan Thomas.

2. Is there any part of the writers' analysis or interpretation of the poem with which you disagree? Explain the basis for any disagreement you have.

3. Research the characteristics of a villanelle. Do the writers of this essay use the term correctly? Do the references to the characteristics of a villanelle in this essay help the reader understand and appreciate the poem being analyzed?

Structure and Style

4. How well have the writers of this essay integrated the analysis of the structure and style of the poem with the analysis of the meaning or content of the poem?

5. Assess the introductory paragraph of this literary essay. How well does it engage the interest of the reader, present a clear statement of the topic or thesis, and provide an overview of the main points to be covered?

6. How have the writers used the six tercets of the poem to create the paragraph structure of this essay?

7. Assess the final paragraph as a conclusion to the ideas presented in this essay.

8. Explain how the writers of this essay have incorporated quotations from the poem into the essay. How do these quotations provide proof for the writers' interpretation of the poem?

Student Essays on Rob Filgate's "Barn Door Detail"

Elements of the Essays

Matt Johnson and Abhijat Kitchlu each provides an interpretation and analysis of the poem "Barn Door Detail" by Rob Filgate. Whose interpretation do you most agree with? Why?

About the Writers

Rob Filgate teaches English on Vancouver Island, British Columbia. He is also poetry editor for *The Claremont Review*, a magazine that publishes the works of young writers, aged 13 to 19.

At the time of publication of this book, Matt Johnson and Abhijat Kitchlu were students at John Fraser Secondary School in Mississauga, Ontario.

Barn Door Detail

Rob Filgate

It has been years since my grandfather stood   1
before this barn door, since his calloused hands

worked free the chain latched on a bent nail.
I wonder what he thought, early on a winter

morning while he forked hay to the animals   5
and drew milk from the eight cows. Or during

the day when he cut down frozen trees by hand,
removed the limbs with an axe, and hooked

the logs to a team of Clydesdales to skid them out
10   on the snow, back to the farm where drifts

hid them until spring. And each night, returning
to the barn by lantern, alone among the animals,

where he talked in a foreign tongue, words
frozen in moonlight, stories of how his sons

15   had drifted away to Edmonton one by one
how the farm had taken the third finger

on his right hand, the cold ache in the hollow
of his bones, his words slipping from stall

to stall, his life hanging in the frigid air
20   like the breath of horses.

Green Milk

Matt Johnson

1   THE TIDES OF LIFE WASH against the shores,
rubbing the rocks of old, and with every new
generation there comes a change. The ambitions
of the Canadian pioneers created business, the baby
boomers perfected that business, and their children
perfected the business of consumption. These
generational ambitions shape and personify the
members of their era, but also serve as the force
disconnecting those children from their fathers and
mothers, forcing their parents into isolation in the wake
of their children's priorities. <u>Poet Rob Filgate exposes
the pain of this loss through the character, setting the
symbolism of his poem "Barn Door Detail."</u>

Introductory
statements to
engage the
reader's interest

Thesis statement;
indication of order
of statement:
"character," "setting
the symbolism"

Main idea of
this paragraph

The <u>central character</u> of Filgate's work is an old   2
father who runs a farm alone, after his young and
ambitious sons "… drifted away to Edmonton one by
one" (stanza 8). He is now doomed to solitude after his
city-seeking children abandoned their father's old way of
life. Alone on his land, the father is unable to
understand the choices his sons have made, and his loss
of them brings him pain, described in the line "… the
farm had taken the third finger on his right hand, the
cold ache in the hollow of his bones" (stanzas 8 and 9).
Living in constant sorrow, his body begins to feel the
cold of his pained heart after his children's
abandonment. But the father is not disconnected from

Proof in the form
of a quotation and
indication of its
source in the poem
integrated into
essay

his sons as a result of their ambition alone. <u>The father
speaks in "… a foreign tongue" (stanza 7), indicating
his migrant status within Canada and further
disconnection from his English-speaking Canadian-born
boys (indicated by their venture into English-speaking
Edmonton).</u> With this disparity in language, Filgate is
able to establish a cultural difference within the
father/son relationship, increasing their emotional
distance from one another while perpetuating the
father's frustration and suffering as he sees his heritage
lost along with the departure of his sons.

Main idea of
this paragraph

Filgate's <u>structural organization</u> in the poem is also   3
effective in mirroring the human disconnection in his
themes. His stanza splices in the following passage
reveal that intention.

> … alone among the animals,

> where he talked in a foreign tongue, …
> (stanzas 6 and 7)

Here the use of a line break in the centre of an
otherwise straightforward sentence mixes the pace of the
poem. By having his theme interact directly with the
form of his work, Filgate provides a physical parallel to
the separation between father and sons.

Main idea of
this paragraph

The <u>symbols</u> throughout Filgate's poem further the   4 clarity of his theme. With reference to the barren objects within the frozen wasteland, the poet is able to clearly expose the complex emotions of the aging father. The words "… he cut down frozen trees …" (stanza 4) explain precisely what the old man feels after his sons' desertion of both their father and his traditions. His hopes and dreams, once bright and blossoming, now stand iced and rigid as they are slowly dismembered through the steady swing of a hacksaw. The father's time in frozen isolation drags on as he tries to remove the memory of his pain. The landscape of the farm provides another symbolic link to the father's pain. Frost rips against the flat farmland and represents the emotional cold snap the father has endured after the loss of his sons. He has become hardened, just as the ice that surrounds him, and as he nears death he seems as disconnected from humanity as the animals he tends to in his last moments, as Filgate shows here: "… his life hanging in the frigid air like the breath of horses" (stanza 10).

5   The <u>unity of character development, form, and metaphor</u> within Rob Filgate's poem perfectly translates the *pain* left after experiencing the generational gap as a father. The poet demonstrates how a father's grip on tradition and misunderstanding of the changing ambitions of his sons has left him with nothing, doomed to freeze in the bleak tundra of his desolation, forever.

Sums up points discussed in the essay "circle-back effect" (returns to a key idea in the introduction)

Analysis of Rob Filgate's "Barn Door Detail"

Abhijat Kitchlu

MODERN MAN DOES NOT often look past the comforts and cushioning of contemporary life to reflect upon the hardships of a bygone era. However, the sacrifice of previous generations cannot be looked on with apathy, as Rob Filgate seeks to reveal in his poem "Barn Door Detail." Through the use of eloquent imagery and the poignant characterization of the narrator's grandfather, Filgate draws attention to the suffering of previous generations and thus forces the reader to re-evaluate his perspective on his progenitors and further appreciate his lifestyle.

The solitary figure of the grandfather is Filgate's primary tool in his portrayal of rural life. The grandfather is depicted as toiling "alone among the animals" (line 12), "by lantern" light. This isolated description creates a sense of empathy and respect in the reader. A character performing strenuous physical labour in lantern-light is a sharp contrast to the modern man's occupation, which is instead often illuminated by the cathode ray tube of a computer monitor. This disparity between past and present forces the reader to find new value in his modern appliances and amenities—a far cry from oil lanterns.

The grandfather is made an even more tragic figure through the description of "his sons [who] had drifted away to Edmonton, one by one" (lines 14 to 15). Filgate uses these sons to point out the disrespect of the new generation that has given up the traditions of agrarian life in favour of the urban lifestyle and work ethic. This tragedy is compounded by the fact that the grandfather is likely an immigrant, as indicated by the fact that he spoke to the horses "in a foreign tongue"; and though he undoubtedly came to this country to create a better life for his sons, they clearly have left him behind in its pursuit. Thus, the grandfather's character is shown to be a relic of a forgotten time, appreciated by neither his progeny nor modern society as a whole.

The poet Filgate seeks to further remedy this lack of appreciation by pointing out the relationship of the grandfather and the narrator. The narrator claims it "has been years since [his] grandfather stood before this barn door" (lines 1 to 2). Moreover, the narrator is forced to "wonder what" (line 4) his grandfather thought, suggesting that the narrator can no longer speak with his grandfather, who has now truly become a ghost of a previous time. This point causes the reader to realize that such a pastoral aspect of society has almost been wiped out by modern ways and that there is very little by which to remember and thus appreciate it.

5   Rob Filgate also uses imagery to generate regard for the past in the reader. The image of "calloused hands" working "early on a winter morning" (lines 2 to 5) lends emphasis to the arduous labour previous farm generations had to perform. The modern reader must then realize his own lifestyle would certainly not demand such diligence and, so, more greatly appreciate his predecessors. The physical image of the grandfather also creates tremendous feelings of empathy in the reader. The grandfather had lost "the third finger on his right hand" (lines 16 to 17) and gained a "cold ache in the hollow of his bones." This agonizing imagery creates anguish in the reader, in turn evoking appreciation for the tribulations of the past, which had no modern medicines to help remedy.

6   Lastly, the transient image of the grandfather's "life hanging in the frigid air like the breath of horses" (lines 19 to 20) adds a sense of fragility to the ways of the past. The image of breath frosting in the air is shown to be parallel to the passing traditions of rural life, which forces the reader to realize how modern progress has endangered the values and work ethic of agrarian life. Such eloquent images emphasize the quiet dignity of the past and how it is inexorably slipping away.

7   Rob Filgate's mastery of beautiful imagery and tragic characterization create a poem that demands that its reader re-examine the trials of rural life and thus learn the value of modern amenities, which are oft taken for granted.

After-Reading Activities

Analyzing the Content

1. Using a chart like the one below, compare the two essays.

	Green Milk	Analysis of Rob Filgate's "Barn Door Detail"
Introduction		
Engagement of the reader		
Thesis statement		
Body		
Conclusion		
Insight into the poem		
Completeness of analysis of the poem		
Use of proof for points made		
Integration of quotations into the writer's text		
Use of "circle-back effect"		

Structure and Style

2. Which of the two essays on "Barn Door Detail" is the most unified? Be prepared to defend your choice.

3. Using the annotations for Matt Johnson's essay as a guide, prepare annotations for Abhijat Kitchlu's essay to illustrate important aspects of the essay.

4. "The grandfather is made an even more tragic figure through the description of 'his sons [who] had drifted away to Edmonton, one by one' (lines 14 to 15)." A change has been made to this line from Abhijat Kitchlu's essay. Explain why a writer would insert "[who]." Explain why the brackets need to be added. What do they tell the reader?

Margaret Atwood's *The Handmaid's Tale*: An Analysis of Chapter 17

Elements of the Essay

"By the Light of the Moon ..." presents a close analysis of Chapter 17 of Margaret Atwood's novel *The Handmaid's Tale* (1986). It focuses on the rhetorical structures, in particular sentence structure and order, and on figurative tools (metaphors, similes, and symbols) that Atwood uses to create the metamorphosis of Offred, the handmaid.

Note: "By the Light of the Moon ..." was originally written by Bonnie Sheppard for her students to follow as a model. To ensure that her students, in their essays, continue to refer back to the craft and style of the writer whose work is under analysis, she instructs them to underline keywords (the "tools") that the writer uses. The notation (S.F.) refers to sentence fragments, which Sheppard allows her students to use, but only if they acknowledge them as intentional. Both underlining and (S.F.) notations appear in this essay to reflect the spirit of her teaching.

About the Writer

Still incurably curious in the twilight of her teaching career, Bonnie Sheppard lives for those teaching moments when she sees "the light go on" as another student grasps a key concept after struggling with how to put those elusive ideas on paper. She teaches both English and art at Clarkson Secondary School in Ontario, and skis as frequently and as fast as she can.

For a biography of Margaret Atwood, see page 9.

Chapter 17 from
The Handmaid's Tale

Margaret Atwood

THIS IS WHAT I DO when I'm back in my room: 1

I take off my clothes and put on my nightgown. 2

I look for the pat of butter, in the toe of my right shoe, where I hid it 3
after dinner. The cupboard was too warm, the butter is semiliquid.
Much of it has sunk into the paper napkin I wrapped it in. Now I'll
have butter in my shoe. Not the first time, because whenever there is
butter or even margarine, I save some in this way. I can get most of the
butter off the shoe lining, with a washcloth or some toilet paper from
the bathroom, tomorrow.

I rub the butter over my face, work it into the skin of my hands. 4
There's no longer any hand lotion or face cream, not for us. Such things
are considered vanities. We are containers, it's only the insides of our
bodies that are important. The outside can become hard and wrinkled,
for all they care, like the shell of a nut. This was a decree of the Wives,
this absence of hand lotion. They don't want us to look attractive. For
them, things are bad enough as it is.

The butter is a trick I learned at the Rachel and Leah Center. The 5
Red Center, we called it, because there was so much red. My predecessor
in this room, my friend with the freckles and the good laugh, must have
done this too, this buttering. We all do it.

As long as we do this, butter our skin to keep it soft, we can believe 6
that we will some day get out, that we will be touched again, in love or
desire. We have ceremonies of our own, private ones.

The butter is greasy and it will go rancid and I will smell like an old 7
cheese; but at least it's organic, as they used to say.

To such devices have we descended. 8

9   Buttered, I lie on my single bed, flat, like a piece of toast. I can't sleep.
In the semidark I stare up at the blind plaster eye in the middle of the
ceiling, which stares back down at me, even though it can't see. There's
no breeze, my white curtains are like gauze bandages, hanging limp,
glimmering in the aura cast by the searchlight that illuminates this house
at night, or is there a moon?

10   I fold back the sheet, get carefully up, on silent bare feet, in my
nightgown, go to the window, like a child, I want to see. The moon on
the breast of the new-fallen snow. The sky is clear but hard to make out,
because of the searchlight; but yes, in the obscured sky a moon does
float, newly, a wishing moon, a sliver of ancient rock, a goddess, a wink.
The moon is a stone and the sky is full of deadly hardware, but oh God,
how beautiful anyway.

11   I want Luke here so badly. I want to be held and told my name. I
want to be valued, in ways that I am not; I want to be more than
valuable. I repeat my former name, remind myself of what I once could
do, how others saw me.

12   I want to steal something.

13   In the hall the night-light's on, the long space glows gently pink; I walk,
one foot set carefully down, then the other, without creaking, along the
runner, as if on a forest floor, sneaking, my heart quick, through the
night house. I am out of place. This is entirely illegal.

14   Down past the fisheye on the hall wall, I can see my white shape, of
tented body, hair down my back like a mane, my eyes gleaming. I like
this. I am doing something, on my own. The active, is it a tense?
Tensed. What I would like to steal is a knife, from the kitchen, but I'm
not ready for that.

15   I reach the sitting room, door's ajar, slip in, leave the door a little
open. A squeak of wood, but who's near enough to hear? I stand in the
room, letting the pupils of my eyes dilate, like a cat's or owl's. Old
perfume, cloth dust fill my nostrils. There's a slight mist of light, coming
through the cracks around the closed drapes, from the searchlight
outside, where two men doubtless patrol, I've seen them, from above,
from behind my curtains, dark shapes, cutouts. Now I can see outlines,
gleams: from the mirror, the bases of the lamps, the vases, the sofa
looming like a cloud at dusk.

16   What should I take? Something that will not be missed. In the wood

at midnight, a magic flower. A withered daffodil, not one from the dried arrangement. The daffodils will soon be thrown out, they're beginning to smell. Along with Serena's stale fumes, the stench of her knitting.

I grope, find an end table, feel. There's a clink, I must have knocked   17
something. I find the daffodils, crisp at the edges where they've dried, limp towards the stems, use my fingers to pinch. I will press this, somewhere. Under the mattress. Leave it there, for the next woman, the one who comes after me, to find.

But there's someone in the room, behind me.   18

I hear the step, quiet as mine, the creaking of the same floorboard.   19
The door closes behind me, with a little click, cutting the light. I freeze: white was a mistake. I'm snow in moonlight, even in the dark.

Then a whisper: "Don't scream. It's all right."   20

As if I'd scream, as if it's all right. I turn: a shape, that's all, dull glint   21
of cheekbone, devoid of color.

He steps towards me. Nick.   22

"What are you doing in here?"   23

I don't answer. He too is illegal, here, with me, he can't give me away.   24
Nor I him; for the moment we're mirrors. He puts his hand on my arm, pulls me against him, his mouth on mine, what else comes from such denial? Without a word. Both of us shaking, how I'd like to. In Serena's parlor, with the dried flowers, on the Chinese carpet, his thin body. A man entirely unknown. It would be like shouting, it would be like shooting someone. My hand goes down, how about that, I could unbutton, and then. But it's too dangerous, he knows it, we push each other away, not far. Too much trust, too much risk, too much already.

"I was coming to find you," he says, breathes, almost into my ear.   25
I want to reach up, taste his skin, he makes me hungry. His fingers move, feeling my arm under the nightgown sleeve, as if his hand won't listen to reason. It's so good, to be touched by someone, to be felt so greedily, to feel so greedy. Luke, you'd know, you'd understand. It's you here, in another body.

Bullshit.   26

"Why?" I say. Is it so bad, for him, that he'd take the risk of coming   27
to my room at night? I think of the hanged men, hooked on the Wall. I can hardly stand up. I have to get away, back to the stairs, before I dissolve entirely. His hand's on my shoulder now, held still, heavy, pressing down on me like warm lead. Is this what I would die for? I'm a coward, I hate the thought of pain.

28   "He told me to," Nick says. "He wants to see you. In his office."

29   "What do you mean?" I say. The Commander, it must be. See me? What does he mean by *see*? Hasn't he had enough of me?

30   "Tomorrow," he says, just audible. In the dark parlor we move away from each other, slowly, as if pulled towards each other by a force, current, pulled apart also by hands equally strong.

31   I find the door, turn the knob, fingers on cool porcelain, open. It's all I can do.

By the Light of the Moon...

Bonnie Sheppard

1   AT THE OUTSET OF *The Handmaid's Tale*, Margaret Atwood's dystopic novel, that nightmarish vision of a totalitarian future, Atwood alerts readers to be aware of "palimpsests" of images, sounds, and meanings (3). In Chapter 17 of the novel, she creates these images, sounds, and meanings using figurative/structural devices to mark a shift in the psychological outlook of Offred, the handmaid. At the literal level, Offred arises from a sleepless bed, crosses to her window, then begins to descend the stairs. At the symbolic level, Offred is hurtled through deep psychological time and space. At last, in Chapter 17, we witness the protagonist's first expression of delight "I like this" (120), marking the handmaid's first tentative steps toward creating her own destiny. Emily Dickinson once wrote, "The Possible's slow fuse is lit/By the imagination," and Atwood illustrates just how true this statement is as she uses simile, metaphor, symbol, and allusion to fire up her protagonist's will to act. Her continued use of these tools reinforces the notion that this power is natural, outside the artificial constructs of politics or religion. Just as music rhythms add a pulse of life to a song's message, so, too, is the evolution of Offred's activism underscored by the rhythms of Atwood's sentence structures: exploratory, decisive, active, or hesitant. The structures mirror the meanings.

I want Luke here so badly. I want to be held and told my name. I want to be valued in ways that I am not; I want to be more than valuable. I repeat my former name, remind myself of what I could once do, how others saw me.

I want to steal something. (120)

Perhaps readers notice the obvious plaintive repetition of the "I want …" structure first as they read this passage, or perhaps they notice the parallel structure of the natural order sentences first. But there can be no question that Atwood has deliberately structured this repetitive, rhythmic passage to alert the reader to its poignant significance. Its rhythm seems to function like a religious chant, a rocking motion. However, perceptive readers notice a movement forward within the structure. The "I" in the first three and one half sentences is merely the passive actor. In the first sentence, "I want Luke here so badly" (120), Luke must come to her; in the second, "I want to be held and told my name" (120), she is again the recipient of actions—"held … told"—not the active agent. In the third, she is inactive once again, desiring to be "valued" by someone else. Yet in the second part of this statement, she begins to reach forward, wanting to be "more than valued" (120). Without putting too fine a point upon it, the change of sensibility from passive to active seems to build in a climactic curve toward the breakthrough "single sentence paragraph" line, "I want to steal something" (120). This climax of her thought suddenly bursts through the passive barrier to an active voice. Offred, the acted upon, becomes Offred, the actor. The sequence almost functions like the child's refrain, "One for the money, two for the show, three to get ready, and four to go!" This bold proclamation "I want to steal something[!]" marks a significant change from the description of self as "buttered … flat … toast" (120), which is the first line of this segment. The movement from the impression of an inanimate object, which has been acted upon and is ready for consumption, to the impression of a motivated, rebellious, actor has been swift, and reinforced both through sentence structure and repetition. But before advancing the reasons for this rapid metamorphosis, let us continue to note the significance of the rhythmic "I want …" passage.

Aside from this repetitive, climactic parallelism and rhythm, the passage also contains one major change in the obvious pattern. The "I want(s) …" are interrupted by the line, "I repeat my former name, remind myself of what I could once do, how others saw me" (120). When Christians end a prayer, a list of requests to God, they generally "sign off" or mark the end of their list by citing His "three part" characteristics. The most frequently used one is, "In the name of the Father, the Son and the Holy Ghost ...." This "sign off" string never calls the God by name, as Christians do not know the name of God. And this closing reminds us of two things: (a) that He once walked freely among us as the Son and (b) of the effect of the inspiring spirit, the Holy Ghost, to work wonders. But in this society of inverted and twisted "religious" values, that has co-opted Biblical passages and stripped Offred of her loved ones, her possessions, and very identity, she cannot possibly turn to *that* god (intentional lowercase) of Gilead. Subsequent paragraphs in this essay will expand on this point. To whom does she turn for strength? Herself (intentional S.F.). Indeed, she *names* herself, but, as God did with Moses at the burning bush when He said, "I am who I am," she keeps her name a secret from us: "I repeat my former name" (120). Moreover, we never learn her "secret" identity at all. In the "reminder" segment of the incantation, she recalls both her power to act freely in the world—"remind myself of what I could once do" (120)—and her reputation as she recites the value others placed upon her—"how others saw me" (91)—to seal the list that recounts the starvation of her heart and spirit. She is now the active agent; the spark of her own divinity lives. Alas, her "inspiration" to steal echoes the only avenue of action granted to the desperate children of Swift's "A Modest Proposal,"* epigraphed at the beginning of *A Handmaid's Tale*. Though stealing might provide a temporary respite, it will not, just as it does not in Swift's satire, eliminate the terrible situation in which the sufferer exists.

6   This brings us to the remarkable metamorphosis. How does Atwood "stage manage" Offred's rapid transformation? In order to intensify the effect of light, it must be placed next to darkness to maximize contrast. And so Atwood creates maximum psychological contrast in three ways. To begin: the end of the first movement of the chapter is marked by the inverted order, periodic sentence, "To such devices we have descended" (120). In other words, in this society we have sunk this low. By reserving the complete meaning to the end of the sentence—descended—the final word acts like a figurative "thunk" at the bottom of the barrel. We can go no lower.

---

*This satirical essay by Jonathan Swift appears on pages 211 to 222 in this textbook.

Atwood reinforces this impression of immobility with the <u>simile</u>   7
"Buttered, I lie on my single bed, flat, like a piece of toast" (120). While
understanding that Offred has been characterized as the inanimate
passive object here, we must also explore the vernacular "I'm toast!" level
of meaning. This effect of helplessness is advanced even more as a detail
in her room is <u>anthropomorphized</u> into a blind companion on high:
"... the blind plaster eye in the middle of the ceiling, which stares down
at me, even though it can't see" (120). To whom do we turn in our
darkest hour? Usually to that all seeing eye-in-the-sky: God (intentional
S.F.). As mentioned previously, in Gilead, God has been usurped and
perverted to suit the needs of the Sons of Jacob, created blind to the
needs of females in this society. The notation "There's no breeze ..."
(120) symbolically hammers this notion home. The wind, <u>figuratively</u>
the breath of God (Cooper 192), is absent. The final image in this
sequence of defeat is the simile "my white curtains are like gauze
bandages, hanging limp, glimmering in the aura cast by the searchlight
..." (120). This image sets an atmosphere of defeat by suggesting that
the curtains are ineffective protection from the wounds inflicted by the
penetration of the searchlight, like the penetration of the commander
she has endured only moments ago. He is the very agent of the men
who have removed family, self, and sympathetic God from her. She is
wounded, heart, and soul. "Thunk!" Just as small change adds up to
respectable sums, these individual similes, <u>metaphors</u>, and <u>symbols</u> add
up to a significant portrait of abandonment, helplessness, and despair.
Can suicide be far behind?

But it is at precisely this point that Atwood begins the transformation   8
of Offred. And she does it with the same figurative and structural tools
that she used to illustrate how far down "down" really is. She literally
flips the "light switch" from artificial—the searchlight—to natural—the
moon, "... or is there a moon?" (120). Not bold enough to echo God's
first words "Let there be light" (Genesis, 1:2), these words are asked
tentatively. Yet, it is enough to stimulate movement, to make Offred rise
from her bed like Lazarus, to seek the truth. Often in life when things
turn bad, people yearn to return to their childhood, to a time when
responsibility did not weigh them down, when anything was possible,
when magic was real. In Christian terms, such a sentiment is expressed
as a desire to wipe the slate clean by being "reborn." In literature,
Shakespeare's Hamlet exemplifies a character who is figuratively reborn
when he returns "naked" and "alone" (4.7.51–52) from the sea to begin

his new journey toward a new manhood. Atwood follows this pattern of figurative rebirth or resurrection as Offred rises from the bed, "… like a child" (120), and moves toward the light. Atwood pegs the image of the child at the window expecting magic by quoting the line from Clement Moore's classic tale of innocent childhood "T'was the night before Christmas": "The moon on the breast of the new-fallen snow" (120). On this undefiled, pure, snow Santa can come, magic *can* happen. In this state of expectation, Offred transcends her surroundings by taking imaginative flight. It is important to note that in the past, Offred has played with words as toys "hold– household … the house is what he holds … the hold of a ship" (99), but then, the ship of imagination did not inspire her to begin her journey to action. This time it does.

9   This time Atwood manipulates another palimpsest of memory to energize the handmaid toward that moment of epiphany that moves her from passivity to action. The whole sequence runs: "… but yes, in the obscured sky a moon does float, newly, a wishing moon, a sliver of ancient rock, a goddess, a wink. The moon is a stone and the sky full of deadly hardware, but oh God, how beautiful anyway" (120). The metaphor of the moon as a floating vessel might very well carry on the childlike state as an oblique reference to the nursery rhyme "Wynkyn and Blynkyn and Nod," but it almost certainly suggests the idea of a journey across the heavens, and it echoes the idea of Offred as the "hold of a ship" (99). Offred may be stationary, but in the unusual word order chosen by Atwood, we are told that Offred recognizes that "the moon does float" (keyword "does"). And she looks to it for inspiration.

10   This brings us to the unusual sentence structure that organizes this progression of images. It is a loose order sentence, main idea up front— "yes, there is a moon" (120)—but the subsequent additions add layers of meaning the way an artist's glazes add a richness of dimension to a flat painting. First, "… a moon does float, newly …" lets us know on a literal level that it is a new moon. Indeed Atwood insists we notice it by placing the unusual adverb "newly" at the end of the main idea. This draws our attention to the observation that it is the beginning of a new cycle. "It also provides analogy for the stages of human development: the new moon is infancy, the crescent is youth and adolescence …" ("Online Dictionary of Symbolism"). On the symbolic level, in terms of Offred's journey, it suggests that the new cycle is about to begin as she is newly born to action and seeks out the moon, imagining its possibilities. And we see that, at the very least, she is up from the bed and dreaming

outside her predicament.

Important to note also is the general <u>symbolism</u> of the moon: "The   11
moon is a feminine symbol, universally representing the rhythm of time
as it embodies the cycle .... In astrology, the moon is a symbol of the
soul, and in the horoscope it determines the subject's capacity for
reflection and adaptation" ("Forum on Symbolism"). In this scene,
Atwood creates Offred's full range of reflection and extrapolation about
this vision of the moon, "a wishing moon, a sliver of ancient rock, a
goddess, a wink" (120). Ending with the "wink" is a nice "conspirators"
touch after the crescendo from wish to goddess.

In the past when Offred wanted to embark on a mental journey,   12
wished to escape her torment at night, she called on Moira: "But the
night is my time out. Where should I go? Somewhere good. Moira ..."
(47). As a sidebar, it is no accident that Atwood named Offred's
inspirational companion Moira, the name given to the oldest Greek
Goddess, who predates even the Olympic gods. It is a name of great
power. "Homer speaks of Fate (Moira)—the goddess of destiny—in the
singular as an impersonal power and sometimes makes its functions
interchangeable with those of the Olympian gods" ("Forum on
Symbolism"). "It makes me feel safer that Moira is here," says Offred to
herself at the Red Center (88). Later, on the way to Angela's birth,
Offred notes "Moira was our fantasy ... she was with us in secret ... in
the light of Moira, the Aunts were less fearsome ..." (167)

But at Offred's point of transformation, Moira is *not* here; the "light   13
of Moira" (167) is *not* here. Offred stands alone at the window in the
light of the new moon, sliver shaped, ancient rock, the controller of time,
tides and all female creatures since time began, before the Moirae, before
the Olympian gods, and before the god of this terrifying theocracy. It is
indeed ancient rock, dependable, unlike the "rock" ("Online Dictionary
of Symbolism") of the church that has failed her and all women in
Gileadean society. Offred thinks of the moon as a "goddess." The
goddess of the moon is Artemis/Diana, ancient Greek/Roman goddess of
the hunt and protector of women, children, and animals ("Analysis of
Mythic and Artistic Symbolism"), who wears the new moon as her
headdress. This is the absolutely most appropriate goddess for Offred,
who is about to go on a "*hunt*," who is indeed a *woman*, and who stands
at the window "like a *child*" (120). This goddess fits her three ways:
hunter, woman, and child. What is the plaintive prayer she offers up in
her own name? The four "I wants ..." mentioned earlier (intentional

S.F.). What is the inspiration that follows? It is the childlike course of action, "I want to steal something" (120). And so we see how Atwood in one sentence has metaphorically, symbolically energized her anguished character toward becoming her own Moira, the master of her own fate—seizing her own destiny under the light of the new moon.

14   At this point, empowered by "the Possible's slow fuse … the imagination," Offred begins her illegal adventure. Atwood underscores the basic animal instincts we all share as she describes Offred sneaking "as if on a forest floor … hair down my back like a mane, my eyes gleaming … letting the pupils of my eyes dilate, like a cat's or an owl's" (120–121). All the <u>similes</u> are comparisons to wildlife, the domain of Artemis/Diana. Aside from the obvious night vision attributes that the owl and the cat share, they are the traditional familiars of female figures of power—witches and goddesses (Walker 148, 754). The gleaming eyes of the questing handmaid contrast brilliantly to the "blind plaster eye" observed so acutely in her room—inactive vs. active. The "fisheye" mirror recalls the phrase "… the round, convex … pier glass, like the eye of the fish" (9) where her reflection was decidedly less powerful than the gleaming-eyed "wild thing" she is now: "and myself in it like a distorted shadow, a parody of something, some fairy tale figure in a red cloak … a sister dipped in blood" (9).

15   We have waited 16 chapters for Offred to take some initiative in this tale of passivity. In one short passage, our protagonist seems to have awakened at last. No prince has kissed her to life; rather she has empowered herself by the light of the moon, that most ancient of female goddesses. She has shown us a flash of wild spirit. In the twist of a few short paragraphs, she is caged once more as Nick informs her of her appointment with the Commander, but for one brief moment she, and her readers, were energized. It is a shock to realize how little has taken place on the surface of things—Offred arose from her sleepless bed, crossed to the window, and began to descend the stairs. Atwood has created the whole symbolic journey, the widened mindscape of the protagonist against these few simple actions. As a student of literature, I slip into the active role now and echo Offred's sentiments, "I like this." I like Atwood's metacognitive use of metaphor, symbol, and allusion as the "fuse" that inspires action, a sense that hope is possible. I like the structural rhythmic swells of exploration, hesitancy, and action that rock the boat of acquiescence and deliver us into uncharted psychological territory with the protagonist.

Works Cited

[The following are Sheppard's notes.]

"Analysis of Mythic and Artistic Symbolism." (17 Aug. 2002)
<http://www.messagenet.com/myths/bios/artemis.html>

Atwood, Margaret. *The Handmaid's Tale.* Toronto: Random House, 1986.

Cooper, J.C. *An Illustrated Encyclopedia of Traditional Symbols.* London: Thames and Hudson, 1982.

"Forum on Symbolism." (17 Aug. 2001)
<http://www.cafearabica.com/wwwboard/social/messages/3637.html>

"Online Dictionary of Symbolism." 17 Aug. 2001.
<http://www.umich.edu/~umfandsf/symbolismproject/symbolism.html/>.

Shakespeare, William. *Hamlet.* Toronto: Harcourt Brace Jovanovich, Canada, 1987.

Walker, Barbara G. *The Woman's Encyclopedia of Myths and Secrets.* San Francisco: Harper Collins, 1983.

After-Reading Activities

Analyzing the Content

1. a) Read Chapter 17 of Margaret Atwood's novel *The Handmaid's Tale.* How does your understanding of it differ from that expressed in the essay?

    b) If you have read the novel, does this essay help you to gain greater understanding of it? If you have not read the novel, does this essay make you want to read it?

2. The analysis of this chapter of the novel emphasizes the meaningful impact of figurative devices (for example, simile, metaphor, symbol, and allusion) as well as sentence structures (for example, parallel structures, sentence order, and sentence fragments). As a class, discuss the extent to which the average reader pays attention to meaning at these levels.

3. Use an Internet search engine to check the meaning of terms such as "dystopic" and to learn more about the goddess Moira. How does the information you find help you understand this essay as well as the novel?

4. Based on the ideas presented in this essay, how would you describe Bonnie Sheppard as a reader?

Structure and Style

5. In your own words, write a thesis statement for this essay.

6. With a partner, discuss the intended reader of this essay (consider level of language, vocabulary, topic, tone). As a class, discuss whether students who have read *The Handmaid's Tale* answered this question differently from those who have not.

7. With a partner, assess the way this essay uses primary and secondary sources to support the interpretations presented. Discuss how the support/proof is presented to the reader and how it is documented so the reader can verify its use in the essay.

Extending the Purpose

1. Rewrite the introductory or concluding paragraph of the essay analyzing the poem "Do Not Go Gentle into That Good Night" to make it an even more effective introduction or conclusion to the essay.

2. Read *The Handmaid's Tale* and write a response to the writer of "By the Light of the Moon ..." agreeing or disagreeing with her interpretation of Chapter 17.

3. Find a literary criticism essay about a work of literature you are studying and finding difficult to understand fully. Explain why the essay is or is not helpful to your understanding of the work.

4. Choose one of the following:
   • Write a literary essay analyzing a poem of your choice or a poem assigned by your teacher.
   • Using "Green Milk" and "Analysis of Rob Filgate's 'Barn Door Detail'" as models, write a critique of "Barn Door Detail" or another poem of your own, or your teacher's, choosing.
   • Write an essay analyzing a key scene or chapter in a longer work of literature such as a novel, a three-act play, or an epic poem.

Elements of the Satirical Essay

A satirical essay is a humorous piece that has an underlying message. Through literary techniques such as irony, exaggeration, caricature, understatement, farce, and mock agreement or disagreement, the writer uses humour to make a critical comment about a person, belief, social issue, or practice. The essay's purpose is to point out a flaw.

Satirical essays are often written in the hope of changing the reader's perspective on the topic by showing how absurd it is. There are numerous examples throughout history where a writer has used this writing strategy to effect social and political change. Jonathan Swift's masterpiece, *A Modest Proposal*, which appears in this section, is one example.

Satire is a technique that also permeates mass media, with many examples to be found in the magazines and newspapers we read, and in the television programs we watch. Good examples of this are the animated television series *The Simpsons*, and the magazine *Mad*.

As you read the satirical essays in this section, ask what social commentary the writers are making. Are they simply poking fun? Trying to effect change? Revealing social problems? Pointing out absurdities?

A Modest Proposal

*for preventing the children of poor people in Ireland from being a
burden to their parents or country, and for making them beneficial to
the public*

Jonathan Swift

Elements of the Essay

One of the best-known satires, Jonathan Swift's *A Modest Proposal* (1729)
uses a naïve persona to propose a horrific solution to the problems in Ireland.
The irony and logic of the arguments create a matter-of-fact tone, masking the
writer's anger, yet magnifying the evil (the English) that he views as the cause
of his nation's problems.

About the Writer

Satirist Jonathan Swift was born in Dublin, Ireland, on November 30, 1667,
and educated at Trinity College. Political turmoil in Ireland led him to England
in 1689, where, for 10 years, he worked with Sir William Temple, a diplomat
who was writing his memoirs. During these years, Swift, too, began to write.
He returned to Ireland in 1699 only to go back to England in 1710. As a writer,
he wrote both poems and prose, the most notable being *Gulliver's Travels*
(1726). Swift died in 1745.

Introduction

Reason a proposal
is needed

I T IS A MELANCHOLY OBJECT to those who walk
through this great town or travel in the country,
when they see the streets, the roads, and cabin doors,
crowded with beggars of the female sex, followed by
three, four, or six children, all in rags and importuning
every passenger for an alms. These mothers, instead of
being able to work for their honest livelihood, are
forced to employ all their time in strolling to beg
sustenance for their helpless infants: who as they grow
up either turn thieves for want of work, or leave their

1

dear native country to fight for the Pretender[1] in Spain, or sell themselves to the Barbadoes.[2]

2   I think it is agreed by all parties that this prodigious number of children in the arms, or on the backs, or at the heels of their mothers, and frequently of their fathers, is, in the present deplorable state of the kingdom, a very great additional grievance; and, therefore, whoever could find out a fair, cheap, and easy method of making these children sound, useful members of the commonwealth would deserve so well of the public as to have his statue set up for a preserver of the nation.

Introduction continues: reason a proposal is needed

3   But my intention is very far from being confined to provide only for the children of professed beggars; it is of a much greater extent, and shall take in the whole number of infants at a certain age who are born of parents in effect as little able to support them as those who demand our charity in the streets.

Introduction continues: background and advantage of the proposer's scheme

4   As to my own part, having turned my thoughts for many years upon this important subject, and maturely weighed the several schemes of other projectors, I have always found them grossly mistaken in the computation. It is true, a child just dropped from its dam may be supported by her milk for a solar year, with little other nourishment; at most not above the value of two shillings, which the mother may certainly get, or the value in scraps, by her lawful occupation of begging; and it is exactly at one year old that I propose to provide for them in such a manner as instead of being a charge upon their parents or the parish, or wanting food and raiment for the rest of their lives, they shall on the contrary contribute to the feeding, and partly to the clothing, of many thousands.

5   There is likewise another great advantage in my scheme, that it will prevent those voluntary abortions, and that horrid practice of women murdering their bastard children, alas, too frequent among us, sacrificing the poor innocent babes I doubt more to avoid the expense than the shame, which would move tears and pity in the most savage and inhuman breast.

Introduction
continues: the
impossibility
of providing for
children of
poor parents

The number of souls in this kingdom being usually   6
reckoned one million and a half, of these I calculate there
may be about two hundred thousand couple whose wives
are breeders; from which number I subtract thirty
thousand couple who are able to maintain their own
children, although I apprehend there cannot be so many,
under the present distresses of the kingdom; but this
being granted, there will remain an hundred and seventy
thousand breeders. I again subtract fifty thousand for
those women who miscarry, or whose children die by
accident or disease within the year. There only remain
an hundred and twenty thousand children of poor
parents annually born. The question therefore is, how this
number shall be reared and provided for, which, as I have
already said, under the present situation of affairs, is
utterly impossible by all the methods hitherto proposed.
For we can neither employ them in handicraft or
agriculture; we neither build houses (I mean in the
country) nor cultivate land: they can very seldom pick up
a livelihood by stealing, till they arrive at six years old,
except where they are of towardly parts, although I confess
they learn the rudiments much earlier, during which
time they can, however, be properly looked upon only
as probationers, as I have been informed by a principal
gentleman in the county of Cavan, who protested to me
that he never knew above one or two instances under
the age of six, even in a part of the kingdom so
renowned for the quickest proficiency in that art.

I am assured by our merchants that a boy or a girl   7
before twelve years old is no saleable commodity; and
even when they come to this age they will not yield above
three pounds, or three pounds and half a crown at most,
on the Exchange; which cannot turn to account either
to the parents or kingdom, the charge of nutriment and
rags having been at least four times that value.

Introduction
continues:
the proposal

I shall now therefore humbly propose my own   8
thoughts, which I hope will not be liable to the least
objection.

I have been assured by a very knowing American of   9

my acquaintance in London, that a young healthy child well nursed is at a year old a most delicious, nourishing, and wholesome food, whether stewed, roasted, baked, or boiled; and I make no doubt that it will equally serve in a fricassee or a ragout.

End of Introduction

10   I do therefore humbly offer it to public consideration that of the hundred and twenty thousand children already computed, twenty thousand may be reserved for breed, whereof only one-fourth part to be males; which is more than we allow to sheep, black cattle or swine; and my reason is, that these children are seldom the fruits of marriage, a circumstance not much regarded by our savages, therefore one male will be sufficient to serve four females. That the remaining hundred thousand may, at a year old, be offered in the sale to the persons of quality and fortune through the kingdom; always advising the mother to let them suck plentifully in the last month, so as to render them plump and fat for a good table. A child will make two dishes at an entertainment for friends; and when the family dines alone, the fore or hind quarter will make a reasonable dish, and seasoned with a little pepper or salt will be very good boiled on the fourth day, especially in winter.

The proposal

11   I have reckoned upon a medium that a child just born will weigh twelve pounds, and in a solar year, if tolerably nursed, increaseth to twenty-eight pounds.

Advantage: supply

12   I grant this food will be somewhat dear, and therefore very proper for landlords, who, as they have already devoured most of the parents, seem to have the best title to the children.

13   Infants' flesh will be in season throughout the year, but more plentiful in March, and a little before and after; for we are told by a grave author, an eminent French physician,[3] that fish being a prolific diet, there are more children born in Roman Catholic countries about nine months after Lent than at any other season; therefore, reckoning a year after Lent, the markets will be more glutted than usual, because the number of popish infants is at least three to one in this kingdom:

and therefore it will have one other collateral advantage, by lessening the number of Papists among us.

Advantage: cost

I have already computed the charge of nursing a beggar's child (in which list I reckon all cottagers, labourers, and four-fifths of the farmers) to be about two shillings per annum, rags included; and I believe no gentleman would repine to give ten shillings for the carcass of a good fat child, which, as I have said, will make four dishes of excellent nutritive meat, when he hath only some particular friend or his own family to dine with him. Thus the squire will learn to be a good landlord, and grow popular among his tenants; the mother will have eight shillings net profit, and be fit for work till she produces another child.

14

Other advantages (paragraphs 15 to 16)

Those who are more thrifty (as I must confess the times require) may flay the carcass; the skin of which artificially dressed will make admirable gloves for ladies, and summer boots for fine gentlemen.

15

As to our city of Dublin, shambles[4] may be appointed for this purpose in the most convenient parts of it, and butchers we may be assured will not be wanting; although I rather recommend buying the children alive, and dressing them hot from the knife, as we do roasting pigs.

16

Distraction from the proposal (paragraphs 17 to 19)

A very worthy person, a true lover of his country, and whose virtues I highly esteem, was lately pleased in discoursing on this matter to offer a refinement upon my scheme. He said that many gentlemen of this kingdom, having of late destroyed their deer, he conceived that the want of venison might be well supplied by the bodies of young lads and maidens, not exceeding fourteen years of age nor under twelve; so great a number of both sexes in every country being now ready to starve for want of work and service; and these to be disposed of by their parents, if alive, or otherwise by their nearest relations. But with due deference to so excellent a friend and so deserving a patriot, I cannot be altogether in his sentiments; for as to the males, my American acquaintance assured me, from frequent experience, that their flesh was generally tough and lean, like that of our schoolboys by continual

17

exercise, and their taste disagreeable; and to fatten them would not answer the charge. Then as to the females, it would, I think, with humble submission, be a loss to the public, because they soon would become breeders themselves; and besides, it is not improbable that some scrupulous people might be apt to censure such a practice (although indeed very unjustly), <u>as a little bordering upon cruelty</u>; which, I confess, hath always been with me the strongest objection against any project, however so well intended.

Irony: isn't this proposal appalling?

18   But in order to justify my friend, he confessed that this expedient was put into his head by the famous Psalmanazar,[5] a native of the island Formosa, who came from thence to London above twenty years ago, and in conversation told my friend, that in his country when any young person happened to be put to death, the executioner sold the carcass to persons of quality as a prime dainty; and that in his time the body of a plump girl of fifteen, who was crucified for an attempt to poison the emperor, was sold to his Imperial Majesty's prime minister of state, and other great mandarins of the court, in joints from the gibbet, at four hundred crowns. Neither indeed can I deny, that if the same use were made of several plump young girls in this town, who, without one single groat to their fortunes, cannot stir abroad without a chair, and appear at playhouse and assemblies in foreign fineries which they never will pay for, the kingdom would not be the worse.

Negative comment on the wealthy

19   Some persons of a desponding spirit are in great concern about that vast number of poor people, who are aged, diseased, or maimed, and I have been desired to employ my thoughts what course may be taken to ease the nation of so grievous an encumbrance. But I am not in the least pain upon that matter, because it is very well known that they are every day dying and rotting by cold and famine, and filth and vermin, as fast as can be reasonably expected. And as to the young labourers, they are now in as hopeful a condition; they cannot get work, and consequently pine away for want of

Others' proposal: how to deal with the elderly

nourishment, to a degree that if at any time they are accidentally hired to common labour, they have not strength to perform it; and thus the country and themselves are happily delivered from the evils to come.

I have too long digressed, and therefore shall return to my subject. I think the advantages by the proposal which I have made are obvious and many, as well as of the highest importance.

20

Support for his proposal, organized as a list

<u>For first</u>, as I have already observed, it would greatly lessen the number of Papists, with whom we are yearly overrun, being the principal breeders of the nation as well as our most dangerous enemies; and who stay at home on purpose with a design to deliver the kingdom to the Pretender, hoping to take their advantage by the absence of so many good Protestants, who have chosen rather to leave their country than stay at home and pay tithes against their conscience to an Episcopal curate.

21

<u>Secondly</u>, the poorer tenants will have something valuable of their own, which by law may be made liable to distress, and help to pay their landlord's rent, their corn and cattle being already seized, and money a thing unknown.

22

<u>Thirdly</u>, whereas the maintenance of an hundred thousand children, from two years old and upward, cannot be computed at less than ten shillings a piece per annum, the nation's stock will be thereby increased fifty thousand pounds per annum, beside the profit of a new dish introduced to the tables of all gentlemen of fortune in the kingdom who have any refinement in taste. And the money will circulate among ourselves, the goods being entirely of our own growth and manufacture.

23

<u>Fourthly</u>, the constant breeders, beside the gain of eight shillings sterling per annum by the sale of their children, will be rid of the charge of maintaining them after the first year.

24

<u>Fifthly</u>, this food would likewise bring great custom to taverns; where the vintners will certainly be so prudent as to procure the best receipts for dressing it to perfection, and consequently have their houses

25

frequented by all the fine gentlemen, who justly value themselves upon their knowledge in good eating: and a skilful cook, who understands how to oblige his guests, will contrive to make it as expensive as they please.

26   Sixthly, this would be a great inducement to marriage, which all wise nations have either encouraged by rewards or enforced by laws and penalties. It would increase the care and tenderness of mothers toward their children, when they were sure of a settlement for life to the poor babes, provided in some sort by the public, to their annual profit instead of expense. We should see an honest emulation among the married women, which of them could bring the fattest child to the market. Men would become as fond of their wives during the time of their pregnancy as they are now of their mares in foal, their cows in calf, their sows when they are ready to farrow; nor offer to beat or kick them (as is too frequent a practice) for fear of a miscarriage.

27   Many other advantages might be enumerated. For instance, the addition of some thousand carcasses in our exportation of barrelled beef, the propagation of swine's flesh, and improvement in the art of making good bacon, so much wanted among us by the great destruction of pigs, too frequent at our tables; which are no way comparable in taste or magnificence to a well-grown, fat, yearling child, which roasted whole will make a considerable figure at a lord mayor's feast or any other public entertainment. But this and many others I omit, being studious of brevity.

28   Supposing that one thousand families in this city would be constant customers for infants' flesh, besides others who might have it at merry meetings, particularly weddings and christenings; I compute that Dublin would take off annually about twenty thousand carcasses, and the rest of the kingdom (where probably they will be sold somewhat cheaper) the remaining eighty thousand.

29   I can think of no one objection that will possibly be raised against this proposal unless it should be urged that the number of people will be thereby much

Other *real* options that should be considered haven't been

lessened in the kingdom. This I freely own, and it was indeed one principal design in offering it to the world. I desire the reader will observe that I calculate my remedy for this one individual kingdom of Ireland, and for no other that ever was, is, or, I think, ever can be upon earth. Therefore, let no man talk to me of other expedients: of taxing our absentees at five shillings a pound: of using neither clothes nor household-furniture except what is of our own growth and manufacture: of utterly rejecting the materials and instruments that promote foreign luxury: of curing the expensiveness of pride, vanity, idleness, and gaming in our women: of introducing a vein of parsimony, prudence, and temperance: of learning to love our country, wherein we differ even from Laplanders, and the inhabitants of Topinamboo:[6] of quitting our animosities and factions, nor act any longer like the Jews, who were murdering one another at the very moment their city was taken:[7] of being a little cautious not to sell our country and consciences for nothing: of teaching landlords to have at least one degree of mercy towards their tenants: lastly, of putting a spirit of honesty, industry, and skill into our shopkeepers; who, if a resolution could now be taken to buy only our native goods, would immediately unite to cheat and exact upon us in the price, the measure, and the goodness, nor could ever yet be brought to make one fair proposal of just dealing, though often and earnestly invited to it.

Therefore, I repeat, let no man talk to me of these and the like expedients, till he hath at least a glimpse of hope that there will ever be some hearty and sincere attempt to put them in practice.   30

Conclusion
(paragraphs 31 to 33)

But as to myself, having been wearied out for many years with offering vain, idle, visionary thoughts, and at length utterly despairing of success, I fortunately fell upon this proposal, which, as it is wholly new, so it hath something solid and real, of no expense and little trouble, full in our own power, and whereby we can incur no danger in disobliging England. For this kind of commodity will not bear exportation, the flesh being of   31 too tender a consistence to admit a long continuance in salt, although perhaps I could name a country which would be glad to eat up our whole nation without it.

32   After all, I am not so violently bent upon my own opinion as to reject any offer proposed by wise men, which shall be found equally innocent, cheap, easy, and effectual. But before something of that kind shall be advanced in contradiction to my scheme, and offering a better, I desire the author or authors will be pleased maturely to consider two points. First, as things now stand, how they will be able to find food and raiment for an hundred thousand useless mouths and backs. And secondly, there being a round million of creatures in human figure throughout this kingdom, whose whole subsistence put into a common stock would leave them in debt two millions of pounds sterling, adding those who are beggars by profession to the bulk of farmers, cottagers, and labourers, with their wives and children who are beggars in effect: I desire those politicians who dislike my overture, and may perhaps be so bold as to attempt an answer, that they will first ask the parents of these mortals, whether they would not at this day think it a great happiness to have been sold for food at a year old, in the manner I prescribe, and thereby have avoided such a perpetual scene of misfortunes as they have since gone through by the oppression of landlords, the impossibility of paying rent without money or trade, the want of common sustenance, with neither house nor clothes to cover them from the inclemencies of the weather, and the most inevitable prospect of entailing the like or greater miseries upon their breed for ever.

The problems in Ireland

33   I profess, in the sincerity of my heart, that I have not the least personal interest in endeavouring to promote this necessary work, having no other motive than the public good of my country, by advancing our trade, providing for infants, relieving the poor, and giving some pleasure to the rich. I have no children by which I can propose to get a single penny; the youngest being nine years old, and my wife past child-bearing.

Disclaimer

Notes

1. James Francis Edward Stuart (1688–1766), son of James II, was exiled after an unsuccessful claim on the throne of England. Irish Catholics were loyal to him, and some even joined him in his exile.
2. Poverty in Ireland led many Irish to the West Indies and other British colonies. To fund their passage, they agreed to work for a stated period for one of the planters.
3. François Rabelais (ca. 1494–1553), a satirist.
4. Slaughterhouses.
5. George Psalmanazar (ca. 1679–1763), a Frenchman who claimed to be Formosan. His fictitious account of Formosa contained a description of cannibalism.
6. Brazil.
7. While under siege by the Roman Emperor Titus, the city of Jerusalem was torn by warring factions.

After-Reading Activities

Analyzing the Content

1. What is Jonathan Swift's "modest proposal"? Make a list of clues left throughout the essay that should help the reader understand that Swift's proposal is not serious. (Hint: Many of these clues will only become obvious once the reader has read the whole essay.)

2. Why does Swift use an "American acquaintance" as the source for information about the "delicious" and "nourishing" properties of year-old and teenage children?

3. a) Explain the serious social issues that Swift is addressing throughout his essay. Use examples from the text to support your explanation.
   b) Research the events that were taking place in Ireland in the early to mid-1700s that would lead Swift to write this essay. Based on your research, what do you think is Swift's purpose in writing this essay?

4. Swift makes a list of viable solutions to the problems in Ireland. Paraphrase his solutions in your own words.

Structure and Style

5. Create an outline for this essay.

6. Satire is similar to an "in-joke" between friends. Who would get Swift's "joke" early in the essay, and who would be left out until the end? Explain both your choices.

7. Make a chart in which you record examples of the following: generalization, hyperbole, understatement, overwhelming with extraneous facts, sarcasm.

8. Explain the effects of Swift's use of a list in paragraphs 21 to 26 to detail the advantages of his proposal.

9. Reread the ""disclaimer" at the end of the essay. Why would Swift add this paragraph?

How to Live to Be 200

Stephen Leacock

Elements of the Essay

Stephen Leacock's satirical essay provides some absurd tips on how a person might live to a "grand, green, exuberant, boastful old age"—without having to exercise or eat healthily. Compare Leacock's style with the other two "how to" essays in this book (L. Rust Hill's "How to Eat an Ice-Cream Cone" (pages 21 to 29) and Eileen Brett's "How to Write a Test" (pages 30 to 34).

About the Writer

One of Canada's best-known humorists and satirists, Stephen Leacock was born on December 30, 1869, in England. He came to Canada in 1876 with his family. He was educated at the University of Toronto and the University of Chicago. In 1908, he became the head of the economics department at McGill University in Montreal. While he wrote on serious subjects in economics and political science, he also wrote satires, for which he became most famous. Through his satires, Leacock poked fun at small-town life and human foibles, notably hypocrisy and pretence. Among his many published works are *Literary Lapses* (1910), *Sunshine Sketches of a Little Town* (1912), and *My Remarkable Uncle and Other Sketches* (1942). Leacock died in 1944.

TWENTY YEARS AGO I knew a man called Jiggins, who had the Health Habit. 1

He used to take a cold plunge every morning. He said it opened his pores. After it he took a hot sponge. He said it closed the pores. He got so that he could open and shut his pores at will. 2

Jiggins used to stand and breathe at an open window for half an hour before dressing. He said it expanded his lungs. He might, of course, have had it done in a shoe-store with a boot stretcher, but after all it cost him nothing this way, and what is half an hour? 3

After he had got his undershirt on, Jiggins used to hitch himself up 4 like a dog in harness and do Sandow exercises. He did them forwards, backwards, and hind-side up.

5   He could have got a job as a dog anywhere. He spent all his time at this kind of thing. In his spare time at the office, he used to lie on his stomach on the floor and see if he could lift himself up with his knuckles. If he could, then he tried some other way until he found one that he couldn't do. Then he would spend the rest of his lunch hour on his stomach, perfectly happy.

6   In the evenings in his room he used to lift iron bars, cannon-balls, heave dumb-bells, and haul himself up to the ceiling with his teeth. You could hear the thumps half a mile.

7   He liked it.

8   He spent half the night slinging himself around the room. He said it made his brain clear. When he got his brain perfectly clear, he went to bed and slept. As soon as he woke, he began clearing it again.

9   Jiggins is dead. He was, of course, a pioneer, but the fact that he dumb-belled himself to death at an early age does not prevent a whole generation of young men from following in his path.

10   They are ridden by the Health Mania.

11   They make themselves a nuisance.

12   They get up at impossible hours. They go out in silly little suits and run Marathon heats before breakfast. They chase around barefoot to get the dew on their feet. They hunt for ozone. They bother about pepsin. They won't eat meat because it has too much nitrogen. They won't eat fruit because it hasn't any. They prefer albumen and starch and nitrogen to huckleberry pie and doughnuts. They won't drink water out of a tap. They won't eat sardines out of a can. They won't use oysters out of a pail. They won't drink milk out of a glass. They are afraid of alcohol in any shape. Yes, sir, afraid. "Cowards."

13   And after all their fuss they presently incur some simple old-fashioned illness and die like anybody else.

14   Now people of this sort have no chance to attain any great age. They are on the wrong track.

15   Listen. Do you want to live to be really old, to enjoy a grand, green, exuberant, boastful old age and to make yourself a nuisance to your whole neighbourhood with your reminiscences?

16   Then cut out all this nonsense. Cut it out. Get up in the morning at a sensible hour. The time to get up is when you have to, not before. If your office opens at eleven, get up at ten-thirty. Take your chance on ozone.

There isn't any such thing anyway. Or, if there is, you can buy a Thermos bottle full for five cents, and put it on a shelf in your cupboard. If your work begins at seven in the morning, get up at ten minutes to, but don't be liar enough to say that you like it. It isn't exhilarating, and you know it.

Also, drop all that cold-bath business. You never did it when you were a boy. Don't be a fool now. If you must take a bath (you don't really need to), take it warm. The pleasure of getting out of a cold bed and creeping into a hot bath beats a cold plunge to death. In any case, stop gassing about your tub and your "shower," as if you were the only man who ever washed.   17

So much for that point.   18

Next, take the question of germs and bacilli. Don't be scared of them. That's all. That's the whole thing, and if you once get on to that you never need to worry again.   19

If you see a bacilli, walk right up to it, and look it in the eye. If one flies into your room, strike at it with your hat or with a towel. Hit it as hard as you can between the neck and the thorax. It will soon get sick of that.   20

But as a matter of fact, a bacilli is perfectly quiet and harmless if you are not afraid of it. Speak to it. Call out to it to "lie down." It will understand. I had a bacilli once, called Fido, that would come and lie at my feet while I was working. I never knew a more affectionate companion, and when it was run over by an automobile, I buried it in the garden with genuine sorrow.   21

(I admit this is an exaggeration. I don't really remember its name; it may have been Robert.)   22

Understand that it is only a fad of modern medicine to say that cholera and typhoid and diphtheria are caused by bacilli and germs; nonsense. Cholera is caused by a frightful pain in the stomach, and diphtheria is caused by trying to cure a sore throat.   23

Now take the question of food.   24

Eat what you want. Eat lots of it. Yes, eat too much of it. Eat till you can just stagger across the room with it and prop it up against a sofa cushion. Eat everything that you like until you can't eat any more. The only test is, can you pay for it? If you can't pay for it, don't eat it. And listen—don't worry as to whether your food contains starch, or albumen, or gluten, or nitrogen. If you are a damn fool enough to want these things, go and buy them and eat all you want of them. Go to a laundry and get a bag of starch, and eat your fill of it. Eat it, and take a good long drink of glue after it, and a spoonful of Portland cement. That will   25 gluten you, good and solid.

26   If you like nitrogen, go and get a druggist to give you a canful of it at the soda counter, and let you sip it with a straw. Only don't think that you can mix all these things up with your food. There isn't any nitrogen or phosphorus or albumen in ordinary things to eat. In any decent household all that sort of stuff is washed out in the kitchen sink before the food is put on the table.

27   And just one word about fresh air and exercise. Don't bother with either of them. Get your room full of good air, then shut up the windows and keep it. It will keep for years. Anyway, don't keep using your lungs all the time. Let them rest. As for exercise, if you have to take it, take it and put up with it. But as long as you have the price of a hack and can hire other people to play baseball for you and run races and do gymnastics when you sit in the shade and smoke and watch them—great heavens, what more do you want?

After-Reading Activities

Analyzing the Content

1. Why would Leacock write an essay that speaks against fitness and health? What do you think is his purpose?

2. What parts of Leacock's essay still hold true today? Do you think that health and fitness have become bigger issues in the last 50 years? If so, why? If not, why not?

Structure and Style

3. Record the points in the essay that are absurd. Explain the impact this technique has on the effectiveness of the essay.

4. Examine the short paragraphs and their content. Agree or disagree with Leacock's use of this technique in developing his point.

5. Describe the aspects of Leacock's essay that qualify it as satire. Look specifically at the language and content. In your opinion, is it good satire?

From Plus-Fours to Minus-Fours

Rohinton Mistry

Elements of the Essay

Rohinton Mistry writes a social and political satire in the form of a fable. Within this framework, Mistry develops his criticisms of the "king," revealing his foolish and self-serving actions through a series of events. "From Plus-Fours to Minus-Fours" was originally part of a convocation address given at the University of Ottawa in 1996.

About the Writer

Born in Bombay, India, in 1952, Rohinton Mistry immigrated to Canada in 1975. He began writing stories in 1983, while attending the University of Toronto. His first published book was a collection of short stories, *Firozsha Baag* (1987). This was followed by a novel, *Such a Long Journey* (1991), which earned him international acclaim as a literary talent. The book was short-listed for the prestigious Booker Prize, and it earned numerous awards, including the Governor General's Award, the Commonwealth Writers Prize for Best Book, and the SmithBooks/Books in Canada First Novel Award. The novel has also been translated into German, Swedish, Norwegian, Dutch, and Japanese. His second novel, *A Fine Balance* (1995), met with equal success, earning him multiple awards internationally. *Family Matters* (2002) is Mistry's most recent novel. All of his books are set in Bombay.

THERE ARE TWO SONGS FROM two musicals of the sixties whose inspirational lyrics might recommend them for an occasion such as this: "Let's Go Fly a Kite" from *Mary Poppins* and "Climb Every Mountain" from *The Sound of Music*. Now it would be grand if the times were such that these two songs—replete with their avian metaphors and energetic images of soaring kites, their exhortations to climb rainbow-swathed alpine peaks and plunge into ice-cold mountain streams—could present us with a full and complete philosophy of life. Unfortunately, the times are not such, and I'm not sure if there ever was a time when the times were such. And so I've had to write a little fable, to complement the two songs.

2   Once upon a time, not so very long ago, in a land that was not at all far away, there lived a people who were considered the most fortunate by the rest of the world. And there was good reason for this: theirs was a land that was blessed in every way. But, what was more significant, theirs was a society that lived by the principles of tolerance and good will and compassion for its members. Now, not all of the citizens were bursting with tolerance and good will and compassion all of the time, but the important thing was: they did their best to *believe* in these values, they believed they were worth striving after.

3   The people of this fortunate land had two passions: kite-flying and mountain-climbing. Some practised one, some the other; many practised both. The most accomplished among them flew their kites from the mountain tops, and it was a truly awe-inspiring sight. The kite-flyers and mountain-climbers had their various teams, the team uniforms were fashioned in fabrics of red and white, and they took great pleasure in friendly competitions and games. But they never forgot their credo of tolerance and good will and compassion.

4   Thus, they were always urging the less agile among them to climb the mountains, and assisting those who had not yet mastered the laws of aerodynamics and glue and paper to fly their kites. Special agencies had even been set up to bring to fruition this vision of a just society. And so the disabled, the feeble, those too poor to buy their mountain-climbing gear or their kite-flying equipment and, most important, their elegant red-and-white uniforms were all looked after and encouraged to participate fully.

5   The wise king of this fortunate land, himself an enthusiast of kites and mountains like his predecessors, gazed upon his kingdom and saw that it was good. He watched his people singing and laughing and playing together, and his eyes moistened with happiness.

6   Now it came to pass that there arose in the land a shortage of cloth. No one could explain exactly why the shortage arose, especially in such a prosperous land, but it had something to do with people who called themselves international fabric-traders, who speculated in the commodity and created artificial deficits. The good king did his best to

ensure that his people would not suffer. He lowered tariffs, raised taxes, tried to impose rules and regulations on the traders, but in the end the fabricated deficits defeated him. The scarcity of cloth made him take the unprecedented step of establishing limits on people's wardrobes.

Most people accepted this modest restriction. They understood that   7
it was fair, equitable, and necessary for the common good. But there were some who protested, especially when their cherished red-and-white team uniforms were unavailable. The dissent spread and, as is inevitable in these situations, brought forth in their midst a challenger who promised he could restore prosperity to the land if he became king.

"Waste in the king's bureaucracy is the reason for this shortage," he   8
said. "I will cut out the waste. I will downsize and restructure and consolidate. I will be lean and mean for a while, but soon you will reap the rewards, trust me."

This is what he said in public. In private, he would stand before his   9
full-length mirror and sing a different song: "Oh-uh-oh yes, I'm the great pretender."

In view of his healthy girth, the need for leanness was self-evident,   10
but why meanness? Alas, no one sought to question him on this point, and then he was already ensconced on the throne of the realm.

The new measures now went into effect. The first proclamation   11
stated that no more fabric would be issued from the royal textile warehouses for uniforms for kite-flyers and mountain-climbers. The new king had no interest in these two groups—he himself was a golfer. Meanwhile, red, white, *and* blue fabric continued to be made available for golf shirts and golf slacks and plus-fours.

The unfairness of it all was not lost on the people. When they   12
complained, the new king said: "Golf is the activity of the nineties. It's a now kind of thing, a global thing. It will bring prosperity to the land, and soon there'll be fabric enough for everyone. It's the theory of trickle-down textiles."

Time passed, but balls—stray golf balls—were all that trickled down   13
the courses. Sometimes they flew at great speed, injuring innocent bystanders. In retaliation, groups of kite-flyers and mountain-climbers began attacking golfers, tearing their clothes off, altering their plus-fours to minus-fours. It became necessary for the king to station his imperial guard on every fairway and green. With their black face visors, body armour and weapons, the guards looked as though they had stepped out of a video game rife with unspeakable violence.

14   The shortage of fabric in the land did not abate. The king went on television and explained that further austerity measures were needed before things could get better. "We have no choice but to issue a downsizing decree," he said. "We are not mean-spirited or heartless, as some of our enemies suggest. We do not enjoy causing pain. But we have to fulfil our promises." Between sentences, the king's lips kept disappearing; he continued: "We will start by saving on skirts and trousers. People's legs will be downsized. Less fabric will then be required to clothe them. Instead of the ankle bone connecting to the leg bone, the leg bone connecting to the knee bone, the knee bone to the thigh bone, and the thigh bone to the hip bone, we will eliminate all the surplus and connect the ankle bone directly to the hip bone. Then everyone can wear very short pants and very short skirts. The savings will be immense."

15   The first cuts began to take effect, and the cries of the people rent the once-tranquil air of the land. The kite-flyers and mountain-climbers pleaded that such drastic measures were not necessary; there were surely better ways to deal with the cloth shortage.

16   "We can't be distracted by special-interest groups," said the king.

17   "But Sire, we will no longer be able to fly our kites and climb the beautiful mountains," said the people.

18   "Nonsense," said the king, unable to control what seemed to be a tiny smirk. "Of course you will. It will be a greater challenge, that's all. Your downsized legs will have to work harder, that's all. My daddy taught me that if I worked hard, I would be able to fly kites and climb mountains as much as I wanted."

19   As the cutbacks continued, the king noticed that things were not proceeding fast enough. He inquired into the delays. The surgeons in charge of downsizing legs said, "We do not have enough operating theatres and hospital beds."

20   "Is that all?" said the king. He met with his advisers. A new decree went forth: the butchers and meat-packers and all the abattoirs in the land were to pitch in. "Same difference," said the king. "They all work with flesh and bone, and use the same tools. We have too much specialization for our own good." He wiped his sweat-beaded upper lip and continued. "While we are at it, let us restructure education. From now on, metal workshop teachers will also teach English—they can recite a sonnet, for example, while giving a welding demonstration. And the English teachers will be retrained as caddies—they'll be more useful on our golf courses."

21   Misery and despair settled like a fog upon the land. And the people

saw that once again the golfers were left unscathed. In fact, the golfers seemed to *grow* in size. The amputated leg bones and thigh bones were being grafted onto the golfers, making them taller and stronger than ever before. Now they were able to stride faster down the fairways, sinking holes-in-one with regularity, completing their eighteen holes in no time.

The kite-flyers and mountain-climbers, their numbers greatly   22
dwindled, crawled to the king in their very short pants and very short skirts and tried to explain that it was not just a luxury or a hobby of which they were being deprived. "All of society suffers, Your Highness, downsizing diminishes us all, including Your Majesty and the members of your royal court."

"And how's that?" asked the king, standing tall.   23

"Kite-flying and mountain-climbing are necessary for our spiritual   24
well-being," said the people. "Kites let you soar as though you had your own set of wings. Your feet stay grounded but you're in flight, so long as you hold tight to the string of your kite."

"Rhyming rubbish and figurative flim-flam," said the king dismissively.   25

"But, Sire, from the mountain top you can see forever, it's like having   26
a glimpse of the paradise that we could share on earth. Kites and mountains—they help us to dream. And you are taking away our dreams, Your Majesty. Without dreams, people perish. Come with us, fly a kite with us, hike up to the mountain top with us. Even a small, teensy-weensy mountain will enrich you."

"Socialist claptrap and metaphorical mumbo-jumbo cannot shake my   27
belief in common sense," declared the king, his lips disappearing completely as he spoke.

And like the king's lips, the art of kite-flying and mountain-climbing   28
also disappeared from people's lives with the passing of time. But it lived on in their hearts and minds, and in their imagination. It helped them to endure, it kept hope alive, for they continued to secretly sing their two songs while waiting for deliverance.

After-Reading Activities

Analyzing the Content

1. Clarify the allegory of this "fable."

2. Originally, this essay was part of a convocation speech. Why is its content appropriate for a graduating class?

Structure and Style

3. Explain Mistry's metaphoric use of kites and mountains.

4. Rohinton Mistry wants his writing to sound like a fable. How has he captured the tone and feeling of the fable form?

5. How does the fable form complement the purpose of this essay?

6. Is the ending of the essay effective? Support your opinion in a series of well-developed paragraphs.

Extending the Purpose

1. In a series of well-developed paragraphs, argue for or against the use of satire as a method of criticizing an aspect of society. Use your experiences with the three satirical essays in this section as well as any other satire you have read previously. Refer specifically to the individual satires when developing your argument.

2. Examine the media (television, newspapers, magazines, radio) for the number of programs, articles, and advertisements that address the subject of fitness. Using your observation and research, write a well-organized argument agreeing or disagreeing with Leacock's point of view in "How to Live to Be 200."

3. a) When writing for a newspaper or magazine, writers must be aware of certain ethics. Using print and electronic sources, find an ethics code for journalists. Take point-form notes on the code, and prepare a report of your findings for the class.
   b) Reread the three satirical essays in this section. Discuss the ethical standard of each of them.

4. Choose a controversial issue in current events, and address it in a satirical essay. Research the topic thoroughly to ensure accuracy in your satire. Use one of the selections from this section as a model for your work.

Unit III

PERSPECTIVES

Perspective Essays

All essays have a purpose. To fulfill its purpose, an essay must convey a clear perspective on its subject matter. Perspectives may be unique, insightful, opinionated, personal, etc. The essays in this unit offer perspectives or viewpoints on academia, the essay form, Shakespeare, vegetarianism, our environment, Canada's First Nations, and work. As you read each essay, consider whether you agree with the writer's perspective, and why. Think of your own perspective on the subject matter.

3.1 On Academia

Of Studies

Francis Bacon

Elements of the Essay

Francis Bacon's "Of Studies" offers his views of studies while praising their virtues. Note the use of parallel structure, repetition, and antithesis. How do they contribute to the expression of Bacon's ideas?

About the Author

One of the great thinkers, Francis Bacon was born on January 22, 1561, in London, England. A philosopher, essayist, lawyer, and politician, he was known for his original ideas. In 1597, he published a series of essays expressing his philosophical thoughts and ideas. Some of these include "Of Studies," "Of Truth," "Of Death," "Of Parents and Children," "Of Love," "Of Goodness and Goodness of Nature," "Of Nature in Men," and "Of Customs and Education." Other major works include *The Proficience and Advancement of Learning* (1605), *Novum Organum* (1620), *Maxims of Law* (1630), and *Reading on the Statute of Uses* (1642).

STUDIES SERVE FOR DELIGHT, for ornament, and for ability. Their chief use for delight, is in privateness and retiring; for ornament, is in discourse; and for ability, is in the judgment, and disposition of business. For expert men can execute, and perhaps judge of particulars, one by one; but the general counsels, and the plots and marshalling of affairs, come best, from those that are learned. To spend too much time in studies is sloth; to use them too much for ornament, is affectation; to make judgment wholly by their rules, is the humor of a scholar. They perfect nature, and are perfected by experience: for natural abilities are like natural plants, that need proyning, by study; and studies themselves, do give forth directions too much at large, except they be bounded in by experience. Crafty men contemn studies, simple men admire them, and wise men use them; for they teach not their own use; but that is a wisdom without them, and above them, won by observation. Read not to contradict and confute; nor to believe and take for granted; nor to find talk and discourse; but to weigh and consider. Some books are to be tasted, others to be swallowed, and some few to be chewed and digested; that is, some books are to be read only in parts; others to be read, but not curiously; and some few to be read wholly, and with diligence and attention. Some books also may be read by deputy, and extracts made of them by others; but that would be only in the less important arguments, and the meaner sort of books, else distilled books are like common distilled waters, flashy things. Reading maketh a full man; conference a ready man; and writing an exact man. And therefore, if a man write little, he had need have a great memory; if he confer little, he had need have a present wit: and if he read little, he had need have much cunning, to seem to know, that he doth not. Histories make men wise; poets witty; the mathematics subtile; natural philosophy deep; moral grave; logic and rhetoric able to contend. *Abeunt studia in mores.* Nay, there is no stond or impediment in the wit, but may be wrought out by fit studies; like as diseases of the body, may have appropriate exercises. Bowling is good for the stone and reins; shooting for the lungs and breast; gentle walking for the stomach; riding for the head; and the like. So if a man's wit be wandering, let him study the mathematics; for in demonstrations, if his wit be called away never so little, he must begin again. If his wit be not apt to distinguish or find differences, let him study the Schoolmen; for they are *cymini sectores*. If he be not apt to beat over matters, and to call up one thing to prove and illustrate another, let him study the lawyers' cases. So every defect of the mind, may have a special receipt.

3.2 On the Essay

The Essay as a Literary and Academic Form: Closed Gate or Open Door?

Margaret Procter

Elements of the Essay

"The Essay as a Literary and Academic Form" was originally a public talk given in January 1999 as part of the University College Symposium on Redefining Literacy. In it, Margaret Procter examines the essay form as it has developed through the ages and looks at what it has become today—a tool that is used to assess students' academic competence. She suggests that in using the essay as such a tool, we are misusing it, and that educational institutions need to rethink how the essay might serve a better purpose in academia. As you read, consider your own experiences with essays and whether or not you agree with Procter's arguments.

About the Writer

Margaret Procter is Coordinator of Writing Support at the University of Toronto. She originally studied and taught literature; now her work focuses on the variety of ways people read and write in learning situations. She coordinates a network of writing centres that help students learn to write different ways in different disciplines, and she also works with professors across the curriculum to help them integrate writing instruction into their courses. She has been a consultant on secondary English curriculum in Ontario, and enjoys visiting high schools to talk with teachers and students about the differences between secondary school and university expectations.

1   Since we're sitting in a classroom talking about literacy, I want to pay some attention to the form or genre that's usually seen as the essence of academic literacy—but one that causes much unhappiness and doesn't always fit the overall goals of the university. It's traditional that students are asked to show their competence in the academic uses of language largely by writing essays, and that faculty members get to say who is literate (or, more forcefully, who is "illiterate") by grading those essays. Students don't get into university unless they can write the essays required by high-school English courses or standardized tests such as the TOEFL. To increase their chances of getting scholarships, they write other essays for their application packages. On arrival, they sometimes have to write sample essays to see if they belong here. Then, in the humanities and social sciences, they keep writing term essays and essay exams to see if they can display what they've learned in their courses. In the sciences they may escape those essays for a while, but then they suddenly need to write a long final-year thesis to demonstrate that they can use the reasoning methods of their discipline. And then, often with some shock, they find that they need to write a personal essay to get into graduate school—even, and especially, into medical school. You know what they write for graduate courses and, in inflated form, for dissertations, not to mention for getting academic jobs and securing tenure. So the essay form at university serves, among other functions, as a gateway—or sometimes it seems to be a portcullis waiting to come down on someone's neck.

2   That's not what essays have been, and continue to be, outside the university. I want to offer a reminder today (a foreshortened one, so that I can get to talk also about what students do here and now) that the essay form has a long history and a large role beyond the ways it has come to be used for education. I'll raise questions about why we use the essay at university, and even suggest that we could make better use of it if we kept remembering what it can be as a mode of writing.

3   Like the novel, the essay has been declared dead a number of times, but the reports are always contradicted—usually in essays. The term "essay" keeps being used and revived because it captures a core function of writing: it lets writers and readers try out something—ideas, feelings, relationships, representations—both for themselves and for other people to read. Montaigne named his short prose writings "*essais*," from the verb "*essayer*," to try or attempt. That's related to the scientific term "assay" (to examine and test, as one might a precious metal), and apparently derived from the Latin "*exagere*" (to weigh) or maybe

"*exigere*" (to examine or test). Note that it's the objects and ideas being tried and tested here, not the writer himself or herself—or indeed the reader's patience or judgement, as with university essays. "Essay" is also the term that Bacon adopted as a modest way of claiming his dues from a patron; that Locke and others used to describe and define modern empirical science; that Addison, Hazlitt, Emerson, Forster, and Leacock used in their times for playing and working with ideas; and that Cynthia Ozick reclaimed in the September 1998 *Atlantic Monthly*, calling the essay form "the movement of a free mind at play" (114). These writers see the essay form not as punishment, but opportunity: an open doorway that lets writers look out, perhaps opening onto a journey (a common metaphor and theme in essays), or perhaps inviting readers in to share a private space. As the name for a genre, then, "essay" evades any claim to ultimate authority, and it promises a process, not a result.

Montaigne, whose dates are close to those of Shakespeare, published   4
his volume of *essais* at a time when the world was changing around him in some of the ways ours is changing now: religion was breaking up and re-forming, wars were raging uncontrollably, political and social structures were shifting, languages were evolving, and text had just adopted a new technology—in his case that of printing. Montaigne's essays show that he used his position as a highly literate person with some leisure and freedom of opinion to think things out for himself, to exercise his motto, "*Que sçais-je?*" (what do I know?), and to try out some answers. (These are all ideals of university education, by the way.) His essays combine quotations and commentary with personal anecdotes and observations, moving from petty topics like the way different people smell to large ones like death. Montaigne revised his pieces repeatedly until he found the particular type of rambling but unified organization he needed. As he warns at the start of the essay "On Repentance":

> The world is but a perennial see-saw. Everything in it—the land, the mountains of the Caucasus, the pyramids of Egypt—all waver with a common motion and their own. Constancy itself is nothing but a more languid rocking to and fro. I am unable to stabilize my subject; it staggers confusedly along with a natural drunkenness. I grasp it as it is now, and this moment when I am lingering over it. I am not portraying being but becoming.... This is a register of varied and changing occurrences, of ideas which are unresolved and, when needs be, contradictory, either because I myself have become different or because I grasp hold of different attributes or aspects of

my subjects. So I may happen to contradict myself but, as Demades said, I never contradict myself. If my soul could only find a footing I would not be assaying myself but resolving myself. (907–908)

5   And he goes on to assert that this changeableness reflects the nature of individual identity:

You can attach the whole of moral philosophy to a commonplace private life just as well as to one of richer stuff. Every man bears the whole Form of the human condition. Authors communicate themselves to the public by some peculiar mark foreign to themselves; I—the first ever to do so—by my universal being, not as a grammarian, poet or jurisconsult but as Michel de Montaigne. If all complain that I talk too much about myself, I complain that they never even think about their own selves. (907–908)

6   Montaigne doesn't want to be seen as preaching, especially on a dangerous doctrinal topic like repentance, but he claims the right to look at that subject in his own terms. "The Fancies of the Muses are governed by art: mine, by chance." Again he is linking this redefinition of authority to the personal nature of the form—rooted in the author as an individual: "But I have one thing which does accord with sound teaching: never did man treat a subject which he knew or understood better than I know and understand the subject which I have undertaken: in that subject I am the most learned man alive.... I speak as an ignorant questioning man: for solutions I purely and simply abide by the common lawful beliefs. I am not teaching, I am relating" (909). Though his essays are monologues, the tone of voice is unlike a sermon. It invites the reader to participate, to join in the testing out of the thoughts. In his dedication, Montaigne makes a joke of this invitation, saying that the book is really only for his family and friends: "If my design had been to seek the favour of the world I would have decked myself out better and presented myself in a studied gait.... And therefore, Reader, I myself am the subject of my book: it is not reasonable that you should employ your leisure on a topic so frivolous and so vain. Therefore, Farewell" (lix). Then follow the three volumes which he had edited and rewritten over many years and had printed for publication.

7   From the start, then, the *"essai"* is unpretentious, the thinking of a seeker, not a preacher, but it isn't just a lightweight or private form: it can and does attempt to think through large issues while rooted in individual self-examination. Montaigne is usually seen as the founder of

one branch of the essay lineage, the kind where form is driven by content, and where personal experience is intertwined with references to reading experience. Nineteenth-century essayists like Hazlitt and Lamb and Emerson are his followers, offering observations and musings, trying out how far they can think through the things of their world. This is the mode in which E.M. Forster gave two cheers for democracy in 1939, and in which Stephen Leacock and Robertson Davies made fun of pretentiousness and hypocrisy. Students in secondary school are allowed to write some expressive and personal essays, and this university pays homage to the tradition by having a few courses in Composition and even one in Expressive Writing. People taking literature courses, however (or Political Science or Archaeology, or Occupational Therapy), would likely be told if they wrote in this mode that their essays lacked thesis statements and topic sentences, and they might even be invited to speak to the dean about their casual way of referring to their sources.

For contrast, Bacon comes along conveniently a few years after Montaigne, writing tightly organized and explicit pieces. He knows the world is changing too, and he is determined to keep safe. He does provide clear initial and final statements giving the point of his essays and neat transitional sentences—though he doesn't employ the kinds of paragraphing we now teach. For him, the "trying out" of ideas is less an exploration than a performance in which he sees how much he can make out of an idea: he will take a traditional saying or make one up, and then set out riffs and variations on it, with consistency no object. You don't come away from a Bacon essay feeling you know the person behind it, but you know you have seen a mind in action. Bacon has a knack for summing things up in pithy phrasing. His essays use words to capture ideas, for a moment at least: "What is truth? said jesting Pilate, and would not stay for an answer" (I); "Men fear death as children fear to go in the dark" (II); "Revenge is a kind of wild justice" (IV); "I cannot call riches better than the baggage of virtue" (XXXIV). Bacon uses his knowledge of classical rhetoric and logic to develop these ideas into tightly controlled chains of reasoning. His descendants are the eighteenth-century essayists who set out to display the glories of the English language in weekly pieces for the new journals, though Addison and Johnson show more engagement with their topics than Bacon did. Perhaps the humour of Leacock and Davies belongs here too, evading personal commitment by irony and understatement, leading readers backwards down ladders of ideas.

8

9   This tradition of using essays for showing off reasoning and language skills has a very evident role in universities. Though present-day students aren't required to write like Bacon, some have already calculated that if they can come up with smart summations of things in crisp sentences, they will reap the rewards of checkmarks in the margins—and perhaps even be able to cover up some lacks of substance.

10   Bacon called for knowledge to be validated by empirical research, but he wasn't the inventor of the research essay. Nor was John Locke, though his "Essay on Human Understanding" (1690 ff.) discusses and demonstrates the ways language should be used for establishing knowledge. Another handy statement of the new ideal for scientific communication is Thomas Sprat's 1667 *History of the Royal Society*. Sprat is writing to define and praise the new organization now meeting weekly in London in an attempt to map out human knowledge step by step. He presents its works in terms that match another side of our ideal for the contemporary university: not just thinking abstractly about problems, but also contributing to the social good. Such an organization works, Sprat says, by drawing together a range of people to observe the world, perform experiments and studies, and talk and write about the results. To keep itself honest, he argues, such an institution must keep presenting individual members' ideas in written form so that they can be subject to open discussion. The philosopher alone in his study, he reiterates, can too easily convince himself that he has found the proofs he wants (103); even the teacher or professor runs risks of becoming too "Magisterial" (60) if he presents ideas only to his students. The regular meetings of the Society take place in London, not in Oxford, include merchants as well as teachers and gentlemen, and then are represented by written pieces in printed Registers.

11   These publications are deliberately set out, Sprat says, "not as compleat Schemes of opinions, but as bare unfinish'd Histories" (115). Any one piece, then, can expect to be replaced and buried (and most have been, from this period and others), but a short clearly written piece of prose, starting with a hypothesis and setting out tests for it, is the right mode for building up trustworthy scientific knowledge. Sprat anticipates Locke in attacking the show of Wit and the displays of Rhetorick and Fancy that have obscured this process in the past, calling instead for clear, concrete, precise style. He and Locke call for an impersonal third-person style as the ideal, so that the scientific processes they set out can be seen as repeatable by anyone who follows the same steps. (In practice,

however, like many current scientific journals, they use first-person singular to indicate the tentativeness of their trials; they also use a range of personal pronouns, including first-person plural, to refer to the community of respondents who will scrutinize their reports.) These pieces are also honour-bound to mention problems and failures, so that the question and hypothesis posed can be seen as genuinely open to inquiry. Like Montaigne's pieces, they were not setting out to prove (except in the root sense of "attempt or try"), but to test. This is the mode of writing that matches inductive inquiry, the one that claims a contribution to objectivity and truth-seeking, as well as to practical applications.

In spite of his stated distrust of rhetorical effects, Sprat gets much humour out of a mocking portrayal of the writer who does not use this mode of communication. He may have been thinking of Descartes here, or any pre-scientific writer, but we might also recognize a contemporary student in the "night-before" mode:

12

> If we follow the Philosopher home into his study; we shall quickly discover, by how many plausible degrees, the wisest men are apt to deceive themselves, into a sudden confidence of the certainty of their knowledge. We will suppose him, to begin his Inquiry, with all the sincerity imaginable: resolving to pass by no small mistake, and to forgive to himself no slight error in the accompt; with these fair purposes, he pitches on some particular subject: This he turns, and tortures every way; till, after much labour, he can make some ghesses at its Causes: upon this, his industry increases: he applies the same matter to several other operations: he still finds the effects answer his expectations: Now he begins to mould some general Proposition upon it: he meets with more and more proofs to confirm his judgment: thus he grows by little and little warmer in his imaginations: the delight of his success swells him: he triumphs and applauds himself, for having found out some important Truth: But now his Trial begins to slacken: now impatience and security creeps upon him: now he carelessly admits whole crouds of Testimonies, that seem any way to confirm that Opinion, which he had before establish'd: now he stops his survay, which ought to have gone forward to many more particulars; and so at last, this sincere, this invincible Observer, out of weariness, or presumption, becomes the most negligent in the later part of his work, in which he ought to have been the most exact. (103)

13 The descendants of Sprat's ideal—not this Philosopher, but the plain-spoken "assayer" of ideas writing for peer review—now form the cadre of scholarly publishing in the sciences and social sciences, with influences on the humanities too. Their genre is now labelled "article," not essay, presumably indicating that each is only one of a set. A research article is not an individual expression, but a construction on a base of piled-up references to predecessors. Any intrusion of personal tone is so unusual as to be dramatic. There's no place for appeals to the reader, either: such articles are set up to be scanned rather than read through—except by graduate students and competitors. The structure attempts to reflect the inductive scientific method, like a lab report, with standardized section headings and a predetermined type of introduction and conclusion. In short, as Cheryl Geisler has recently pointed out, the essay has given up its amateur origins and taken on a professional form. Only high-level professionals can write it, and only professionals can or would read it.

14 And yet universities now expect student writers to turn out apprentice versions. It's the scientific article—respected but unloved, and depending on highly technical knowledge—that seems to provide the main model for most essays written in educational institutions. I think our respect for this form is greater than the actuality deserves. It breeds more scenes of the person working alone in his or her study (or upstairs in the computer room of the University College Library) spinning out ideas to fill a form, and losing sight of its purpose. The school essay—the kind that people are taught in high school, and use for essay exams, and often come here thinking of as "the university essay"—is expected to fit into a structure (or a format, as students often say) that indicates argumentation, and to use referencing and other markers of a professional mode.

15 As most students experience it—though very committed ones have always been able to make it work otherwise—the format and practical constraints of this type of essay contradict the purpose of demonstrating good reasoning and forbid real discussion of a genuinely open issue. The school essay as written for exams and even to sum up a research project can't have a truly inductive structure posing a question and following it through. That would be too messy, and too difficult to grade. Instead, it is expected to take what textbooks call a deductive form, with the point of argument stated first and "proved" by example and explanation in the body of the paper—just what Sprat was mocking.

16 The firmest rule of this type of essay is that it must be organized around a thesis statement, a term related to the professional mode of

graduate-student writing, though a degradation of the scientific and logical term "hypothesis." (If you don't know what a thesis statement is, you've just betrayed your age. I had to learn it about 15 years ago in order to teach from composition textbooks.) Everyone writing an academic essay in North America (not elsewhere) knows that the thesis statement is a sentence of generalization, given resoundingly at the end of the first paragraph, after a few sentences of even bigger generalization that serve as decoys. Students are sure that the essay must go on to give precisely three points of support, each in a paragraph with topic sentences fore and aft; then it must end with a final paragraph that repeats everything, only backwards. You will note that there's no space available for more than a passing glance at complexity or disagreement. (Compare this to the weekly exercise written in French lycées, which follow the pattern thèse, antithèse, and synthèse. Artificial too, but at least based on a recognizably logical pattern.) "Discuss," the typical prompt, is also a mockery since only the student's voice is asked for. The rule against using "I" is absolute, students think, because the prose has to claim that it contains objective truth uncontaminated by emotion or engagement.

As a timed test of literacy, like the thirty-minute Test of Written English for international students, or the old one-hour English Proficiency Test that the University of Toronto used to give, this type of essay has an even weaker foundation: it has to be built on what students already know, but they can't mention most of that because they realize that teachers (or those even more distant markers hired by Educational Testing Services of Princeton, NJ) won't accept that as real knowledge— and teachers are the only people who can be conceived of as reading these pieces. As take-home work, the essay of this type can most efficiently be built up by taking scraps from what you can find in the library or on the Web, a practice that is seen to be legal as long as you use footnotes (again, a technique from nineteenth-century German scholarship; our current practice of using parenthetical references only makes the seams a bit more evident). Students' perennial problem is transitions: you have to think about covering up the joins, rather than what your structure is built of. In practical terms, you might as well buy the content as borrow it.

This type of essay has in fact been devised to make testing easier. It arose within the past thirty or so years alongside the expansion of universities and the worries within universities that maybe not all those people belonged there. The University of Toronto began to ask for this type of essay in the early 1980s, along with other Ontario universities, as

17

18

the basis of the English Proficiency Test administered to all incoming students. Borrowing from U.S. textbooks, themselves based on the requirements of other standardized tests, we gave out directions to Ontario high schools that a five-paragraph argumentative essay "on a general topic" was what universities wanted: that is, a formulaically organized set of words based on no specific reading or knowledge, and written to no particular reader. Such essays can be scanned quickly to check for the requisite elements and to see whether the student loses his or her nerve during the hour or so of writing. The main purpose of such essay tests, students seem to think, is to provide many chances to make grammar errors. And those errors do indeed happen, to everyone's dismay, as one might predict when students are writing to nobody about nothing in no real language. With personal engagement forbidden, "trying out" of ideas replaced by the need to make a definite point early and often, and the reader turned into a spectral marker, the school essay hardly deserves the name: it is a sad falling off from the real nature of the literate transaction embodied in Montaigne, Locke, Hazlitt, and Davies.

19   Fortunately, this type of essay isn't really central to the function of the university, at least if we agree that our purpose includes letting people think about things and work out individual and common understandings. That noble goal was shared by some educators in the mid-nineteenth century, and it underlies the reasons that essays first became part of university practice. As with Montaigne, essays were brought in to allow for new kinds of thinking and learning; and as with Sprat's ideals, they also responded to new social realities. Before that, since the Middle Ages, university students had concentrated on construing Latin or Greek texts line by line to paraphrase or translate them. Students also memorized texts for oral recitation (still a word for test in some American dialects). For final summations, before going on to become lawyers and clergymen, they created orations based on their study of rhetoric and logic and theology. They might debate ideas orally, too, though public debates tended to bring out dangerous ideas and were often left to student voluntary societies. Examinations in specific subjects were oral interrogations of individual students in the presence of their peers. In his novel *Childhood, Boyhood, Youth*, Tolstoy depicts the terror of being called up to the table of examiners, after realizing from previous students' experience that one wasn't ready, and being subjected to rapid-fire questions and equally rapid scorn and dismissal. Exchange and transfer students from Europe tell me they are still examined this way.

University students in the unreformed universities always seemed to   20
find places to write and learn writing outside the curriculum: poets often
developed early in the relatively leisurely pace of university life, and
aspiring thinkers formed essay-writing societies like the Apostles at
Cambridge—a club that required members to write regular essays and
read them to other members, not unlike the Royal Society meetings two
centuries earlier. Of course students could and did talk about ideas among
themselves and with their tutors. But for a long time, requiring students to
write reflectively about ideas was too dangerous (since the ideas could get
out of hand), too inconvenient (because of lack of paper and lighting,
for instance), and too troublesome to monitor (a challenge we still face).

Essay writing began to replace oral exams and speeches at the time   21
when new disciplines were defining themselves (English out of Classics,
then a host of others). It was also a time when the intellectual
environment was coming to recognize open questions—even about texts
like the Bible, not to mention scientific theories such as evolution or the
facts of dizzying social changes around them. The Harvard history
department manual of 1888–1889 affirmed high aims for student
research essays: "The purpose of the system is to train students in
finding things out for themselves. It will … interest them in the
unsettled questions of our history" (Russell 85). More practically, writing
was also needed as practice for employment examinations. After 1860
writing essay examinations was the only way to obtain jobs in the British
and colonial civil services. (That had been the case for centuries in
China.) There were administrative reasons too: once teaching started to
be given in specified courses by lecture according to the German model
of specialization in order to handle increasing enrolment, there was a
need for individual demonstrations of knowledge that wouldn't take up
as much class time as speaking individually. So the motives for asking
students to write were both practical and idealistic, and the changes
seem to have happened quite quickly over a range of institutions.

In Scottish and U.S. universities, the writing of essays became a subject   22
in itself, integrated with Rhetoric and Logic, subjects retained (and
renewed) from the medieval curriculum. In Edinburgh and Cambridge,
Massachusetts alike, studying the art of persuasion was seen as essential
preparation for taking part in public life and for maintaining freedom of
expression. The composition programs in elite U.S. universities, starting
with Harvard in the 1850s, come directly from that tradition. They still
combine teaching of essay writing with teaching of civic awareness.

Egerton Ryerson would have liked to see Canadian higher education develop a rhetorical focus, but he lost that round of the culture wars.

23   In Canada as in England, as the discipline of English defined itself, rhetoric as a subject died out, and literary studies won the day. But even as the study of writing faded off the calendar pages between 1850 and 1880 (books by Robin Harris and Henry Hubert trace this process at the University of Toronto and other Canadian institutions), essay writing became one of the main things students did in most subjects at university, both for tests and in courses—and thus grading them the main things professors did, at least if they couldn't hire enough teaching assistants to do it for them. The newly formed English Department at the University of Toronto made its compromise early. It was very ready to use essay writing in conjunction with large lecture classes, and to allot some marks that way, but it refused to teach composition. In 1900 it devised a system that lasted until the late 1960s: it required four "original essays" per year from all students taking its literature courses, but gave a separate course credit for writing them (English 1a, 2a, etc.). Here is the note that appeared in calendars from 1900 to the late 1960s. It makes clear that composition was not a subject to be taught by professors, but a requirement to be met by students. One may note the stiffer resolve of the 1960s not to give any second chances, as well as the new reliance on handbooks to do the dirty work.

24   From the 1921-2 Arts & Science calendar, English section:

> Composition: In the first two years of the undergraduate course original essays are required during the session from students taking the Pass and Honour Courses in English, even from those who have received dispensation from attendance upon lectures. These essays, after being carefully examined, are returned with suggestions and criticisms, and the marks assigned are reckoned in determining standing in the May examinations. Throughout the course Composition shall be regarded as a subject distinct from literature, and candidates failing to secure the necessary standing in these essays are required to repeat the work of the year in English Composition.

25   From the 1966-7 Arts & Science calendar, English section:

> Composition. In each year of the undergraduate course original essays are required during the session from students taking the general, pass or honour courses in English, even from those who

have received dispensation from attendance at lectures. These essays, after being carefully examined, are returned with suggestions and criticisms, and the marks assigned are reckoned in determining standing at the annual examinations. The student is required to obtain a suitable dictionary and a textbook of composition from a list supplied by the instructor. Candidates who have failed to secure standing in these essays will receive no credit for the examinations in the corresponding courses in literature, 100, 104, 110, 200, 201, 300, 301, 404, 405 and will be required to repeat the work of the year in English. See page 50.

Other departments followed similar patterns for using but not teaching the academic essay. It's hard to pin down exact evidence for its use, because it's the kind of thing people take for granted rather than talk about, especially if they don't want to teach it directly. It is a matter of record that most courses in Canadian universities until the 1950s required essay answers in course exams and written "theses" for graduation. It's not quite so clear that all departments asked for essays during term, though some records and examples exist. At Harvard near the turn of the century, I read, Henry Adams required his History students to write out debates on questions he set; William James in Psychology asked his students to list and comment on inconsistencies in the course readings. Another of his classes was asked, "Make idealism as plausible as you can in two or three pages" (Russell 84).

26

This kind of assignment causes work for everybody, and I suspect that the realities of actual assignments in most classes rarely matched the ideals stated. Professors can be heard from the beginning complaining about students' bad writing, and "correction" soon became the word for the responses they made. Robert Scholes, for instance, cites an early comment that the "spelling, grammar, and other beggarly elements" of early graduates from Brown University were "far from impeccable" (5). One of the first moves of W.J. Alexander on being appointed chair of the English Department at the University of Toronto in 1889 was to request funding for a teaching assistant to help with the "arduous work" of reading student essays (Harris 32). A.S.P. Woodhouse, too, in what are now thought of as the golden days of the 1950s, lamented the inability of first-year students to write coherently or correctly (Harris 122), and instituted a "temporary" course in remedial English to fix them up. And from the start, humanities departments grumbled that they were being exploited in a service function just because they paid attention to writing

27

in their courses (Graves, Miller, Russell, Scholes, passim).

28   Stephen Leacock sets a number of levels of irony in play and mocks a central assumption of liberal education in his 1921 essay "Oxford as I See It" when he cites an informant (not himself, of course) as saying that studying at Oxford consists merely of going to a tutor's rooms regularly for four years and being smoked at while the tutor goes over one's exercises. "A well-smoked man," he concludes sardonically, "reads and writes English with a grace that can be acquired no other way" (80). We have a no-smoking policy now at University College, but still seem to believe in that method of high expectation and indirect instruction.

29   So we can keep wondering just why we have the essay as the form that people depend on to guarantee university literacy, to sum up what writing and reading are really for. If professors don't use it, they seem to feel guilty, and students are well aware which courses give essays. They either run from them so they won't get caught, or flock to them so they can claim they faced the challenge. I see professors in even huge classes of 1000 asking their students to write essays, because everybody knows that essays are good for you. In the light of what I've been saying about both potential and reality, I'd like to suspend judgement on that.

30   I do agree that the essay as a genre represents some essential aspects of literacy, and that essay assignments can embody the aims of a university. In fact I see a number of indications now, as we adapt to another period of social and cultural and technological change, that this university, at least, is restoring the essay (though not always called that) as a way of thinking and communicating, not just a way of making difficulties for everyone concerned. One heartening sign, for instance, is the restoration of the pronoun "I." It's actually encouraged in some carefully framed essays in Women's Studies and Sociology, inviting students to base their analysis of ideas on self-reflection. Where else, indeed, could it start when people are writing about aspects of their own lives? It happens in the journal responses I see a number of English professors asking their students to keep about their course readings. I also see personal writing used in Geography and Engineering and Medicine when students are asked to recognize and analyze practical problems based on what they have actually seen and experienced, and sometimes to take into account what they thought and felt while they were seeing and doing. *"Que sçais-je?"* (what do I know, and how?) is still a real question for science and social science as well as the humanities. The writing that comes from these activities may or may not be called

essays, but it is related to Montaigne's form.

What's more, to fulfill Sprat's tradition, the question is regaining its   31
central place in essays, guided by instructors who are tired of
prematurely authoritative statements and weak evidence, and by those
who are still excited themselves at the idea of keeping questions open
long enough to try out various answers. It happens as much in
Philosophy as in the sciences, and in the social sciences too, as it should.
But it always depends on taking time to think, consider, and discuss,
and that's not a commodity easily available for either students or faculty.

Another adaptable assignment type is the critique: a new name and a   32
new way of asking for close and analytic reading of sources. To write a
critique, students look closely at an individual scholarly text and
comment on it, usually bringing in some of their prior knowledge—
perhaps personal experience, and certainly knowledge of other texts or
approaches in the discipline. The critique takes both summary and
analysis of other texts, and leads students toward the realization that
texts represent not just information, but ways of putting it. Nobody
wants to call this rhetoric, but that's what it is all the same.

A new type of assignment takes the typical essay prompt "discuss"   33
quite literally. Using e-mail in a class listserv or Web forum, students
talk to each other in and outside of class—in the best instances, giving
everyone a chance to contribute an individual viewpoint, and letting
students themselves take responsibility for the direction of discussion.
And this kind of talk is in writing; what's more, "the reader" isn't an
abstraction, but a peer who may jump in and ask what you mean and
what about some other viewpoint. Again, this is a lesson in rhetoric
without the label.

And as a final example, I see short focused assignments, repeated   34
regularly, that not only develop writing skills but give students a chance
to practise specific moves of reading and discussing. That happens in an
English Poetry course where students write periodic analyses of specific
passages and then bring them to class to read in groups. I've seen that
same practice in Sociology, where students also study the way their
groups interact in doing the group work, and in science-based courses
like Environmental Studies, where the assigned questions on readings or
labs often turn out to be much more open-ended than students first
realize. If exercises like that can bring people together with their peers to
try out ideas in terms of language, then they deserve to be seen as part of
the "essay" category too.

35   The common factor in all of these innovations is that reading and writing are being used to learn something and to think, not just to demonstrate knowledge or even skill with language. I'm not saying that these particular adaptations will solve all problems or make everyone delighted to write or read at university. Papers will remain a pain to finish by the deadline, and a burden to read en masse. Not everyone who writes inventive assignments will enjoy the process, and those who read the resulting pieces may well start to notice that they're also illogical or pedagogically flawed, and have to reinvent innovative assignments once again. The formulaic school essay will doubtless survive for teaching purposes, and there will even be times when we'll decide that, after all, it's better than multiple-choice questions. But if we can keep believing that writing is a valuable way to explore ideas and set up connections between writers and readers, then we'll keep finding a place for essays under one name or another.

Bibliography

[The following are Procter's notes.]

Allen, Peter. *The Cambridge Apostles: The Early Years.* New York: Cambridge University Press, 1978.

Bacon, Francis. *The Essays,* ed. John Pitcher. London: Penguin, 1985.

Bizzell, Patricia. "Arguing About Literacy," *College English,* 50 (February 1988), 141-153.

Geisler, Cheryl. *Academic Literacy and the Nature of Expertise: Reading, Writing, and Knowing in Academic Philosophy.* Hillsdale NJ: Laurence Erlbaum, 1994.

Good, Graham. *The Observing Self: Rediscovering the Essay.* New York: Routledge, 1988.

Graves, Roger. *Writing Instruction in Canadian Universities.* Winnipeg: Inkshed Publications, 1994.

Harris, Robin S. *English Studies at Toronto: A History.* Toronto: University of Toronto Press, 1988.

Heilker, Paul. *The Essay: Theory and Pedagogy for an Active Form.* Urbana IL: National Council of Teachers of English, 1996.

Hubert, Henry A. *Harmonious Perfection: The Development of English Studies in Nineteenth-Century Anglo-Canadian Culture.* East Lansing: Michigan State University Press, 1994.

Hubert, Henry A. "Babel After the Fall: The Place of Writing in English," *University of Toronto Quarterly* 64 (Fall 1995), 381-397.

Leacock, Steven. *My Discovery of England.* 1922. Toronto: McClelland and Stewart, 1961.

Miller, Thomas P. *The Formation of College English: Rhetoric and Belles Lettres in the British Cultural Provinces.* Pittsburgh: University of Pittsburgh Press, 1997.

Montaigne, Michel. *The Complete Essays*, trans. M. A. Screech. London: Penguin, 1987.

Olson, David R. "From Utterance to Text: The Bias of Language in Speech and Writing," *Harvard Educational Review*, 47 (August 1977), 257-281.

Olson, David R. "Writing: The Divorce of the Author from the Text," in *Exploring Speaking-Writing Relationships: Connections and Contrasts*, ed. Barry M. Kroll and Roberta J. Vann. Urbana IL: National Council of Teachers of English, 1981.

Olson, David R. "An Introduction to Understanding Literacy," *Interchange* 18 (Spring/Summer 1987), 1-8.

Ozick, Cynthia. "SHE: Portrait of the Essay as a Warm Body," *Atlantic Monthly*, September 1998, 114-118.

Russell, David. *Writing in the Academic Disciplines, 1870-1990: A Curricular History*. Carbondale, IL: Southern Illinois University Press, 1991.

Scholes, Robert. *The Rise and Fall of English: Reconstructing English as a Discipline*. New Haven: Yale University Press, 1998.

Sprat, Thomas. *History of the Royal Society* [1667], ed. Jackson I. Cope and Harold Whitmore Jones. St. Louis: Washington University Studies, 1959.

Tolstoy, L.N. *Childhood, Boyhood, Youth*, transl. Rosemary Edmonds. Toronto: Penguin, 1964.

University of Toronto Calendar, Arts and Science, 1921–2 and 1966–7.

3.3 On Shakespeare

Shakespeare, Prince of Light

Pablo Neruda

Elements of the Essay

In this essay, Pablo Neruda explains why Shakespeare is "the greatest of all human beings" and the "Prince of Light." Note Neruda's poetic language, imagery, and syntax. What effect do they have on his writing? Are you convinced by his claims? Why or why not?

About the Writer

Born on July 12, 1904, in Parral, Chile, Pablo Neruda (Neftalí Ricardo Reyes Basoalto) was a poet, political activist, and diplomat. From 1927 to 1943, he worked as a foreign diplomat, travelling and living overseas. Political events, such as the Spanish Civil War, led him to political activism. Two years after he returned to Chile, he was elected a senator and he joined the Communist Party in Chile. Neruda became renowned for his love poems, and he used his fame to bring attention to social injustices. In 1971, he won the Nobel Prize in Literature. His poetry collection, *Twenty Love Poems and a Song of Despair* (1924), has sold over a million copies worldwide. Neruda died on September 23, 1973. By the time of his death, he was considered the most celebrated literary and political figure in Chile.

1   GONERIL, REGAN, HAMLET, Angus, Duncan, Glansdale, Mortimer, Ariel, Leontes ...

2   These names from Shakespeare were part of our childhood; they crystallized and became the substance of our dreams. Even when we could scarcely read, we knew that behind the names lay a continent with rivers and kings, clans and castles and archipelagos, that someday we would explore. The names of these somber, or radiant, protagonists revealed to us the texture of poetry, the first peal of a great bell. Later,

much later, come the days and years when we discover the lines and lives of these names. We discover suffering and remorse, martyrdom and cruelty, beings of blood, creatures of air, voices illuminated for a magic feast, banquets attended by bloodstained ghosts. All that action, all those souls, all those passions—all that life.

In every epoch, one bard assumes responsibility for the dreams and wisdom of the age: he expresses the growth, the expansion, of that world. His name is Alighieri, Victor Hugo, Lope de Vega, Walt Whitman. 3

Above all, his name is Shakespeare. 4

These bards amass leaves, and among the leaves one hears birdcalls; beneath these leaves roots grow. They are the leaves of great trees. 5

They are leaves, and eyes. They multiply and gaze down on us, insignificant men, through all the passing ages, they gaze on us and help us discover ourselves: they reveal to us our labyrinths. 6

In the case of Shakespeare, there is a third revelation, as there will be others: that of the sorcery of his distilled poetry. Few poets are so compact and secret, so secure in the heart of their diamond. 7

The sonnets were carved from the opal of tears, from the ruby of love, from the emerald of jealousy, from the amethyst of mourning. 8

They were carved from fire, made from air, sculpted from crystal. 9

The sonnets were uprooted from nature so whole that, from first to last, one hears how water flows, how the wind dances, and how, golden or flowering, the cycles of the seasons and fruits follow one after the other. 10

The sonnets hold an infinity of keys, of magic formulas: static majesty, speeding arrows. 11

The sonnets are banners that one by one rise to flutter from the castle tower. And though exposed to weather and to time, they conserve the magenta of their stars, the turquoise of their half-moons, the splendor of their blazing hearts. 12

I have read Shakespeare's poetry for many years; the poems, unlike the plays, do not tell of lives, of battles, of derring-do. 13

There is the stark whiteness of the page, the purity of the road of poetry. Along that road glide endless rows of images, like tiny ships laden with honey. 14

Amid this excess of riches in which the driving power of creativity moves in time with intelligence, we see, we can almost feel, an unwavering and flourishing Shakespeare, and note that the most striking aspect of his poems is not their abundant power but their exacting form. 15

My name is written in my copy of the *Sonnets*, along with the day 16 and the month in 1930 when I bought the book on the island of Java.

17   It has been with me, then, for thirty-four years.

18   There, on that far-off island, it was my model, the purest of fountains, deep forests, a fabulous multitude of hitherto unknown myths; it was crystalline law. Because Shakespeare's poetry, like that of Góngora and Mallarmé, plays with the light of reason, imposes a strict, if secret, code. In a word, during those lost years of my life, Shakespeare's poetry kept open a line of communication with Western culture. By Western, naturally, I mean Pushkin and Karl Marx, Bach and Hölderlin, Lord Tennyson and Mayakovsky.

19   Of course, poetry recurs throughout the plays as well, in the towers of Elsinore, in the castle of Macbeth, on Prospero's ship, among the perfume of pomegranates in Verona.

20   A phantasmagorical wind blows through the tunnel of each play. The oldest sound in the world, the sound of the human heart, is the matter from which these unforgettable words are formed. Fantasy and humanity appear in all the plays, along with the parlance of the common man, the signs of the marketplace, the vulgar voices of parasites and buffoons, all accompanied by the steely ring of suits of armor locked in crazed combat.

21   But what I like best is to follow the extravagant flow of Shakespeare's poetry, a harmony painted on the wall of time in blue, enamel, and magic seafoam, an amalgam imprinted on our eternity.

22   As an example, in the pastoral idyll *Venus and Adonis*, published in 1593, there is the flickering of cool shadows on flowing waters, the insinuating green of singing groves, cascades of rippling poetry, and myth fleeing into the greenery.

23   Then suddenly a steed appears, dissipating fantasy with its pounding hoofs, as "His eye, which scornfully glisters like fire, shows his hot courage and his high desire."

24   Yes, if a painter were to paint that horse: "His art with nature's workmanship at strife, as if the dead the living should exceed." There is no description that can equal that of his amorous, furious horse galloping with real hoofs through marvelous sextets.

25   And I mention it, though Shakespeare's bestiary contained traces of many beasts, and his herbarium retains the color and scent of many flowers, because that pawing steed is the theme of his ode, the generative force of nature captured by a great synthesizer of dreams.

26   This autumn I was given the task of translating *Romeo and Juliet*.

27   I accepted the request with humility. With humility, and with a sense

of duty, because in fact I did not feel capable of decanting that passionate love story into Spanish. But I had to do it, since this is the anniversary of Shakespeare's birth, the year of universal veneration of the poet who opened new universes to man.

Translating with pleasure, and with honor, the tragedy of those star-crossed lovers, I made a discovery.   28

I realized that underlying the plot of undying love and inescapable death there was a second drama, a second subject, a second principal theme.   29

Romeo and Juliet is a great plea for peace among men. It is a condemnation of pointless hatred, a denunciation of the barbarity of war, and the solemn consecration of peace.   30

When Prince Escalus, in moving and exemplary language, reproaches the feudal clans who are staining the streets of Verona with blood, we realize that the Prince is the incarnation of enlightenment, of dignity, and of peace.   31

When Benvolio reproaches Tybalt for his warlike temperament, saying: "I do but keep the peace; put up thy sword," the fierce swordsman replies: "What! drawn, and talk of peace? I hate the word …"   32

So, peace was despised by some in Elizabethan Europe. Centuries later, Gabriela Mistral—persecuted and insulted for her defense of peace, dismissed from the Chilean newspaper that had published her articles for thirty years—wrote her famous phrase: "Peace, that accursed word." One sees that the world and the press continued to be governed by Tybalts, by swordsmen.   33

One reason more, then, to love William Shakespeare, the greatest of all human beings. There will always be time and space to explore in Shakespeare, to lose ourselves, or begin the long journey around his statue, like the Lilliputians around Gulliver. And though we may go a long way without reaching the end, we always return with hands filled with fragrance and blood, with flowers and sorrows, with mortal treasures.   34

At this solemn moment, it is my pleasure to open the door of tributes, raising the curtain so the dazzling, pensive figure of the Bard may appear. And across four centuries I would say to him: "Greetings, Prince of Light! Good health, sir itinerant actor! We are the heirs to your great dreams; we dream them still. Your words do honor to the entire world."   35

And, more quietly, I would whisper into his ear: "My friend, I thank you."   36

3.4 On Vegetarianism

The Harvest, the Kill

Jane Rule

Elements of the Essay

Jane Rule's essay, "The Harvest, the Kill," is critical of the "hygiene, myth and morality" that prevent people from eating certain foods, whether plant or animal. Illustrating her points with personal experiences and vivid images, Rule challenges her readers' perception of their place in the complex food chain.

About the Writer
Born in New Jersey in 1931, Jane Rule moved to Canada in 1956. She taught at the University of British Columbia until 1976 and came to be known as one of the best fiction writers in the province. Her works, which often explore feminist and social issues, include the novels *Desert of the Heart* (1964) and *After the Fire* (1989). She currently lives in Baliano Island, BC.

1   I live among vegetarians of various persuasions and moral meat eaters; therefore when I have guests for dinner, I pay rather more attention to the nature of food than I would, left to my own imagination.

2   The vegetarians who don't eat meat because they believe it to be polluted with cancer-causing hormones or because they identify their sensitive digestive tracts with herbivore ancestors are just cautious folk similar to those who cross the street only at the corner with perhaps a hint of the superstition found in those who don't walk under ladders. They are simply taking special care of their lives without further moral deliberation.

3   Those who don't eat meat because they don't approve of killing aren't as easy for me to understand. Yesterday, as I pried live scallops from their beautiful, fragile shells and saw them still pulsing in the bowl, ready to cook for friends for whom food from the sea is acceptable, it felt to me no less absolute an act of killing than chopping off the head of a chicken. But I also know in the vegetable garden that I rip carrots untimely from

their row. The fact that they don't twitch or run around without their heads doesn't make them less alive. Like me, they have grown from seed and have their own natural life span which I have interrupted. It is hard for me to be hierarchical about the aliveness of living things.

There are two vegetarian arguments that bear some guilty weight for me. The first is the number of acres it takes to feed beef cattle as compared to the number of acres it takes to feed vegetation. If there ever were a large plan to change our basic agriculture in order to feed everyone more equally, I would support it and give up eating beef, but until then my not eating beef is of no more help than my eating my childhood dinner was to the starving Armenians. The second is mistreatment of animals raised for slaughter. To eat what has not been a free-ranging animal is to condone the abuse of animals. Again, given the opportunity to support laws for more humane treatment of the creatures we eventually eat, I would do so, but I probably wouldn't go so far as to approve of chickens so happy in life that they were tough for my table.

4

The moral meat eaters are those who believe that we shouldn't eat what we haven't killed ourselves, either gone to the trouble of stalking it down or raising it, so that we have proper respect for the creatures sacrificed for our benefit.

5

I am more at home with that view because my childhood summers were rural. By the time I was seven or eight, I had done my share of fishing and hunting, and I'd been taught also to clean my catch or kill. I never shot anything larger than a pigeon or a rabbit. That I was allowed to use a gun at all was the result of a remarkably indulgent father. He never took me deer hunting, not because I was a girl but because he couldn't bear to shoot them himself. But we ate venison brought to us by other men in the family.

6

I don't remember much being made of the sacredness of the life we took, but there was a real emphasis on fair play, much of it codified in law, like shooting game birds only on the wing, like not hunting deer with flashlights at night, like not shooting does. But my kinfolk frowned on bait fishing as well. They were sportsmen who retained the wilderness ethic of not killing more than they could use. Strictly speaking, we did not need the food. (We could get meat in a town ten miles down the road.) But we did eat it.

7

Over the years, I became citified. I still could and did put live lobsters and crab in boiling water, but meat came from the meat market. Now that I live in the country again, I am much more aware of the

8

slaughter that goes on around me, for I not only eat venison from the local hunt but have known the lamb and kid on the hoof (even in my rhododendrons, which is good for neither them nor the rhododendrons) which I eat. The killers of the animals are my moral, meat-eating neighbors. I have never killed a large animal, and I hope I never have to, though I'm not particularly tenderhearted about creatures not human. I find it hard to confront the struggle, smell, and mess of slaughter. I simply haven't the stomach for it. But, if I had to do it or go without meat, I would learn how.

9   It's puzzling to me that cannibalism is a fascinating abomination to vegetarian and meat eater alike, a habit claimed by only the most vicious and primitive tribes. We are scandalized by stories of the Donner Party or rumors of cannibalism at the site of a small plane crash in the wilderness, a boat lost at sea. Yet why would it be so horrifying for survivors to feed on the flesh of those who have died? Have worms and buzzards more right to the carcass?

10   We apparently do not think of ourselves as part of the food chain, except by cruel and exceptional accident. Our flesh, like the cow in India, is sacred and taboo, thought of as violated even when it is consigned to a mass grave. We bury it to hide a truth that still must be obvious to us, that as we eat so are we eaten. Why the lowly maggot is given the privilege (or sometimes the fish or the vulture) denied other living creatures is a complex puzzle of hygiene, myth and morality in each culture.

11   Our denial that we are part of nature, our sense of superiority to it, is our basic trouble. Though we are not, as the producers of margarine would make us believe, what we eat, we are related to what we harvest and kill. If being a vegetarian or a moral meat eater is a habit to remind us of that responsibility, neither is to be disrespected. When habit becomes a taboo, it blinds us to the real meaning. We are also related to each other, but our general refusal to eat our own flesh has not stopped us from slaughtering each other in large and totally wasted numbers.

12   I am flesh, a flesh eater, whether the food is carrot or cow. Harvesting and killing are the same activity, the interrupting of one life cycle for the sake of another. We don't stop at eating either. We kill to keep warm. We kill for shelter.

13   Back there in my rural childhood, I had not only a fishing rod and rifle, I had a hatchet, too. I cleared brush, cut down small trees, chopped wood. I was present at the felling of a two-thousand-year-old redwood

tree, whose impact shook the earth I stood on. It was a death more simply shocking to me than any other I've ever witnessed. The house I lived in then was made of redwood. The house I live in now is cedar.

My ashes may nourish the roots of a living tree, pitifully small compensation for the nearly immeasurable acres I have laid waste for my needs and pleasures, even for my work. For such omnivorous creatures as we are, a few frugal habits are not enough. We have to feed and midwife more than we slaughter, replant more than we harvest, if not with our hands, then with our own talents to see that it is done in our name, that we own to it.

The scallop shells will be finely cleaned by raccoons, then made by a neighbor into wind chimes, which may trouble my sleep and probably should until it is time for my own bones to sing.

Vegetarianism: Going Green!

Julie Cameron

Elements of the Essay

While Jane Rule's essay examines some principles around vegetarianism, Julie Cameron's essay simply presents the fact that she is "going green" and has become a vegetarian. She provides reasons for her choice and offers suggestions on how to be a healthy vegetarian. What are your own perceptions on vegetarianism vs. meat eating?

1   WHEN I TOLD MY MOTHER I was going to be a vegetarian she didn't try to discourage me, she simply said, "fine, but I'm not making two dinners." She thought it was a phase, something that I would grow out of. After all, who can live their entire life without eating a hamburger, a hot dog, or the traditional turkey at Thanksgiving? Turns out, lots of people can.

2   You have to realize, two of my uncles are butchers and they keep much of my family in discount meat. For me to waltz into my parents' kitchen and inform my mother that I would no longer be participating in family steak night was, well, unexpected to say the least.

3   Much to my mother's dismay, I turned out to be one of thousands of vegetarians in Canada who was under voting age. Some people thought I did it to be cool, some people (like my mother) thought I did it for shock value. But I was always asked the one-word question, so many times I should hand out flyers explaining it: WHY?

4   Why? Lots of reasons. I was never a big steak fan, loved animals, and when I was little I had a friend who lived on a dairy farm. If you have ever named a cow, you will understand how difficult it is to sit down to a hamburger. But there was, of course, one fateful encounter that pushed me to my dinner of destiny.

5   My mother had a friend named Jen. Jen had long brown hair down

to her calves. I'm not exaggerating, it was down to her calves. She insisted we go to the Natural Foods Store in our town so she could get organic vegetables and soymilk. I had never even known what soy was, or that there was a difference between vegetables from the grocery store and vegetables from a natural foods store. And I was amazed. Not only did she have hair down to her calves, but she also knew about foods I had never even heard of. My decision was made.

I feel very fortunate to be a vegetarian in an age where there are so many meat alternatives. My friends and family appreciate that I don't try to force my food choices on them—there is nothing worse than a holier-than-thou vegetarian. 6

If you are thinking about becoming a vegetarian, it's important to do a little research first and make sure you maintain a healthy diet. I have met so many junk-food vegetarians (a self-proclaimed vegetarian who doesn't eat meat, but doesn't eat anything healthy or remotely close to a vegetable, unless potato chips and French fries count), that I'm not surprised most people think eating vegetarian isn't healthy. It is extremely important to make sure that your nutrition is balanced, especially since you have to find alternatives to getting your protein, iron and zinc from something other than meat. 7

Be sure to take in healthy doses of beans/pulses and rice (or grains) together to get the full complement of essential amino acids. Without the beans, some essential protein building blocks are missing and the body will not be able to make proper muscle tissue, and other tissues in the body and you could lose muscle and gain fat. Soy protein is a good way to get the protein needed. Veggie soy dogs and soy burgers are often the easiest way with a busy schedule! 8

To meet these needs it is recommended that vegetarians:
- Eat at least 5 servings of a calcium rich food every day.
- Get at least 20–30 minutes of direct sunlight 2–3 times each week for vitamin D.
- Eat a food item that is fortified with vitamin B-12 and iron every day. This means that a vitamin or mineral has been added to a food item. A good source of this would be a fortified breakfast cereal.
- Eat a variety of whole-grain products every day; this will boost the intake of zinc.
- Enjoy a vitamin C fruit or juice with meals to help the body absorb iron.

Types of vegetarians:

Veganism
Excludes the consumption of all food of animal origin except human breast milk.

Rastafarian Veganism
In general the diet excludes all red meat, milk, fats and oils of animal origin, but it may include fish depending on the nationality of the Rastafarian.

Macrobiotic
A diet that does not totally exclude but strictly limits foods of animal origin.

Fructarianism
The diet is confined to foods such as fruit, nuts and certain vegetables, where harvesting allows the parent plant to flourish.

Polo-vegetarianism
Form of vegetarianism that includes the consumption of chicken.

Lacto-vegetarianism
Form of vegetarianism that includes the consumption of milk.

Lacto-ovo-vegetarianism
Form of vegetarianism that excludes red meat, poultry and fish but includes the consumption of dairy products and eggs.

Pesco-vegetarianism
Form of vegetarianism that includes the consumption of milk and eggs, and, occasionally, fish.

Semivegetarian (demi-vegetarian; quasi-vegetarian)
A self-classification amongst people who claim to have eating habits which focus on vegetarian foods, but they eat some kind of meat on an occasional basis. Red meats are usually excluded.

Reduced meat-eaters
People who classify themselves as reducing their overall meat consumption.

3.5 On Our Environment

A Sense of Wonder

David Suzuki

Elements of the Essay

Scientist David Suzuki argues that we have become so disconnected from our environment that we no longer hold a sense of wonder about the world around us. Rather, we look to worlds of fantasy and outer space to draw joy. Do you agree with his assessment?

About the Writer

David Suzuki was born in Vancouver in 1936. As Japanese-Canadians, Suzuki and his family were interned during World War II. After attending university in the United States, Suzuki joined the University of British Columbia in 1969 and won the Steacie Memorial Fellowship as "Outstanding Canadian Research Scientist Under the Age of 35." While still active in his own research in genetics, Suzuki took on the popularization of scientific issues as his mission. As a popular public figure, a status gained primarily through his work on CBC TV's *The Nature of Things*, Suzuki continues to seek to raise awareness of scientific and environmental concerns.

H UMANS, I BELIEVE, ARE naturally drawn to lives and worlds outside of our own. We revel in the existence of creatures and even whole societies beyond what we ourselves experience in our everyday lives. But have we gone so far in creating worlds of fantasy that we are missing the joy of other worlds that already exist all around us? 1

One doesn't have to look far to see examples of the attraction to other worlds in science. From the explorers who first mapped the earth, to researchers trying to understand the inner workings of the human genome, to those seeking to find out whether life, of some kind, exists on Mars, scientists certainly share this sense of wonder. But they hardly hold a patent on it. 2

3   Indeed, the trait seems universal. Look at the popularity of fantasy literature, or movies like *The Lord of the Rings* and *Star Wars*. Or the escapism of video games like *Myst* where other worlds are created for us to explore. This innate sense of curiosity and wonder draws us to each other, to the world around us and to the world of make-believe.

4   As a child, my escape to another world was a swamp near our house in London, Ontario. It was a wondrous world filled with amazing, bizarre and beautiful plants, insects, amphibians, birds and mammals. Every day in that marsh I could always count on finding something new; some exciting new creature or world to discover. Today, that swamp is entombed by a huge parking lot and shopping mall. The vast diversity of life has been replaced by an enormous array of consumer products. What does that mean for youths who spend their time there now?

5   Eminent Harvard biologist E.O. Wilson has suggested that human beings possess a trait he called "Biophilia"—that is, an innate desire to bond with and understand other life forms. That was certainly true from my own experiences. But I didn't grow up in a world of computers, video games and the Internet. I bonded with my family, friends and the creatures I found in my swamp. Today's youths, especially in big cities, often lead more isolated, insular lives and can be so far removed from the natural world that they can't even identify the common plants and animals that live around them.

6   Researchers at the University of Cambridge recently found that out when they surveyed British schoolchildren. They asked 109 children (boys and girls) to identify creatures depicted on a series of 20 flashcards. Ten cards were pictures of common British plants and wildlife—things like rabbits, badgers and oak trees. The other 10 cards were pictures of creatures from the popular children's trading cards series, television show and video game, Pokémon.

7   The researchers discovered that at the age of four, children could identify about 30 per cent of the wildlife and a handful of Pokémon. But by age eight, children were identifying nearly 80 per cent of the Pokémon, and barely half of the common wildlife species (they were not asked to be terribly specific with the wildlife—in many cases answers like "beetle" would have sufficed).

8   I think this example shows how powerful the need to understand other people, worlds and life forms really is. When we are deprived of meaningful interaction with the world around us, and sometimes even our families and friends, we seek to understand and interact with things

that only exist in our imaginations or on a computer screen.

Not that the world of make-believe is necessarily bad. The ability to immerse people in a different world through words, images and sounds is what gives good stories, books and films their power. And this power is a wonderful thing. The sharing of common stories and experiences can even help us bond with each other as human beings.   9

But when the world of fantasy, of television, video games and computers becomes the only outlet for our sense of wonder, then I think we are really missing something. We are missing a connection with the living world with which we share common histories, life cycles and even segments of our genetic code. Fascinating other worlds exist all around us. But even more interesting is that if we look closely enough, we can see that these worlds are really part of our own.   10

3.6 On Canada's First Nations

Seeing Red over Myths

Drew Hayden Taylor

Elements of the Essay

Who are First Nations/Native/Aboriginal/Indigenous peoples? Drew Hayden Taylor points out that within these general terms are a variety of Aboriginal groups and cultures that differ from one another. Non-Natives, however, do not appreciate or recognize that such diversities exist among the group of people that we have come to generalize and lump into one—"First Nations," or whatever the term might be. Taylor argues that such generalization has made dealing with "Native" issues difficult precisely because people don't see that there are differences among Native cultures.

About the Writer

Ojibwa playwright, scriptwriter, and journalist Drew Hayden Taylor was born at the Curve Lake Reserve, Ontario, in 1962. Although he has worked in both television and film, he is primarily recognized for the work he has done for stage. In 1989, he won the Chalmers Award for *Toronto at Dreamer's Rock*, and in 1990 he received the Canadian Authors Association Award for *Bootlegger Blues*. Taylor's most popular work is the play *Someday* (1993), which has been performed across the country. His two most recent plays are *Only Drunks and Children Tell the Truth* (first performed in 1996) and *400 Kilometres* (1999), both of which have received rave reviews.

1   A YEAR AND A HALF AGO, my Mohawk girlfriend and I (a fellow of proud Ojibway heritage) found ourselves in the history-rich halls of Europe, lecturing on Native issues, the propaganda and the reality, at a university deep in the heart of northeastern Germany. Then one young lady, a student at this former communist university, put up her hand and asked an oddly naive question, something like, "Do Indian women shave their legs and armpits like other North American

women?" (This was not the strangest question I've had put to me. I keep a list, which includes, "I'm phoning from Edinburgh, Scotland, and am doing research on natives in the 1930s. Can you send information?" or "Where can I get my hands on some Inuit throat singers?")

But unbeknownst to me, the shaving of extremities in Europe is a largely unexplored area of female hygiene; evidently this topic warranted investigation as to its possible Aboriginal origin. But the question presented a rather obvious example of the issue that permeates North America: The myth of pan-Indianism. The young lady had begun her question with "Do Indian women …?" Sometimes the questioner substitutes First Nations/Native/Aboriginal/Indigenous for Indian; however it's worded, it reveals a persistent belief that we are all one people.

Within the borders of what is now referred to as Canada, there are more than 50 distinct and separate languages and dialects. And each distinct and separate language and dialect has emerged from a distinct and separate culture. I tried to tell this woman that her question couldn't be answered because technically, there is no "Indian/First Nations/Aboriginal." To us, there is only the Cree, the Ojibway, the Salish, the Innu, the Shuswap, etc.

I find myself explaining this point with annoying frequency, not just in Europe, but here in Canada, at the Second Cup, Chapters, the bus station. The power of that single myth is incredible. When people ask me, "What do First Nations people want?" how do I answer? Some of the Mi'kmaq want to catch lobster; some of the Cree want to stop the flooding and logging of their territory in Northern Manitoba, Alberta and Quebec; the Mohawk want the right to promote their own language, and I know bingo is in there somewhere.

That's why every time I see a TV news report talking about the plight of the Aboriginal people, I find myself screaming "Which 'People'? Be specific!" That's why I never watch television in public.

Such is the power of myths. By their very definition, they're inaccurate or incomplete. Now you know why we as Native people (see, I do it myself) prefer not to use the term "myth" when referring to the stories of our ancestors, as in "The Myths and Legends of Our People." There is something inherently wrong about starting a traditional story with "This is one of the myths that was passed down from our grandfathers …" Literally translated, it means, "This is a lie that was handed down by our grandfathers …"

The preferred term these days is "teachings"—as in, "Our teachings say ..." It's certainly more accurate, because it recognizes the fact that most myths exist for a purpose—that there's some nugget of metaphor or message within the subtext. And in the Native (there I go again!) way, we like to accentuate the positive. (N.B. The word "legend" can also be used instead of "teachings," provided you have oral permission from a recognized elder, or written permission from an Aboriginal academic—any Nation will do).

8   The myth of pan-Indianism is not the only one rooted in the Canadian psyche. A good percentage of Canadians believe that there's a strong Aboriginal tradition of alcoholism. In Kenora, a decade or so ago, someone told me that in one month alone there had been almost 300 arrests of Aboriginals for alcohol-related offences. And Kenora's not that big a town. The statistic frightened me ... until it was explained that rather than confirming the mind-boggling image of 300 drunken Indians running through the Kenora streets, it signified the same dozen people who just got arrested over and over and over again. It's all in how you read the statistic. And nobody told me how many white people had been arrested over and over again. It's all in how you read that statistic.

9   While acknowledging that certain communities do, indeed, suffer from substance-abuse problems (like many non-Native communities, I might add), I can safely say that neither myself, my girlfriend, my mother, my best friend and most of the other people of Aboriginal descent I consider friends and acquaintances, are alcoholics. Which makes me wonder why this myth is so persuasive.

10   It's also believed by a good percentage of Canadians that all Native people are poor. Unfortunately, many communities do suffer from mind-numbing poverty, as do many non-Native communities. But contrary to popular belief, capitalism was not a foreign concept to Canada's earliest inhabitants. There were levels of wealth and status back then; today, instead of counting their horses, the rich might count their horsepower.

11   Several weeks ago, a Toronto newspaper attacked a rumour about a coalition of Aboriginal people who had expressed interest in buying the Ottawa Senators. The columnist thought the idea preposterous: "These are the same people who can't afford to pay tax on a deck of smokes; the same people who are so poor they claim government policy is forcing them to live in neighbourhoods where a rusted car with more than one flat tire is considered a lawn ornament."

12   The ratio of rusted-car-on-lawn to no-rusted-car-on-lawn is so disproportionate it's hardly worth mentioning.

Yes, there are some wealthy Native people out there (I wish I knew   13
more of them personally). But their existence is a hard idea to accept
when the media only feature First Nations stories on the desperate and
the tragic.

So where does this leave us? I was asked to write an essay on the   14
"myths of a common Indian identity." Which, as I translate it, means
that I was asked to comment on lies about something that doesn't exist.
That sounds more like politics to me. But if you're still curious about
whether Indian women shave their legs and armpits ... you'll have to ask
one. I'm not telling.

3.7 On Work

Stupid Jobs Are Good to Relax With

Hal Niedzviecki

Elements of the Essay

Generally, people are advised that no matter what the job, or how menial or tedious, one should always do his or her very best. Hal Niedzviecki's essay offers a counterargument as he suggests how a person might deal with "stupid jobs." Are you convinced by his central argument?

About the Writer

Hal Niedzviecki was born in Brockville, Ontario, and raised in Ottawa and Washington, DC. As the co-editor of *Broken Pencil: The Guide to Alternative Culture in Canada*, Niedzviecki has been both a voice in and a close observer of emerging cultural and literary trends. He has written three books: *Smell It* (1998), a collection of short short stories; *Lurvy: A Farmer's Almanac* (1999); and *We Want Some Too: Underground Desire and the Reinvention of Mass Culture* (2000). Niedzviecki also edited the anthology *Concrete Forest: The New Fiction of Urban Canada* (1998).

1   Springsteen kicked off his world tour in Toronto's Massey Hall a while back. Along with record company execs and those who could afford the exorbitant prices scalpers wanted for tickets, I was in attendance. As Bruce rambled on about the plight of the itinerant Mexican workers, I lolled in the back, my job, as always, to make myself as unapproachable as possible—no easy feat, trapped as I was in a paisley vest and bow-tie combo. Nonetheless, the concert was of such soporific proportions and the crowd so dulled into pseudo-reverence that I was able to achieve the ultimate in ushering—a drooping catatonia as close as you can get to being asleep while on your feet.

But this ushering nirvana wouldn't last long. For an usher, danger   2
takes many forms: wheel-chair-bound patrons who need help going to
the inaccessible bathroom, vomiting teens, and the usher's worst
nemesis, the disruptive patron. And yes, there she was: well-dressed,
blonde, drunk, and doped up, swaying in her seat and … clapping.
Clapping. In the middle of another one of Springsteen's interminable
solo dirges.

Sweat beaded on my forehead. Her clapping echoed through the hall.   3
The Boss glared from the stage, his finger-picking folkiness no match for
the drunken rhythm of this fan. Then, miracle of miracles, the song
ended. The woman slumped back into her seat. Bruce muttered
something about how he didn't need a rhythm section. Placated by the
adoring silence of the well-to-do, he launched into an even quieter song
about an even more desperate migrant worker.

I lurked in the shadows, relaxing my grip on my flashlight (the usher's   4
only weapon). Springsteen crooned. His guitar twanged. It was so quiet
you could hear the rats squirreling around the ushers' subterranean change
rooms. The woman roused herself from her slumber. She leaned forward
in her seat, as if suddenly appreciating the import of her hero's message.
I wiped the sweat off my brow, relieved. But slowly, almost imperceptibly, she
brought her arms up above her head. I stared, disbelieving. Her hands
waving around in the air until … boom! Another song ruined, New York
record execs and L.A. journalists distracted from their calculations of
Bruce's net worth, the faint cry of someone calling: Usher! Do something!

For several years now, I have relied on stupid jobs to pay my way   5
through the world. This isn't because I am a stupid person. On the
contrary, stupid jobs are a way to avoid the brain numbing idiocy of
full-time employment. They are the next best thing to having no job at
all. They will keep you sane, and smart.

I'm lazy sometimes. I don't always feel like working. On the stupid   6
job, you're allowed to be lazy. All you have to do is show up. Hey, that's
as much of an imposition on my life as I'm ready to accept. Does The
Boss go to work every day? I don't think so. He's The Boss.

Understanding the stupid job is the key to wading your way through the   7
muck of the working week, and to dealing with such portentous concepts
as The Youth Unemployment Crisis and The Transformation of the
Work Place. So sit back and let me explain. Or, as I used to say: Hi, how
are you this evening? Please follow me and I will show you to your seat.

8   The reality for the underemployed, over-educated young people of North America is that the stupid job is their future. As the middle-aged population continues to occupy all the "real" jobs, as the universities continue to hike tuition prices (forcing students to work and study part-time), as the government continues to shore up employment numbers with make-work and "retraining," there will be more stupid jobs than ever.

9   These stupid jobs won't be reserved for the uneducated and poor. In fact, the fertile growth of the stupid job is already reaping a crop of middle-class youngsters whose education and upbringing have, somehow, given away to (supposedly) stalled prospects and uncertain incomes. These are your grandchildren, your children, your sisters, your cousins, your neighbours. Hey, that might very well be a multi-coloured bow-tie wrapped around your neck....

10   I took a few tentative steps down the aisle. All around me, people hissed in annoyance and extended their claws. Clapping woman was bouncing in her seat. She was smiling. Her face was flushed and joyous. The sound of her hands coming together was deafening. I longed for the floor captain, the front of house manager, the head of security, somebody to come and take this problem away from me. I hit her with a burst of flashlight. Taking advantage of her momentary blindness, I leaned in: Excuse me Miss, I said. You can't do that. What? she said. That clapping, I said. Listen, she slurred. I paid three hundred dollars to see this. I can do what I want.

11   My flashlight hand wavered. Correctly interpreting my silence for defeat, she resumed her clapping. Springsteen strummed louder. I faded away, the darkness swallowing me up. For a blissful moment, I was invisible.

12   A lot of young people think their stupid jobs are only temporary. Most of them are right, in a way. Many will move on from being, as I have been, an usher, a security guard, a delivery boy, a data co-ordinator, a publishing intern.

13   They will get marginally better jobs, but what they have learned from their stupid jobs will stay with them forever. I hope.

14   If I'm right, they will learn that the stupid job—and by extension, all jobs—must be approached with willing stupidity. Set your mind free. It isn't necessary, and it can be an impediment. While your body runs the maze and finds the cheese, let your mind go where it will.

Look at it this way: You're trading material wealth and luxury for   15
freedom and creativity. To put it simply: while you may have less money
to buy things, you will have a lot more time to think up ways to achieve
your goals without buying things. You're making so many dollars an
hour, but the on-the-job perks include daydreams, poems scribbled on
napkins, novels read in utility closets, and long conversations about the
sexual stamina of Barney Rubble.

How much is an idea worth? An image? A moment of tranquility? A   16
bad joke? The key here is to embrace the culture of anti-work. In other
words, don't let your brain get all used up memorizing the gallery's obscure
seating arrangements or how the boss prefers you to drive the route.

Sometime after the Springsteen debacle, I was on a delivery, dropping   17
off newspapers at various locales. I started arguing with my co-worker,
the van driver, about work ethic. I suggested we skip a drop or two,
claiming that no one would notice and even if they did, we could deny
it and no one would care.

He responded by telling me that no matter what job he was doing, if   18
he accepted the work, he was compelled to do it right. I disagreed. Cut
corners, I argued. Do less for the same amount of pay. That's what they
expect us to do, I said. Why else would they pay us so little? Not that
day, but some weeks later, he came to see things my way.

What am I trying to tell you? To be lazy? To set fire to the corporation?   19
Maybe. Our options might be limited, but they are still options.
Somewhere in the bowels of Massey Hall it has probably been noted in
my permanent record that I have a bad attitude. That was a mistake.
I wasn't trying to have a bad attitude. I was trying to have no attitude.

For a couple of years I hired on as a security guard at the One of a Kind   20
Craft Show, held twice a year in Toronto's Automotive Building at the
CNE. Here the middle classes (whoever they are) flocked to buy baubles
that were priced outrageously under the guise of being handmade. The
most successful craftspeople were the ones who sold items that all looked
exactly the same. The Christmas Tree Ornament Lady packed in the big
money. What she made in one hour, I made in two days. Her handcrafted
mass-produced ornaments were a kind of torpid corollary to the long
hours I spent trolling the aisles watching the employed hordes buy.

The people who worked with me were fascinating. We were all   21
university graduates (or students) with artistic pretensions. We loved to tell
jokes on our walkie-talkies. There was a lot of pot smoking. The use of

code words over the radio was predominant. Whenever something had to be done, it was difficult to track one of us down. Many of us were outside in the parking lot getting high. We worked fifteen-hour days. The pay was low, but the hours amassed. I didn't have to explain my stupid jobs philosophy to anyone there. They were way ahead of me. They were my professors. Like the ushers at Massey Hall, they were painters and artists and designers and musicians. But many of them had no skill, no craft: this latter group deserves special mention in the stupid jobs pantheon. These are urban creatures, aberrant socialites well-versed in anarchist thought, the best punk bands in Saskatchewan, and what's on cable at 3:30 A.M. They can't imagine working nine to five, have strange ideas, and probably deserve paycheques just for being their loquacious selves.

22   What I should have told my friend in the delivery van was that when working the stupid job, passivity is the difference between near slavery and partial freedom. It's a mental distinction. Your body is still in the same place for the same amount of time (unless you're unsupervised). But your mind is figuring things out. Figuring out how many days you need to work to afford things like hard-to-get tickets to concerts by famous American icons. Or wondering why it is that at the end of the week, most people are too busy or tired to do anything other than spend their hard-earned dollars on junk they don't really need. Personally, I'd take low level servitude over a promotion that means I'll be working weekends for the rest of my life. You want me to work weekends? You better give me the rest of the week off.

23   Meanwhile, it's not like my life is all that great. I might claim to have determined the best way to live, but I remain—like so many other would-be social engineers—caught in the trap of my own contradictions.

24   Every year at the end of the Craft Show the worst offenders were barred from ever working the Craft Show again. I didn't get banned. I'm still a little embarrassed about that.

25   My father's plight is a familiar one.

26   He started his working life at thirteen in Montreal. He's fifty-five now. His employer of twelve years forced him to take early retirement. The terms are great, and if he didn't own so much stuff (and want more stuff) he could live comfortably without ever working again. But he feels used, meaningless, rejected.

27   On his last day, I helped him clean out his office. The sight of him stealing staplers, blank disks, and Post-it note pads was something I'll

never forget. It was a memo he was writing to his own soul (note: they owe me).

But the acquisition of more stuff is not what he needs to put a life of   28
hard work behind him. I wish that he could look back on his years of labour and think fondly of all the hours he decided not to work, the hours he spent reading a good book behind the closed door of his office, or skipping off early to take the piano lessons he never got around to. Instead of stealing office supplies, he should have given his boss the finger as he walked out the door. *Ha ha. I don't care what you think of me. And by the way. I never did.*

Despite his decades of labour and my years of being barely employed   29
(and the five degrees we have between us) we've both ended up at the same place. He feels cheated. I don't.

Extending:
Exploring Perspectives

1. One of the underlining issues in "Jurassic Conservation?" (pages 142 to 145), "The Harvest, The Kill" (pages 260 to 263), and "A Sense of Wonder" (pages 267 to 269) is the relationship between humans and nature. Write an essay describing the different perspectives on the relationship between people and nature developed in these essays, or write about your own perspective on the issue in response to the perspectives presented in these essays.

2. The essay "Vegetarianism: Going Green!" (pages 264 to 266) is accompanied by additional information in boxes. Would this information be better integrated into the essay? What is the difference between the information in the essay and in the boxes? What is the connection between the information in the essay and in the boxes?

3. In light of the information in "Vegetarianism: Going Green!" and "The Harvest, the Kill," debate the following resolution: Be It Resolved That There Is No Virtue in Being a Vegetarian. Additional research may be necessary.

4. Write an essay presenting a personal perspective on one of the following topics:
   - the best education to prepare a person for life in the twenty-first century
   - the role of the essay in society
   - the condition of spoken and written English today
   - the most important person of the last millennium
   - vegetarianism
   - genetically modified foods
   - multiculturalism in Canada: a model for the world?
   - salaries and income of pop culture (sports, music, film, and television) stars
   - a topic of your own, or your teacher's, choosing

Index of Titles

Index of Authors

Acknowledgements

Am I Blue? from *Living the Word: Selected Writings 1973-1987* by Alice Walker, copyright © 1986 by Alice Walker, reprinted by permission of Harcourt, Inc. Lyrics from **Am I Blue?** by Grant Clarke and Harry Akst. Copyright 1929 Warner Bros. Inc. (renewed). Used by permission. All rights reserved. **Through the One-Way Mirror** by Margaret Atwood. Originally published in *The Nation,* March 22, 1984. Copyright © 1984 Margaret Atwood. Reprinted by permission of the author. **Hollywood vs. Canada** by Elizabeth Renzetti. Copyright © Elizabeth Renzetti. **How I Caused that Story** by Doris Kearns Goodwin. From *Time,* February 4, 2002. Copyright © 2002 Time Inc. Reprinted with permission. **How to Eat an Ice-Cream Cone** from *How to Do Things Right* by L. Rust Hills. Reprinted with permission of the author. **How to Write a Test** by Eileen A. Brett from *Contest: Essays by Canadian Students,* 2nd edition, edited by Robert Hookey © 1994. Reprinted with permission of Nelson Thomson Learning, a division of Thomson Learning. **Television Addiction** from *The Plug-In Drug,* revised and updated by Marie Winn, copyright © 1977, 1985, 2002 by Marie Winn Miller. Used by permission of Viking Penguin, a division of Penguin Putnam Inc. **Eye Tricks** by Mark Kingwell. *Queen's Quarterly* 108/4 (Winter 2001), pp. 593-602. Copyright © Mark Kingwell. Reprinted with permission. **Victims and Agents** by Martha Nussbaum. Copyright © 1998 Martha Nussbaum. First published in *Boston Review.* Reprinted with permission. **It's Only a Paper World** by Kathleen Fury. First published in *Working Woman,* August 1986. **Of Weirdos and Eccentrics** by Pico Iyer. *Time,* January 18, 1988. Copyright © 1988 Time Inc. Reprinted with permission. **Some Notes on Parody** from *Parodies: An Anthology from Chaucer to Beerbohm – and After* by Dwight Macdonald. Published by Random House, 1960. **Barbie and Her Playmates** by Don Richard Cox. Reprinted by permission of *Journal of Popular Culture,* Volume 11:2, Fall, 1977. Introduction from **Fast Food Nation: The Dark Side of the All-American Meal** by Eric Schlosser. Excerpted and reprinted by permission of Houghton Mifflin company. All rights reserved. First published in the *Atlantic Monthly.* **After the War Is Over** by Renata Salecl. Reprinted with permission. **A Home at the End of the Journey** by Allen Abel. First published in *Maclean's,* January, 1995. Reprinted by permission of the author. **Anecdotes of Racism: A View Across the Aisle** by Miguna Miguna. First published in *The Toronto Review,* Volume 19, No. 1, Fall 2000. Reprinted with permission of the author. **Double Vision in a New Old World** by Naomi Shihab Nye. Reprinted with permission. **If Black English Isn't a Language, Then Tell Me, What Is?** by James Baldwin. Originally published in *The New York Times.* Reprinted with permission of *The New York Times.* **Jurassic Conservation** by Malcolm Tait. From *The Ecologist* (December 2000/January 2001). Reprinted with permission of the author. Excerpt from *Fragile Freedoms: Human Rights and Dissent in Canada* by Thomas Berger. Published by Stoddart. © Thomas Berger. Reprinted with permission of the author. **We're Mesmerized by the Flickering Tube** by Philip Marchand. Reprinted by permission of *The Toronto Star Syndicate.* **Thunderstrokes and Firebolts** by Janice McEwen. Copyright © Janice McEwen. **Food for Sloth** by Carol Krenz. Originally appeared in *Montreal Magazine,* Jan./Feb. 1990. Reprinted with permission of the